Rock Music in Performance

Rock Music in Performance

David Pattie
University of Chester

palgrave
macmillan

First published 2007 by
PALGRAVE MACMILLAN
Houndmills, Basingstoke, Hampshire RG21 6XS and
175 Fifth Avenue, New York, N.Y. 10010
Companies and representatives throughout the world

PALGRAVE MACMILLAN is the global academic imprint of the Palgrave Macmillan division of St. Martin's Press, LLC and of Palgrave Macmillan Ltd. Macmillan® is a registered trademark in the United States, United Kingdom and other countries. Palgrave is a registered trademark in the European Union and other countries.

ISBN-13: 978-1-4039-4746-8   hardback
ISBN-10: 1-4039-4746-5   hardback

This book is printed on paper suitable for recycling and made from fully managed and sustained forest sources. Logging, pulping and manufacturing processes are expected to conform to the environmental regulations of the country of origin.

A catalogue record for this book is available from the British Library.

A catalog record for this book is available from the Library of Congress.

10   9   8   7   6   5   4   3   2   1
16   15   14   13   12   11   10   09   08   07

Printed and bound in Great Britain by
Antony Rowe Ltd, Chippenham and Eastbourne

Contents

Introduction   vii

Part I: Performance and the Practice of Authenticity   1

1   4Real: Performance and Authenticity   3

2   Performance and Mediation: Performance, Space
    and Technology   21

3   Performance, Gender and Rock Music   40

Part II: Performance, Authenticity and History   57

4   The 1960s   59

5   The 1970s   81

6   The 1980s   104

7   The 1990s   127

8   The 21st Century   152

Notes   164

Bibliography   172

DVD List   177

Video List   179

Websites   180

Index   181

Introduction

This study grew from an article, originally published in 1999 ('4Real: Rock, Authenticity and Performance', *Enculturation*, Vol. 2, No. 2). The initial article explored a paradox which, it still seems to me, lies at the heart of the live performance of rock music. The rock musician, as commonly imagined, must be 'real'; he or she must perform in such a way as to convey and confirm a sense of authentic investment in the music played, or in the worldview that the artist embraces. But, as soon as we accept the idea that authenticity is performed in the live event, we open up an area which is, to say the least, ambiguous: how is it possible to perform authenticity? Performance, after all, is commonsensically regarded as a mediation (and perhaps, also, a distortion) of reality; the idea that it is somehow possible to capture a moment of authenticity through the medium of performance seems paradoxical at best.

And yet (as demonstrated below) such an idea exists, and conditions both musicians' and the fans' responses to live performance; and, what is more, this paradox seems to have been largely ignored by those who write about popular music. In fact, the whole idea of popular music as performance is, as noted in Quirk and Toynbee (2005), strangely underrepresented in the field. There are interesting discussions of the performance styles of various genres and bands (cf. Auslander 2006; Fast 2001; Weinstein 2000; Macan 1997). There are relatively few attempts to provide a taxonomy of the nature of the event itself (indeed, I was rather surprised, while researching this book after a few years' writing and thinking about other matters, to find my 1999 article cited in Quirk and Toynbee (2005) as one of the few texts available). There are exceptions: Allan Moore has some very insightful things to say about the expression of the self in the performance of music, and his work is used below; Philip Auslander has attempted to analyse the impact of mediation on live performance (although, as Chapter 2 demonstrates, I have severe reservations about the argument he puts forward). Mainly, though, performance is treated as an adjunct to the creation and dissemination of music: Shuker (2001) barely mentions it; *The Cambridge Companion to Pop and Rock* (2001) is similarly mute; George McKay's detailed and otherwise exemplary *Glastonbury: a Very English Fair* (2000) is only tangentially concerned with the fact that, somewhere in the complex socio-political matrix he describes, a band on stage are playing.

Such a gap cannot be filled by one book alone; and I have not attempted it. This book has a narrower focus. It deals with the paradox outlined in the 1999 article: how do rock musicians negotiate the tension between authenticity and performance when playing live? Chapter 1 establishes the nature of the paradox, and begins to demonstrate it in action. Chapter 2 (which engages in a number of close readings of U2 in performance) looks more specifically at the complex mediations through which the paradox is filtered. Chapter 3 looks at the creation of gender – especially maleness – in performance. The second part of the book looks at the way in which the paradox has been expressed in various styles and at various times. Although I follow a loose timeline, I have not attempted to include every example; there are omissions – simply because a book which listed all the manifestations of the paradox would be too long to publish, and too heavy to pick up. Throughout, I have on purpose focused on the performer, the stage and the technology which drives the event: there are many excellent discussions of the nature of fandom (see, for example, Cavicchi 1998; Schippers 2002) which I utilise, but much remains to be done on the performer's role in the event, and it is here that I have focused my attention. The book finishes with two studies of contemporary performance: the Stones, engaged in yet another massively successful world tour (and, in doing so, breaking a cultural taboo – performing age rather than youth), and a trio of bands (Gorillaz, Radiohead and The White Stripes) who have all managed to use the live event to manifest a liberating ambiguity, based firmly on the idea of performance as both mediated and real. If the paradox, established in the late 1960s (when rock, seriously and self-consciously, declared itself as an art form), persists through to the early years of this century, then it is probably fair to say that it has not lost its hold over musicians and audiences. This book is an attempt to deal with the reasons behind the longevity of the paradox, and an attempt to catalogue some of its manifestations – in a performance style which remains, stubbornly, 4Real.

Part I
Performance and the Practice of Authenticity

1
4Real: Performance and Authenticity

Playing 4Real

One of the iconic moments of 1990s rock occurred in a profoundly unlikely location: the backstage area of Norwich Arts Centre, in the aftermath of a Manic Street Preachers gig. An *NME* reporter, Steve Lamacq, had been critical of the Preachers: in particular, he had accused them of traducing the spirit of rock, of shamelessly mining rock history for their music and attitude, and of committing the ultimate rock crime of inauthenticity:

> 'I know you don't like us,' [Ritchie] says steadily, 'but we are for real. When I was a teenager, I never had a band who said anything about my life, that's why we're doing this. Where we came from, we had nothing.'
>
> As he's talking, from somewhere he finds a razorblade. Turning unnervingly serious, he takes the blade and slowly and deliberately carves '4 Real' into his left arm ...
>
> He had 17 stitches, apparently. What a dumb way to end an evening ...[1]

Edwards' act of self-mutilation is extreme, but not extreme enough that it cannot be fitted into a recognisable framework of rockstar behaviour. It carries the same charge as Jim Morrison's self-exposure in front of a Miami audience, or Iggy Pop's numerous self-inflicted in-concert woundings (lashing himself with the microphone stand, dripping hot wax over his chest). As a plea for final understanding, it mirrors and reverses Johnny Rotten's despairing epitaph on the Sex Pistols ('ever get the feeling you've been conned?') delivered at the end of their final gig in San Francisco's Winterland Ballroom. It allies Edwards, at the beginning of the band's public life, with all the tortured rock poets, all the 'real' stars, who have to fight the industry, the cynicism of the press, and the indifference of the public in order to reach their ideal audience; a group loosely configured as those who will understand them – those who have nothing, not even a band to give them a voice.

Edwards' gesture conforms to accepted rock iconography: but it also exceeds it, moves beyond it, into rather more troubling territory. Iggy Pop may have harmed himself spectacularly, but he did so in public, as part of the Stooges' assaultative stage show. Edwards' act is semi-private. It takes place in front of the public's putative representative, the one who will relay the experience of the concert to a wider audience than could necessarily attend the gig itself: but he is also involved in a conversation, making the exchange private as well as public. One might say that Pop's acts are outer-directed, aimed to the audience, and to the wider audience of those who invest themselves in rock music. Edwards' act is directed, first of all, to himself. It takes a public concern – the authenticity or otherwise of the Manics as a group – and turns it into a private, desperate act of self-confirmation, as though the only way that Edwards has to convince himself that he is not, ultimately, a charade, is to inscribe his authenticity, slowly and painfully, on his own skin.

But Edwards does not simply create an unambiguous symbol of his desire to be believed. He inscribes '4Real'; the word can be accepted, but the numeral seems both less and more than the word it represents. It weakens the declarative power of the act; the choice of 4 rather than 'for', a substitution familiar from Prince's song titles and lyrics (for example, 'I would die 4 U' from *Purple Rain*) might be thought of as too self-aware, as a too-knowing sign of Edwards' investment in both the history and the spirit of rock. In contradiction to this, though, it might be seen as an attempt to expand the scope of Edwards' declaration, through a punning reference to the composition of the band; '4Real' decoding as 'we, all four of us, are authentic rock artists'.

Both readings are possible; what is interesting, though, is the fact that Edwards chose the act and the terminology in the first place. The act is private, but has public consequences; the sign is authentic, but archly so, calling attention to itself as an artificial statement as it declares its reality. In other words, Edwards' act is both declaration and performance; it calls attention to itself as artificial, *and* it takes itself seriously, as a statement of real intent.

Thinking 4Real

> Rock discourse is rife with discussion of a quality which has come to be identified as 'authenticity' ... The distinction is ... one between what is 'authentic' and what is 'commercial'. Over the past thirty years, it has become increasingly clear that this distinction is illusory, if only because rock music requires some accommodation to commercial pressures (as represented by the record labels to which rock bands are signed) in order to reach any audience beyond their local one. Illusory or not, audiences nonetheless feel the need to ascribe authenticity to particular artists.[2]

The idea of authenticity – of realness, of faithfulness to an original intent, and to aesthetic honesty – runs like a ground bass through the practice and study of rock music. Even though the notion itself is at best profoundly slippery, and at worst extremely problematic (and even though the term itself is worn through overuse – according to Quirk and Toynbee (2005), the delegates attending the 2004 Experience Music Project conference booed every time authenticity was mentioned – and it is very difficult to blame them) it is inescapable. As Moore notes above, audiences continue to ascribe authenticity to the work of certain performers, and to dismiss others as merely entertainers; bands and musicians, too, tend to define their output in terms of its imputed reality. This happens, for example, between musicians; the well-documented battles between Oasis and Blur, and Nirvana and Pearl Jam, and, paradigmatically, between John Lennon and Paul McCartney are all essentially battles over authenticity. It is also clearly demonstrated in the attitude of musicians to technology. For example, when Franz Ferdinand came to record their second album, they rejected the armoury of tone-altering software available to modern musicians:

> People use it to correct everything and in doing so, they strip their music of its idiosyncrasies, its uniqueness. And that's not something I like to do.[3]

Pro tools are dangerous to the serious musician, because they encourage cheating; in fact, for some musicians, the whole process of contemporary recording is a threat to the authenticity of the music. Taken to the extreme, the same impulse drives Jack White to record on equipment that is at least thirty years old; Franz Ferdinand might not go quite as far, but at base they and The White Stripes, it seems, share the same fear – that their authentic voice will get lost somewhere in the process of recording.

The term is there; it is part of the everyday vocabulary of musicians, critics, audiences and academics; and it does not show any signs of disappearing – no matter what the external and internal pressures brought to bear on the form. As later chapters will demonstrate, authenticity in rock has always existed in crisis; rock music was declared dead (with theatre cited as the murder weapon) almost at the moment of its birth, and groups like The Stooges, The Clash, The Pogues, Metallica, Nirvana, Radiohead and The Libertines have, in their various ways, played on the trope of the last gang in town (The Clash even wrote a song with that title on their second album). Indeed, it might be said that rock musicians and fans need this sense of crisis, because it is a powerfully generative narrative; rock music as a form needs to be under threat – from the industry, from the presence of musical forms which betray too closely the influence of commerce, from burn-out, from the pressures of fame, from the ever-present nightmare of musical differences, from the very fact of success itself, and so on, and so on.

This does not mean that rock music is not an industrialised process; it does not mean that rock stars are any more or less constructed than any other stars (for example, Fred Goodman's *The Mansion on the Hill* (1997) is a useful corrective to any lingering notions of the unfettered creativity of a musician like Bruce Springsteen – more of whom later in the book). What it does mean is that the precise nature of authenticity in the practice of rock can never be defined. There is always a new crisis; therefore, there is always a new idea of authenticity that takes account of the crisis and opposes it. This means that authenticity is endlessly recalibrated and reconsidered and that apparent truisms which seem unshakeable to one generation of critics and fans might be comprehensively overturned when the need arises. Abba and Pink Floyd represented the inauthentic backdrop to punks' ingrained authenticity; two decades later, they had been recuperated – Abba as exponents of pure pop (as opposed to the manufactured pop of Take That or The Spice Girls), and Pink Floyd as early explorers of ambient musical space (in the style of The Orb). Authenticity can be lost between albums, even though the music and image of the band might not have changed that much. *Parklife* (1994) establishes Blur as The Kinks of the 1990s, even though the album demonstrates a far wider range of musical influences; *The Great Escape* (1995) is, if anything, even more in thrall to Ray Davies – but it is now measured, not against the remnants of grunge, but against Oasis (who are working-class, Northern, and in thrall to John Lennon; and who are in their turn superseded – see below). Even tones move in and out of authenticity: as Moore notes in the article cited above, it is impossible to rank sounds in order of 'realness'. A roughened vocal texture might suggest authentic emotional investment (as it might for Bruce Springsteen or Michael Stipe), or that the singer has lived the life described in the songs (Tom Waits would be the most obvious example to cite here). However, this vocal texture can be learned (as, arguably, Bob Dylan learned the power of roughened vocals from Woody Guthrie); and it can also be surgically implanted (Bonnie Tyler's performance in 'Total Eclipse of the Heart' was only possible after she had undergone surgery to place nodes on her vocal chords). What is true for voices is equally true for instruments. Synthesised or electronic instruments are at first the enemies of authenticity: in 1977, the *NME Encyclopaedia of Rock* describes Kraftwerk's music as technologically arid ('The precise clean beat of the electronic pads simulates [the] gadget-ridden advanced technological environment that their fans presumably live in'[4]). Two decades later, a new division emerged, at least in some parts of rock, between analogue and digital instruments; digital instruments were now cold avatars of inhuman, inauthentic technology, and, for a neo-progressive band like Ozric Tentacles, the superseded analogue synthesiser was warm and reassuringly human (see Macan 1997) – or, for Brian Eno, endearingly textured and imprecise (Tamm 1995). Moore is right to note, in the title of his short essay, that authenticity is constructed: but the building work will never be completed, because the house is always being redesigned.

Given this, it is not surprising that two of the more recent interventions in this debate have attempted to take the inherently unstable nature of authenticity in rock into account. Keir Keighley, in a useful essay in *The Cambridge Companion to Rock and Pop* ('Reconsidering Rock'), identifies rock's drive toward authenticity as a persistent feature of the form:

> The persistent belief that rock somehow emerges outside the mainstream, prior to the involvement of the record industry, mass media, or large audiences, expresses a widespread feeling that, despite its success, rock remains magically untainted by 'the mass'. Rock's mythical, originating 'elsewhere' is neither a time or place, though. Instead, it designates the distinctive identity rock carves out of the centre of mass culture.[5]

For Keighley, this identity is carved out in two main ways: ones which conform either to Romantic or Modernist notions of art. He provides a helpful list[6] of the different tendencies associated with each lineage:

Romantic authenticity tends to be found more in –	Modernist authenticity tends to be found more in –
Tradition and continuity with the past	*Experimentation and progress*
Roots	*Avant-gardes*
Sense of community	*Status of artist*
Populism	*Elitism*
Belief in a core or essential rock sound	*Openness regarding rock sounds*
Folk, blues, country, rock 'n' roll styles	*Classical, art music, soul, pop styles*
Gradual stylistic change	*Radical or sudden stylistic change*
Sincerity, directness	*Irony, sarcasm, obliqueness*
'liveness'	*'recorded-ness'*
'natural' sounds	*'shocking' sounds*
hiding musical technology	*celebrating technology*

As Keighley notes, these are tendencies rather than absolutes, and the terms themselves are helpfully capacious – it is hard to think of a rock performer whose work does not coincide with these definitions at some point. And herein lies part of the problem: it is hard to think of any musician who could not be typed at some point against at least some of these definitions. Robbie Williams displays the sincerity, directness and the sense of community required by romantic authenticity; his work also drips with irony and obliqueness, and he ranges over power ballads, rap, film scores, and (on *Intensive Care*) the kind of layered guitar rock most closely associated with The Smiths. Even when the terms are applied rather more rigorously, to musicians more commonly listed as part of rock, the process of application is rather difficult. Morrissey, an arch modernist lyrically, is in these definitions an arch romantic musically; David Bowie, over the course of a long career, has managed to produce work that could fit into nearly all of the tendencies described above (and he also managed in the mid-1980s to drop out of authenticity altogether, only to be recuperated in the 1990s). Keighley's broad definitions are very useful (they provide, for example, a commonsensical explanation of the presence of Joy Division,

Bjork and The KLF in the discourse of rock), but they are not broad enough to prevent substantial leakage from one set of tendencies to the other.

Another recent attempt at defining authenticity (Auslander 2003) similarly seeks to capture a concept which is always on the move. The article deals with the recurrence of 1950s musical styles in the music of the late 1960s and early 1970s; whereas Keighley posits authenticity as a matter of shifting tendencies, Auslander takes examples from the period and maps their authenticity[7] across a sliding scale:

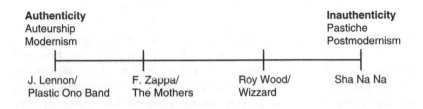

Auslander goes on to relate these twin poles to modernism (the concern for authenticity, and the expressive power of the individual artist) and postmodernism (the pole where we find inauthentic pastiche). This argument is, usefully, relational. If authenticity and crisis go together this suggests a constant process of comparison. The terms only make sense in relation to their implied opposites: I am an artist, or a real musician, and you are faking it, or you have sold out. However, it might be a useful arrangement of a number of musicians at the turn of the 1970s, but it is contingent. As noted above, ideas of authenticity shift continually; there is no reason to assume that Roy Wood (a musician who was in touch with musical history, a musician so committed to his work that he played almost all the instruments on Wizzard's albums, a reclusive figure, hiding behind the image he created) might not be subject to the same process of recuperation as Brian Wilson. Today's purveyor of pop fluff might very well be tomorrow's intuitive genius. Indeed, a review of a Roy Wood compilation in *Mojo* in May 2006 describes him as 'a witty songsmith with a track record of whimsical English eccentricity'.[8] It is even possible to imagine Sha Na Na (a parody/pastiche of basic 1950s rock, and a band whose members constructed their identities) as an authentic expression of the simple pleasures of simple music. After all, a few years after the period Auslander describes, exactly the same trick worked for The Ramones. There is no reason to assume that the concrete examples that anchor Auslander's continuum will automatically stay in place; it might be hard to imagine

John Lennon being shaken loose from his position, but, as I have just noted, it is very easy to imagine Sha Na Na's journey to authenticity (and to provide examples of similar transformations). It is even easier to imagine Roy Wood and Wizzard as far more authentic, in the argument that Auslander makes, than Frank Zappa (whose attitude to 1950s doo-wop was as hard to type as his attitude to any of the forms of music he employed).

In other words, authenticity will not stay still. Both Keighley and Auslander helpfully describe it as a process, but even their attempts to capture the effects of the discourse in the practice of popular music are not fluid enough to take account of what happens in the creation and reception of the music itself. Perhaps a more useful definition is provided by Allan Moore, in his 2002 article 'Authenticity as Authentication', which begins by asking what seems to me to be the right question – not how is authenticity constructed within and around music, but how and why is authenticity ascribed to particular types of music by performers and by audiences? Moore argues for a typology of authenticities which operate within and around the performance of music: first-person authenticity (in which the audience is aware of the presence of a creative musician in the performance of the music, and responds to the music as an expression of the artist); second-person authenticity (in which music is used by a listening group as a way of authenticating its own experience); and third-person authenticity (when performer and audience agree that the style of music performed is correctly aligned with a pre-existing musical tradition). The usefulness of this typology is its openness; as Moore notes, even the most unlikely contenders can be ascribed authenticity if the conditions are right (S Club 7, for example, are undeniably an example of second-person authenticity for Moore's young daughter, for example).[9] By the article's end, Moore has effectively shifted the terms of the debate, from authenticity inscribed in music to authenticity ascribed to music:

> Academic consideration of authenticity should thus, I believe, shift from consideration of the intention of various originators towards the activities of various perceivers, and should focus on the reasons they might have for finding, or failing to find, a particular performance authentic.[10]

Moore's typology is useful; as with the definitions given above, it is flexible and capacious – but this is not a problem for Moore (as it is for Keighley and Auslander) because for Moore that malleability is the point. Everything is, in this argument, recuperable for authenticity.

Before moving the discussion back to live performance, I wish to add one more argument. In 'A Star is Born and the Construction of Authenticity', Richard Dyer pointed out that:

There is a whole litany in the fan literature surrounding stars in which certain adjectives endlessly recur – sincere, immediate, spontaneous, real, direct, genuine, and so on. All of these words can be seen as relating to a general notion of 'authenticity'. It is those qualities that we demand of a star if we accept her or him in the spirit in which she or he is offered. Outside of a camp appreciation, it is the star's really seeming to be what she/he is supposed to be that secures his/her star status, 'star quality' or charisma. Authenticity is both a quality necessary to the star phenomenon to make it work, and also the quality that guarantees the authenticity of the other particular values a star embodies … It is this effect of authenticating authenticity that gives the star charisma.[11]

In other words, for Dyer it is not enough that the star is real; he or she must act realness. The qualities that Dyer identifies as the signs of authenticity – genuineness, spontaneity, immediacy, etc. – are all qualities associated with performance. To be said to exist, they have to be demonstrated; they have to become clearly visible to an audience. The paradox contained within this formulation is not that an audience accepts as real that which is patently unreal; rather it is that an audience accepts reality, or authenticity, as a performance, without necessarily accepting that its status as performance invalidates it as a true expression of the star's authentic self. The audience, it could be said, believes in the star's performed self, while being aware that that self is itself a performance, and must be judged as a performance. The crucial question for both the performer and the audience seems to be one of belief: the spontaneous expression of both the audience's and the performer's faith in the act seems, at least for some performers, to confirm that the connection between performer and audience can be termed authentic, no matter how transparently fake the trappings of the performance are.

For Dyer, the guarantee of Judy Garland's performed authenticity is the way in which she transforms an artificial film moment (the moment in which a musical number overwhelms a film's narrative development) into a private moment, shared on screen only with her musicians: the audience become interlopers, observing an act which is not meant for them, and are therefore able to read Garland's performance as a direct expression, both of her filmed and her real self. In this example, the music is simply the vehicle through which a performer reveals him/herself. In rock, the position of the music is rather more crucial:

> [Bono] talks about embracing irony, the stupid glamour of rock & roll, the mirror balls and limousines – without abandoning the truth at the heart of the music itself. He compares it to Elvis Presley in a jump-suit singing 'I Cant Help Falling in Love with You' to a weeping woman in Las Vegas. It might have been hopelessly kitsch, but if the woman believed in the song *and Elvis believed in the song*, it was not phoney. Maybe rock & roll was at its truest in the space between these apparent contradictions.[12]

What Bono describes as a contradiction is, it seems to me, simply a restatement of a standard rock trope: that the music contains within itself a pre-existing truth, and that it is the task of both performer and audience to rediscover and re-express that truth. The music, it seems, is the fixed element in an otherwise infinitely transformable set of relations between the star, the audience, and all the trappings of performance. In rock music, therefore, the elements that Dyer associates with the persona of the star are slightly recast. The audience does not simply gauge the star's performance against what it knows of the star's persona: in rock, if Bono is correct, both the audience and the performer look to the music to provide the ultimate validation, the ultimate proof of authenticity. It is as though the music itself contains, beyond the meanings attached to a particular chord structure and rhythm, a single set of lyrics or a specific delivery, the ability to organise the audience's and the star's perception of it as inherently truthful.

This view, unsurprisingly, comes from a vocalist steeped in rock lore; a man who described the instrumentation of his group (guitar, bass, drums) as an attempt to return to the three primary colours of rock; a man who claimed, during the performance of an accredited rock classic that 'All I have is a red guitar/three chords, and the truth'.[13] It is a view that comes directly from the history of the form; rock, the common narrative asserts, derives from the blues, and therefore derives from a form that grew directly, unmediated, from the lives of those who sang and played it. It does not matter that, in Bono's example, both Elvis and the woman are situated on the heartland of American Kitsch: they believe in the song – and their belief is strong enough to transcend their surroundings, and to unite them in an almost religious moment of revealed truth.

The hold that this idea has over the imaginations of both rock performers and those who report and write about rock music should not be underestimated. It exists as a shared, communal myth about the power of a music that carries within itself the mystical power to speak, and to speak truthfully, about the lives and experiences of those who listen and of those who play; a music that both relies on and transcends the individual performer, and that also provides a shared language that allows the performer and the fan to communicate. Rock, therefore, is more than a specific musical style, or a specific series of performance conventions: it is itself an icon, a prize to which both the performer and the audience aspire. All the indicators that Dyer notes in the construction of the authentic Hollywood star – the spontaneity, the directness, the sheer unguardedness of the performance – are indicators that can be used in a discussion of rock stars in performance. However, in rock the authentic bedrock against which the star is judged is the music; the persona of the performer is important, but only in so far as it reflects his or her investment in the music. It is as though, behind the tripartite typology outlined by Moore, there is a fourth-person authenticity quietly operating: one in which the idea behind the form, rather than the music itself, is a touchstone for both fans and musicians. Ritchie Edwards' act was, and remains, extreme, but it can be read (and Edwards undoubtedly wished it to be read) as a sign of his investment in the central myth of rock as an authentic, and authenticating language. In the rest of the study, I will argue that the manifestation of this language in performance is through a series of tropes: gestures, poses, characteristic tones and images, which, in the eyes of an engaged audience, metaphorically suggest the presence of the authentic performer.

Never coming down: the 4Real performer

So far, I have used the terms 'star' and 'audience' in a rather loosely inclusive way: even the blanket use of the term 'rock' is profoundly problematic, given the myriad sub-genres that have proliferated since the term was first employed in the late 1960s. Popular music is, after all, more liable than most popular cultural forms to obey a logic of fragmentation, driven both by the market's need to generate an audience, and the tendency, on the part of some sections of the audience, to reposition themselves against the form of music currently perceived as dominant. The troubles experienced by Oasis after the release of their third album are a salutary example of this. Their record company (Creation Records) confidently assumed that demand for the album *Be Here Now* would meet and exceed that for the multi-million selling previous album *What's the Story (Morning Glory)?* In accordance with this view, the record company treated the release of the third album with the kind of secrecy normally accompanying the election of a new pontiff. The album was hyped, while its contents were jealously guarded; the feverishly expectant atmosphere surrounding the album's release was heightened by the media's interest in the activities of the Gallagher twins (activities that, once again, conformed to the accepted standards of rock transgression: Noel Gallagher, the surly, iconoclastic generational spokesman, and Liam, the wild man of rock).

However, the album's performance, and the performance of the singles taken from it, did not meet the expectations of the group or of the record label. Partly, this is because of the very success of the marketing strategy, which ensured that those interested in the group spent their cash on the album very quickly (the album sold over half a million copies in its first week of release). However, this coincided with the activation of a backlash against the group, conducted simultaneously by the music press (the *NME*, in particular, turned against the group, dismissing them as bloated and self-indulgent) and, more interestingly, by sections of the fan base itself (see the contemporary letters columns of the *NME* and *Melody Maker*). Oasis were no longer deemed to be the spokesmen of a particular generation, sharing that generation's particular view of the world; that role had passed on – to Radiohead, and more particularly to their lead singer Thom Yorke (a tortured rock poet, in the lineage of Kurt Cobain and Leonard Cohen), to the Manic Street Preachers, newly sanctified after Ritchie Edwards' disappearance, and finally, to Richard Ashcroft and The Verve (of whom more below). The identity of the authentic rock musician is, therefore, not fixed: to an extent it is at the mercy of a particular audience (the people, in Edwards' formulation quoted above, who need a band to speak for them), and it is also subject to a process of commodification, as the 'real' musician is positioned in the marketplace. If, as I have suggested above, the performer and the audience find a moment of authentic communication in a commonly held idea of rock music as an unspecific but accessible real language, then it is important to note that, in practice, that language changes – and changes quickly. Perhaps, therefore, the extent to which a group or a musician is able to establish themselves as authentic depends on the extent to which their target audience accept that they are able to balance the performance of authenticity with the practice of authenticity, as reflected in the band's/musician's and the fans' idea of the music as it exists at that particular time.

As an example of this, it might be instructive to analyse a review of a 1997 Verve concert by the *NME* editor Steve Sutherland. The band, after a rather difficult period in which they had split up and reformed, had released a new album, *Urban Hymns*, and a couple of 'landmark anthems', 'Bittersweet Symphony' and 'The Drugs Don't Work'. The video for

'Bittersweet Symphony' had placed Richard Ashcroft, the band's lead singer, in archetypal opposition to the everyday; he walked down a scrupulously ordinary street, singing directly to camera, while the rest of the world (it seemed) moved unconsciously to impede him. The concert's opening moments seemed to be a reflection of the attitude contained within the video: this band did not require the more obvious trappings of performance. In fact, they seemed to position themselves squarely against any idea of the theatrical:

> There is no fuss. No bother. No big intro. Just numbers on a screen counting down, then Richard lopes on, removes his parka, takes off his shoes, silently screams and shakes his fist at the crowd. There is no giant telephone box. No Rolls-Royce drum-riser. Just the Verve and their calamitous beauty, getting down to business. The band in the shadows, Richard up front. Not a performance as much as an experience.[14]

For Sutherland, The Verve are not engaged in a performance, as the term is normally understood. The unadorned simplicity of their stage set-up is contrasted against Oasis' set (which contained a Rolls-Royce drum-riser and a giant telephone box): Oasis have, it seems, forfeited their right to communicate with the audience because they have uncritically accepted the idea that rock performance is firstly a performance, rather than a moment of authentic communication between performer and audience. In other words, they need their props because they are faking it: they no longer believe in the fans and in the music.

At the same time, though, the moments that Sutherland praises are themselves unambiguously theatrical. Ashcroft's entrance is prepared for by a count-down: it is hard to imagine a more transparently artificial technique for securing an appropriately tense, expectant response from an already self-selectedly enthusiastic audience. Ashcroft's entrance is itself archetypal. The underdressed performer, who wears his authenticity in his everyday clothing, enters and readies himself to perform, removing his coat and his shoes in a gesture that can be read as both public and private. It is a public gesture, readying Ashcroft for an appropriately energetic performance: but it also seems unguarded, spontaneous, as though Ashcroft regards the location as if it were his home. In this light, the paragraph's final sentence is interestingly phrased. Performance is the negative term, because it connotes a communication that is one-way, in which the performer controls the performance and the audience merely receive it: experience is the positive term, because it connotes an event that may have some elements of performance to it, but that uses those elements to create a direct communication between the performer and the audience. The public performance must be superseded by a private act of communion.

'Urban Hymns' has had its time to bed inside our consciousness. We know it off by heart and are ready now to participate in a couple of hours of being The Verve. Now ... we too have drained the elixir, we too are Richard, eyes closed, head thrown back, throat muscles taut with the pain of singing. These are our songs too and we each have personally interpreted their shadowy lyricism, have taken each line about cats in bags and butterfly chasing and have impregnated them with our own memories.[15]

The music, here, is more than a simple point of connection; it is the vehicle for a moment of transformation (an example of second-order authenticity, to use Moore's typology), but strongly suggesting both first- and third-person authenticity as well. The band and audience, it seems, become one. This moment, a moment of transformation, where the boundary between the performer and the audience no longer seems to exist, has been described by Jon Savage as the goal of any successful rock performance (1997: 250). Although it might not be possible to theorise such a transformation (to do so would be to move across the discursive boundary separating theorist from fan), it is at least possible to discuss its constituent elements, as described in Sutherland's review.

Firstly, there is a loss of control. Ashcroft is, it seems, unable to contain his response to the music. It pushes him beyond the conventional response of the performer to an audience; he seems impatient with their applause, precisely because it is a response appropriate to performance but not to the communion that both band and audience are (supposed to) achieve. His singing style, too, seems to signal an unconscious response to the music: he (and the audience alongside him) sings with his eyes closed, his head thrown back, his 'throat muscles tense with the sweet pain of singing'. Secondly, there is an unpremeditated quality about the performance as described. The performance is one where, in Sutherland's words, 'The Verve get it right'[16]; all the elements of a successful performance have fallen into place, with the strong implication that this is a matter of this band, performing at this time, in front of this audience, who respond in this particular way. The description carries the powerful, yet unstated implication that the success of this performance is strictly unrepeatable, even though the response to the band might be equally as rapturous elsewhere. Thirdly, it is profoundly private: we (a pronoun employed for full emotive effect) share this experience with Richard; the first name, and the intimacy it connotes, is casually assumed as a sign of Ashcroft's and the audience's shared experience of the event.

These three categories – loss of control, unpremeditation and privacy – are the three categories that Dyer assigns to the authentic performance of the star in classical Hollywood cinema: they are present here, but they are expressed in terms of both the singer's and the audience's in-depth knowledge of the songs. The audience does not eavesdrop on the spontaneity of the star; the audience also loses control, acts unpremeditatedly, and shares in the essential privacy of the star's performance, by recognising and performing the music with the same kind of commitment as Ashcroft himself displays. By the review's end, we have reached the logical endpoint of the rhetorical development strongly suggested in the section quoted above. Sutherland suggests that, by the time that the final song is reached, there is no difference between Ashcroft and the audience: more than this, that both have shared the same experience of the world, and have come to share a common attitude to that experience:

> Richard is singing what happened to The Verve as a metaphor for our whole generation. Lost without any idea of what to believe in, he offers us the best he can; the shared experience that we are all fuck-ups and it's ok. By the time the band are cranking up into 'Come On' at the very end, Richard has no need to hector us into sharing his reverie. We are right up there with him, howling at the moon, It's a high place to be. Ain't never coming down.[17]

Transformation has been replaced by apotheosis. Ashcroft is now the chosen representative of his generation, the latest in a line of such spokesmen; the slighting references to Oasis in the review are an indication that the burden of responsibility of speaking for his peers has passed directly from the Gallaghers to The Verve.

A standard rock trope – the generational representative – has been rearticulated, and in this rearticulation the terms of the trope have altered. Oasis, for example, spoke both for a confident, laddish, unrepentant British working-class masculinity, and for the classes excluded during the Thatcherite 1980s:

> Scratch the hedonistic surface and there's sharp social observation; not for nothing is leader Noel Gallagher the first lyricist to mention The Big Issue in a hit song.[18]

Before Oasis, and a profound influence on both the young Gallaghers (Liam Gallagher's stage persona is loosely adopted from Ian Brown, the

Roses' lead singer), The Stone Roses spoke for the contradictory yet transformative aspirations of the late 1980s love generation:

> 'Time! Time! Time! The time is now,' Ian Brown shouts as The Stone Roses come out on to the massive stage at Spike Island ... The Manchester groups have succeeded in capturing and stimulating an ambience which is delicately balanced between ambition and solidarity, between radicalism and conservatism, between hedonism and idealism, between androgyny and laddishness, between gentleness and violence[19]

only to find that the contradictions embedded in their initial reception had been flattened out once Suede's image established itself in the early 1990s:

> Suede presented a severe androgyny, all 1970s waisted angles and pouting, with lyrics that told stories of explicit gay sex – 'The Drowners', 'Animal Nitrate' – or at least went in for a good blurring, like on 'Moving': 'so we are a boy we are a girl'.[20]

It is not that the music industry, the groups, the writers, and the audience are prone to acts of communal amnesia, in which the lauded achievements of the previous year become the monolithic mistakes of the present: rather, it is that a group identified as authentic are rarely defined as possessing a single identity. In the extracts quoted above, The Stone Roses and Oasis are the focus of contradictory readings; of their personae, their music, and their relation to the lived experience of those who listen and of those who write. Even Suede, who undoubtedly blur gender codings in their music and in performance, have been held to reflect a variety of contradictory experiences – suburbia against the city, glamour against sleaze, etc., etc. The group's image is not entirely open (one cannot imagine a gender-bending Oasis track, for example), but it is dialogic; as argued above, in performance, rock groups attempt to achieve direct communication, if not communion, with their audiences – but this is not to say that the experience is judged identically by everyone who participates in it. After all, the focus of the performance for both the performer and the audience is not the performer's image but the music the performer produces, and that music is not reducible to a single, canonical interpretation. It is this that enables a particular group to establish, at a particular time in their careers, a wide, generational appeal; the discursive inclusivity of music allows both musicians and audience to invest it with their own meanings, while still engaging in a shared moment of communion.

Sutherland's review of The Verve at Glasgow Barrowlands is not an isolated moment of journalistic ecstasy; something of the same tenor can be found in accounts and reviews of other bands of the same period: The Stone Roses at Spike Island in 1990; Oasis at Maine Road in 1995; Blur at Alexandra Palace in 1995; Pulp at Glastonbury in 1995; Radiohead at Glastonbury in 1997; The Verve themselves at Wigan in 1998. Each performance is more than a performance; it is the moment when the audience achieve communion with the group, in the contradictory, inherently dialogic way described above. As Sutherland describes it, the successful performance is a performance that denies that it is a performance; the moment of communion itself therefore rests upon a contradiction, in which overtly theatrical moments (the countdown, the initial disrobing/preparation) are described as though they are displays of Ashcroft's authentic, untheatrical self. Moreover, the exact nature of the communion is itself vague: Sutherland describes 'our whole generation' as consisting entirely of 'fuck-ups', without specifying the exact nature of the term (there are as many ways to fuck up, after all, as there are people on the planet). And yet, if Sutherland's account of the audience's response is trustworthy (and there is no reason to assume that it is not) then, perhaps, we should look for the meaning of the event, and the meaning of rock performance in general, not in the vague and contradictory effects of a performance, but in the process of the performance itself, and in the shared performative language constantly rearticulated in each encounter between performer and audience.

Conclusion

The experience of pop music is an experience of identity; in responding to a song, we are drawn, haphazardly, into emotional alliances with the performers and with the performer's other fans ... Somebody else has set up the conventions, they are clearly social and apart from us. Music ... stands for, symbolises and offers the immediate experience of collective identity.[21]

Simon Frith's account of music's construction of identity as contradictory – both individual and collective – is, I think, persuasive: but if we are to account for the experience of rock performance, the opposition that Frith sets up has, I think, to be taken further, to embrace not only the contradictions inherent in the audience, but also the contradictory nature of the rock performer, and the contradictory response to that performer on the part of the audience. All share the sense that a good rock performance must contain a central contradiction – that it must be 4Real, both constructed and authentic, both theatrical and spontaneous; but that the theatrical, constructed elements of the performance always exist in opposition to that which is authentic and spontaneous, while at the same time those theatrical elements are subsumed within the spontaneity of the event. Performance is permissible, it seems, if the performance is a performance that is real: if the act is an act that can be treated as though it is not an act. The contradiction, therefore, both does and does not exist. The experience addressed in rock performance is always general, communal, and the community formed in performance is an inherently dialogic and active one. There is no metalanguage of fandom to which the individual audience member surrenders; there is no deeply articulated structure of participation that governs all responses to the event. The performer does not entirely control the event: the audience are not entirely constructed by their place in the event. The fluid and flexible use of a constructed authenticity, as outlined by Moore and Dyer, operates for both bands and fans. Both, as argued above, find justification for their participation in the event in the idea of rock as a myth of authenticity, but the experience that the music authentically expresses is not the same from group to group, nor from audience to audience, nor even from reviewer to reviewer; all rely on the music to speak for and through them – and that reliance is, in turn, based on a myth that music, if believed in, is inherently authentic.

It is within these contradictions that, finally, Edwards' act of desperate self-mutilation can be placed. It cannot be read as entirely theatrical: it cannot be read as entirely spontaneous (the 4 is far too obviously a constructed sign). It is both a private act, a moment of bizarre intimacy between Edwards and Lamacq; but it has a strongly public element to it – it is, after all, the most visible sign possible that the Manics' public image was an authentic one, and it is hard to imagine any other statement carrying the same emotional impact of Edwards' desperate, last-ditch assertion of authenticity. For me, Edwards' act is remarkable, not only for the sheer physical impact of the act itself, but also because it does call attention to, and in doing so it rearticulates and reforms, the central contradiction in the public performance and reception of rock music and the public persona of the rock star; both rest on the contradiction between the constructed and the unpremeditated, and both rely for their ultimate validation on the open, dialogic status of music as a performance language.

2
Performance and Mediation: Performance, Space and Technology

Performance and liveness

As noted in the Introduction, there are precious few examples in the academic literature on popular music where live performance is treated as performance, rather than as an expression of sub-cultural solidarity or as an incidental part of the industrial processes of popular culture. One of the few writers who treats the process with anything like the attention it deserves is Philip Auslander, whose book *Liveness: Performance in a Mediatized Culture* (first published in 1999) deals with live music as an important, culturally indicative form in itself, and also as a clear example of a process which is overtaking all forms of performance:

> [When] we go to a concert with a large video screen, for instance, what do we look at? Do we concentrate our attention on the live bodies or are our eyes drawn to the screen, as Benjamin's postulate of our desire for proximity would predict? At an industrial party I attended recently, I found the latter to be the case. There was a live band, dancing, and a video simulcast of the dancers on two screens adjacent to the dance floor. My eye was drawn to the screen, compared to which the live dancers … had all the brilliance of fifty-watt bulbs.[1]

In other words, live performance is necessarily collapsing into mediatised representation: any special cultural claims that 'liveness' – the once and once only event, that disappears the moment it is over – could make are no longer valid in a culture that prizes replication over uniqueness.

Auslander's text is a polemic against a particular strain in performance studies, most notably expressed by Peggy Phelan in *Unmarked: the Politics of Performance* (1993). Phelan valorises performance as perhaps the only art form that can't be entirely commodified: it can't be bought or sold, because the moment of performance's incarnation – the moment it happens – is also the moment of its death:

> Performance's only life is in the present ... To the degree that performance attempts to enter the economy of representation it betrays and lessens the promise of its own ontology. Performance's being ... becomes itself through disappearance.[2]

Performance, therefore, is the last, best and indeed the only guarantee of authenticity in a world given over to the power of the image. Auslander, however, argues that the relation between live and mediatised performance is nowhere near as simple; liveness has always been bound up in the processes of mediation – and, as such, liveness is as open to the 'economy of representation' (in that characteristically damning phrase) as any other cultural artefact. In a society which prizes the image over the event, even something as apparently evanescent as live performance has to fall into line:

> Currently, mediatized forms enjoy far more cultural presence and prestige – and profitability – than live forms. In many instances, live performances are produced either as replications of mediatized representations or as raw materials for subsequent mediatization.[3]

Live music – the guarantor of authenticity, the place where the real musician and his or her real fans meet in a real space to see and hear the music recreated, uniquely and unrepeatably – is, in an environment created and policed by MTV, revealed as the profoundly mediatised event that it always really was. In a cultural space where representation precedes and determines performance, any lingering romantic attachment to the authenticating power of liveness is simply untenable. Auslander makes much of the scandal surrounding Milli Vanilli in the early 1990s; not only did the group lip-synch to vocal tracks in performance, but the voices they mimed weren't even theirs. Effectively, Milli Vanilli give the game away. Liveness in popular music has never been live (at least, not in the sense that Phelan intends). It has always been a simulated event; and a simulation, according to Baudrillard, is a representation which does not refer to a presentation. All that has happened, for Auslander, is that the logic which has always governed live performance has finally become apparent.

It is easy, in 2005, to pick holes in Auslander's argument; to note that his examples shift from rock music (Eric Clapton) to pop (Milli Vanilli) when the argument requires it; to point out that, for the traditional rock ideologue he identifies, Milli Vanilli might stand as confirmation of the inauthenticity of pop, and as a back-handed confirmation of the authenticity of a contemporaneous rock group like Nirvana; and to remind oneself that the scandal he describes finished Milli Vanilli's career. One could go further; as the rest of the book will argue, there has been no lessening of the grip of the 'ideology of authenticity' in live performance – indeed, after the cycle of boy and girl bands initiated by the Spice Girls in the late 1990s played itself out, the next evolution of the form married the boy band to the rock band, with Busted and McFly making much of the fact that they could actually play.

More abstractly, one might say that both Auslander and Phelan implicitly rely on the idea that liveness and replication are in some way implacably opposed. For Phelan, they exist in a binary dialectic in the world; for Auslander, they exist in a binary dialectic within the event. However, it makes more sense (as the rest of the chapter will argue) to see these terms not as opposed, but as engaged in a multi-stranded dialogue. As noted in the previous chapter, in rock music the idea of authenticity is not opposed to the idea of performance; rather, the two terms are part of a conversation that fans, critics and musicians have around the true nature of the live event. Similarly, in the performance of rock music, liveness and replication exist in dialogue – and that dialogue is not simply between the authentic and the mediatised. Rather, the dialogue is between the performers, the technology that surrounds them (and the complex processes of authenticity and mediation that the technology opens up), the audience, the industry, the wider culture, the history of the band, of the event, and of the form. Auslander is correct in noting (as other critics have before and after him) that the precise location of authenticity in the processes of rock music is almost impossible to discover; he is wrong in arguing that mediatisation destroys the romantic ideology of authenticity merely by exercising its logic on the event. Mediatisation, as he points out, has already happened; it was there from the beginning; however, it has already been incorporated in the dialogue described above. The event, in other words, always exhibits both liveness and replication; and it does so as part of a far wider, far more complex network of relations than Auslander allows – one that, as discussed in the previous chapter, foregrounds 4Realness (that is, the sense that performance is both constructed and authentic).

Auslander is wrong, therefore, but he is usefully wrong: he calls attention to a tension within the live event, which can be broadened out into a fuller discussion of the characteristic dynamics of that event. To follow through the implications of that discussion, I'll trace the relation between liveness and replication in the performances of an archetypally authentic band, who figured tangentially in the first chapter. U2 have a long performance history, in which they have repeatedly demonstrated a commitment to the idea of the truth of the music they play. However, as anyone who knows the band's history is aware, U2 have also plunged headlong into the mediatised world. Perhaps no other band has explored the tension between the live and the replicated so openly; arguably, also, no other band has managed to expose and illuminate the basic processes of the live event. U2 know their history, and the history of the form; this makes them an illuminating case study, because they lay bare the tensions between the live and the replicated in performance; and because they also provide a good example of the way in which these tensions are resolved – or usefully exposed – in performance.

Performance and narrative

The DVD of U2's *Vertigo* tour (*U2: Vertigo, Live from Chicago*) begins with a track from the current album ('City of Blinding Lights', from the album *How to Dismantle an Atomic Bomb*). The performance starts in semi-darkness, the stage illuminated by what appear to be hanging red lampshades; taped voices resolve themselves into the repeated word 'everyone', as the lampshades are slowly drawn upward. Then, as a cheer signals the presence of the musicians, spotlights shine from the back of the stage, silhouetting Adam Clayton, Larry Mullen, and The Edge. Then, as beaded LED strips descend to surround the stage, Bono climbs up on to the walkway that stretches in a sweeping arc into the auditorium, at the furthest point from the rest of the band, and stands in a spotlight, his head and arms raised as strips of paper, red on one side and white on the other, float down around him. He turns and walks back to the main stage; as The Edge plays the main guitar figure from the track, white spotlights at floor level shine briefly and brightly, directly into the audience. The general tenor (and the general order) of the band's first appearance – group, music, lighting change, then Bono – has, by 2005, become pretty much fixed. It is a version of the industry standard; a high profile suggests a delayed (and perhaps overtly theatrical) entrance; the first song will be from the new album, or from a recent one – unless the group has been touring for so long that the performance is dominated by the history that the group and its audience share; it will begin to reveal the possibilities inherent in the technology; it will declare that the band are there, and that the show will be a good one.

U2 have declared themselves, and the concert proper can begin. It is worthwhile asking, though, precisely which version of U2 the audience are watching. For Auslander, following the argument laid out above, the answer to this question is simple; this is a moment of false authenticity, where both band and audience engage in a consensual hallucination of communion. Both band and audience are mediated and mediatised; U2 are a simulation of themselves – a rock band harking back to a never to be recovered moment of revealed truth, found somewhere in the discredited ideology of rock. However, this is arguably far too simple. As noted above, Auslander is right to note that replication is bound up in performance; however, he does tend to assume that the experience of authenticity is an inherently static one – that, no matter when the gig happens, there is a simple pleasure to be had from the thought that these musicians and no others are up there on stage. However, it could be argued that any live musical performance, especially one by a group of such longevity as U2, is a narrative that at no point resolves itself into a moment of unmediated self-presence. The concert tells a story of the development of the form, and the positioning and pacing of a performance; and the concert also tells the story of the various versions of the band, and the various ways in which those versions have been successively revealed and linked in performance.

If I were to characterise the development of a performance narrative, as revealed by the DVD record of the *Vertigo* tour (which is assembled from two nights' footage, but which mirrors the shape of an individual show almost exactly), it is in terms of a repeated movement toward the audience. Firstly, and characteristically, a pair of fast tracks, the first anthemic, the second ('Vertigo') more intense, composed of distorted power chords in the chorus and midsection against an emptier sonic picture of drums, bass and staccato muted guitar in the verses. During these, the characteristic performance style of the group is re-established: three musicians as workmen, Bono as theatrical focus. During the first couple of songs, Bono sings between the The Edge on his right and Adam Clayton on his left, and directly in front of the drum kit (a formation so frequent for four-piece guitar bands as to be almost paradigmatic). However, he is not rooted to the spot: the energy of his performance moves him beyond the main stage monitors, impels him to lean over the front rows of the audience, and, two-thirds of the way through 'Vertigo', to move back out on to the catwalk which will take him directly into the heart of the auditorium. In the first moments of the performance, Bono reconfirms a characteristic performance style; an outer-directed sincerity, which, at the same time, includes overtly theatrical, illustrative performance choices. The fans take pictures of him, and he mimes taking pictures of them; at the end of 'City of Blinding Lights' he sinks down to the stage, overwhelmed, only to bounce back up immediately to lead the band and crowd through the Portuguese count-in to 'Vertigo'. Both performance modes – sincerity and theatricality – are played directly to the audience, implicitly requesting a response; the sense that Bono's performances are overt invitations to dialogue is well-established in the backstory that U2 have generated. For example, Eamon Dunphy's *Unforgettable Fire* (1987) (which deals with the band's ascent to international stardom) documents many such moments:

> Sometimes Bono had to work hard. He'd look early on for a vote of confidence in the audience; he'd ask them to clap and if they did he was rolling. Or he'd make a statement about music, the world they lived in, the town or hall they were in that night. If the hall responded the band's confidence grew. If not, things would get desperate.[4]

Given U2's secure fan base and commercial position, the nature of such a direct address has necessarily changed. Now, it is paradigmatic; the direct offer of the performance to the audience has to be part of the dynamic of the event. It is how U2 operate; it is known; it is the necessary initial confirmation of a renewed desire for connection between band and audience.

From here, the conversation develops through an invited response ('Elevation', stripped back to vocals and effect-laden guitar for half its length, gives Bono and the audience the first opportunity to engage in communal singing); back into the past that, it is implied, the band and the audience share ('The Electric Co.', a track from the band's first album, is dedicated to those who came to see them in Chicago over two decades ago); back into Bono's own past (he recalls his father, and remembers listening to jazz in Chicago, on tour at the age of 24); through the invitation Bono extends to two audience members to join him in performance (a boy, for 'Into the Heart', and a young woman for 'Mysterious Ways'); through the invitation to political activism that precedes the performance of 'One'; through the other band members' increasing willingness to travel along the catwalk into the audience; and, finally, in the closing moments of the gig, as all four band members stand in a line on the catwalk, leading the audience through a version of 'Yahweh', before returning to the main stage for a long farewell, each musician leaving separately, leaving the audience singing the chorus of '40'. At the end of the concert, Bono shines a hand-held spotlight on the audience; in a gesture of unmissable obviousness, he bathes them in the same light that bathes him.

This much is, it seems clear, intended to be an authentic recreation of unproblematic identity, of the kind that Sutherland (in the previous chapter) celebrates and Auslander derides. At the same time, though, the performance achieves something else, something far less easily assimilable into an ideology of authentic self-presence. Part of the show's dynamic is certainly toward communion; however, there is another dynamic, which takes both audience and band through moments of consciously constructed theatre. As noted in the previous chapter, there is a tension between real presence and performance at the heart of live rock music, which allows both performer and audience to recover even the most overtly performative gestures for authenticity. However, merely to say this doesn't determine the location and nature of those performative elements. Any type of performance requires a vocabulary of performative gestures that marks it out as distinct for audiences and performers. These gestures – agreed behaviour modes which are eternally renegotiable, but at the same time inherently characteristic of particular forms – serve to locate both audience and performers within a particular performance event.

These gestures are part of what Richard Schechner has termed the framing of the event:

> There is an 'axiom of frames' which generally applies in the theater: the looser an outer frame, the tighter the inner, and conversely, the looser the inner, the more important the outer. Thus the improvisational actor is freed from both director and drama, but s/he will therefore have to make fuller use of conventions (stock situations and characters, audience's expectations etc.) and the physical space. The actor will also find himself directly confronting his own limitations: there will be little mediating between him and his audience.[5]

If we substitute musician for actor here, we can begin to determine the constraints that make certain performance gestures (like the ones described above) appropriate in this context. There are no fixed characters for the performers to inhabit (the question of the performer's persona is a complex one, and we will return to it later). Even though the performance has a structure (in this case a conventional one for U2 – new material at the beginning and at the end, more familiar material gradually accumulating from the midpoint of the concert, and heavily featured in the first of the two encore slots), this does not amount to a drama, at least not in the way that Schechner employs the term. However, this performance has a tight inner frame – comprised of characteristic, tropic gestures which serve to locate the performance in a shared history that links the band and the fans (see Chapter 1).

There are three strands to this. Firstly, and most obviously, there are the small performative gestures; the fact that Bono's microphone stand is slightly taller than it needs to be, so that the microphone is angled down: that The Edge wears a hat, and Adam Clayton wears glasses (items of every-day wear rendered significant by their appearance in performance after performance); that Bono's microphone is held up and out to the audience when he invites them to sing; that, during the first two songs, Bono drags the microphone stand down to an angle of roughly 45 degrees to the floor; that The Edge's Les Paul is white, with black bordering. It is of course hard to determine how many of these gestures are picked up by individual audi-ence members, or by the audience as a whole. What is undeniable is that all these gestures connote a general sense of what can only be termed 'U2ness'. There may be performance choices that reflect the performance of the form as a whole (when a chord needs to be attacked, The Edge will execute the downward forearm chop of the generic rock guitarist), but each one of these gestures is mediated through the performance history of U2; there may be a performance language more or less common to many rock musicians, but only U2 speak this language in this particular way.

Secondly, there are those choices which are, in conception and execution, more overtly theatrical. The costuming on the *Vertigo* tour is in the same general style as that adopted for the previous tour (*Elevation*, 2000–1):

> *Elevation* walked the streets, blending easily, moving freely. I wanted the costumes to be in context with the music, speaking the same language … I decided I wanted to maintain their personalities from the street to the stage and back again. I didn't want one overall designer look. I liked the idea that they could walk from stage into a bar and blend in; that they were clothes the audience could relate to … At the same time, how-ever, the show's clothes had to be aspirational. They had to project.[6]

The gestures described above are, it might be said, unconsciously charac-teristic, part of the muscle-memory of the musician; costuming, even when it is chosen to reflect the performer's real self, is chosen to make a point (both about that real self and about the status of the band). It is con-sciously performative, in other words; it positions the band on this tour at this time in their history and reflects upon this position. This general style is carried forward to the *Vertigo* tour; the costumes are similarly a heightened version of the performers' selves, but they also reflect the new material – Bono's leather jacket is marked with red stripes, replicating

How to Dismantle an Atomic Bomb's album cover. Much the same logic governs those moments in the performance where the performative interplay between band and audience shades into overtly staged moments of theatre. 'Bullet the Blue Sky', for example, has been a staple of U2 performances since *The Joshua Tree*; during both the *Zoo TV* and *Popmart* tours, it has been a backdrop for a lightly sketched-in characterisation, Bono appearing as a caricatured representative of US military power. On the *Vertigo* tour, the persona adopted is different. During 'Love and Peace or Else', one of the stage crew hands Bono a bandanna, on which are the religious symbols of Judaism, Islam and Christianity. During 'Bullet the Blue Sky', Bono pulls the bandanna over his eyes and kneels in front of the drum kit, his hands raised and crossed above his head as though they were tied together. As the guitar solo finishes, he fumbles his way toward the microphone; instead of delivering the final monologue, he sings a version of 'When Johnny Comes Marching Home' which describes soldiers coming home to Illinois. Other performative gestures relate directly back to U2's performance history. 'Zoo Station' begins with a quick reprise of the information-overloaded videos of the *Zoo TV* tour, before Bono emerges in quasi-military uniform, goose-stepping and snapping his arm into a *Dr Strangelove*-inspired Nazi salute. During the song, he executes a peculiar sideways leap, his feet together, his arms curved above his head. Each one of these performance choices exactly replicates the performance of the song on the original tour. The gestures have become iconic; they comprise the performance that mediates the song.

I will have more to say about the relation between performance and technology below; but for the moment we should note that the third strand that relates band and audience to a history of performance is staging. This is perhaps more overt in U2's case than it is in the histories of other bands: however, it is probably true to say that, the longer lasting the band, the more self-referential the staging is likely to be (REM's developing predilection for overtly tacky glitter; the baroque staging, and the showers of rose petals, at Rolling Stones gigs; the circular screen, a feature of Pink Floyd's live act from *Dark Side of the Moon* through to *Pulse*; the mock-presidential American crest on the wall behind the drum kit at Ramones gig after Ramones gig, and so on). In U2's case, since *Zoo TV*, each set has grown from the previous one. *Zoo TV* was itself an attempt to rewrite U2's performance vocabulary (which had, up to that point, consisted of relatively simply lit performances in an expanding series of 'generic stage boxes')[7] in the light of the band's discovery of postmodernity. *Popmart* extended the postmodern logic of *Zoo TV* (a bigger screen, a more overt satirical referencing of consumer culture). The *Elevation* tour, a self-conscious return to direct communication, took the central feature of the *Popmart* set – the central arch – and tipped it forward into the auditorium, creating a walkway that embraced the audience. *Vertigo* takes the design of *Elevation* and reimagines it as a series of expanding circles, that begin in the middle of the main stage and stretch past a circular, audience-embracing catwalk to the tiered seating around the venue. An implied history, therefore, is suggested to the audience from the moment that they enter the performance space.

This show, then, comprises a series of narratives; and it is true that at least one of these narratives aspires toward the kind of unmediated authenticity that Auslander sees as characteristic of the form. However, there are others, equally important, that demonstrate the band's willingness to mediate themselves, consciously and unconsciously, for the audience. The performance history shared by band and fans cannot help but play itself out each time a new performance happens; when a band appear on stage, they are already mediated – by the tropes habitual to the genre, and to the band's own history. These operate as a set of strong internal frames (to use Schechner's terminology), structuring the loose narrative of performance.

Performance and persona

In Quirk and Toynbee (2005), Tim Quirk provides an interesting description of a moment of absolute authenticity in performance – a moment where, he argues, it is clearly apparent that Pete Townsend has crossed a performative border between the kind of stage tricks expected of him and true self-transcendence. It occurs during the performance of 'Young Man Blues' at the Isle of Wight; and occurs when Townsend is at his most nakedly iconic – when his arm, once again, windmills around his body before striking the guitar:

> The windmill is now such an iconic gesture that not only does it have a name, but the very footage that so impressed me is featured in a montage sequence in *School of Rock*, when Jack Black is teaching his students how to look and move on stage. If you're like me, though, you notice two types of Pete Townsend windmills when you watch that clip. They look exactly the same, but they feel different. The first is the 'I'm-doing-this-cuz-all-you-fuckers-expect-me-to' windmill. And the second is the 'I'm-doing-this-because-I-can't-help-myself' windmill.[8]

Any performer will recognise this moment: the moment in performance where you seem to get to where you want to go without a clear idea of how you got there. However, Quirk's argument begs a question. Given that both windmills look the same, how does he know that one is more authentic than another? What is it about a performance that convinces an audience that the musician means it? The first chapter began to answer this question: the idea of performance as fundamentally and always inauthentic, as opposed to the reality of spontaneous action, isn't one which has that much purchase in the creation and reception of the music. It is worthwhile, though, spending a little more time on that apparent paradox: what are the factors that enable an audience to make the kind of emotional connection with a performative gesture (and, whether it is conscious or unconscious, Pete Townsend's windmilling arm is a performative gesture) that Quirk describes?

To ask this question is to ask about the relation between the audience and the various personae that performers adopt on stage. As a way into the question, I'll examine two contrasting yet similar performances of a track that has featured in U2's set intermittently for the past two decades. 'Sunday Bloody Sunday' turns up in various versions over the years: a full-band performance (at Red Rocks in 1984; at Slane Castle in 2001); a solo version, sung by The Edge (on the *Popmart* tour); and a duet between voice and guitar which expands to include bass and drums (*Rattle and Hum*). The version caught on *Rattle and Hum* is prefaced, in the film, by an apologetic Bono, wondering out loud whether the version should stand: it was played in the immediate aftermath of the bombing at Enniskillen, and people watching the film might not understand the anger behind the performance. In concert, Bono introduces the song by talking about the Irish in America; some have left for economic reasons, some to escape the Troubles. The song itself, as noted above, starts off with vocals and guitar; Larry Mullen gives time, beating his sticks together. The full band enters immediately after the second chorus, pushing the song forward at a substantially faster pace than the album version. After the guitar solo, Bono, on a platform on the right-hand side of the stage, delivers an impassioned speech about Irish American support for the IRA, climaxing on the shout 'Fuck the revolution!' On the final verse, he returns to the main stage, finishing the song on his knees, his hands grasping the microphone stand. At Slane Castle, on the other hand, there is no introduction: the song follows 'Out of Control' without a break, the crowd cheering as they recognise the opening drum beat. Bono sings the song on the main stage; again after the guitar break, he ties the song to the current state of the Troubles. A ceasefire has been in place for a number of years, so his speech, rather than damning those who support violence without understanding its impact, takes the form of a call and response with the audience, in which both he and they declare their determination not to go back (and, for those fans of the band with long memories, engages the audience in a recreation of the chants first heard during the song's performance at Red Rocks in 1984). He reminds the crowd, though, that it is three years since the bombing at Omagh; and as the song finishes, he reads through a list of the names of the Omagh dead. It is a long list; the other musicians have finished and the lights are dimming before he comes to the end of it.

Both of these performances are passionate: that, of itself, doesn't automatically prove that the passion is meant. In fact, if Auslander's argument above is to be believed, the question can be resolved the other way; there might have been an original action, an original moment of anger that carried Bono through the song, but by the time the recorded performances are circulated, those actions have by necessity taken their place in the chain of mediatisation that binds even the most apparently authentic act. Why, then, would we, on balance, want to follow the audience (and particularly the enthusiastic, then hushed, audience at Slane) and assign a meaning in reality to Bono's reworking of the song?

The answer to this, perhaps, can be found in the moment-to-moment formation of the singer's performance persona. As a means of establishing just how complex this persona is, we'll take, for the purposes of the discussion, the performance continuum mapped out by the theorist Michael Kirby in 1990.[9]

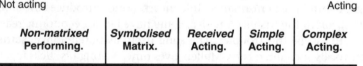

Not acting				Acting
Non-matrixed Performing.	*Symbolised Matrix.*	*Received Acting.*	*Simple Acting.*	*Complex Acting.*

Kirby describes the move from not-acting to acting as the acquisition of a series of details; the performer, onstage presenting a version of himself, gradually becomes an actor through the amassing of an increasingly complex network of performance elements; costuming, emotional and intellectual ambiguity, relation to a complex text or stage image, and so on. In some forms of theatre the actor begins on the right-hand side of this line, and stays there for pretty much the entire performance – a complex character in a complex world; in other forms of performance we might expect that the performer will stay firmly on the left-hand side of the line (the Noh stage hand is a vital part of the performance, and yet he is, conventionally, invisible; his performance persona is predicated on disappearance). If, as Auslander states in a recent article on Suzi Quatro, the rock singer is an actor, then the nature of that act must be reflected somewhere along Kirby's continuum.

And yet, it is very hard to find where; Bono's performance is never still. There are features of both performances that would fit neatly into a symbolised matrix; that is, the simple adoption of some signifying elements (in both cases, the costume he adopts would be a good example; the braces, the high-waisted trousers and the bare chest in 1987 suggest the poor farmer, or the exploited sharecropper; the costuming in 2001 represents Bono, as the costume designer notes above). Other features might push the performance toward received or simple acting: the speeches in each case are imbued with a fair amount of rhetorical power, and in both cases bear some unspecified relation to evangelical preaching – the sudden, abrupt shifts in volume, the invitation to the audience to shout their responses, the overt performance of passion, in which the whole body is involved. However, if we treat all of Bono's on-stage actions as the manifestation of a particular persona – Bono Vox, rather than Paul Hewson – the whole performance, from first entrance to last exit, is a sustained piece of complex acting. On the other hand, we might note that there are moments in each performance that have to be spontaneous – if only because no experienced performer would consciously include them. Bono forgets the words to the second verse in 2001; in 1987, during the most impassioned part of his speech, he strays too close to a speaker and triggers a burst of high pitched feedback. In other words, one might describe Bono's performance in both versions of the track as an unstable mediation. It is very hard to figure out the precise relation of the performance to the person; it is equally hard to figure out the precise relation of the performer to the song (it is delivered with consciously enacted passion: but the passion and the performance cannot be easily distinguished). As the singer commented to John Waters:

> Like most things in our stage show, there are accidents, and if they work you repeat them … It's important to know, and it's something that's hard for a seated writer to spot – but performing to me is like having a twitch. It just kind of comes on. You're *there*, so you *do* something. And if you're on, that spontaneous thing will come off. And if you're not, it really won't.[10]

And in this idea of the repeated accident – the moment of spontaneous performance that works, and then is repeated – we can see the origin of the trope; and in the tension between action and repetition we have, once again, a reaffirmation of the 4Realness of live rock performance.

Performance and technology

Perhaps the most famous, and certainly the most striking, evolution in U2's performance history was the shift between the *Love Town* tour (1989–90) and *Zoo TV* (1991–3). During the 1980s, U2 had established a particular performance style, one which relied on simple lighting and simple stage design. This simplicity was a point of pride: during the *Joshua Tree* tour, The Edge commented:

> With U2, it's the music that makes the atmosphere. There's no laser shows, no special effects. And we always make sure that the sound is as good at the back end as it is down the front. If we succeed or fail, it's definitely down to our own ability to communicate the music.[11]

However, on the next two tours everything changed (bar the commitment to keep the sound as clear as possible, even in the biggest venues). At a time when currents in American rock were pulling performers back toward overt simplicity and direct engagement, U2 charged toward the media-saturated contemporary world with not even a backward glance. Both *Zoo TV* and the *Popmart* tour that followed it used video technology, not only to create stunning images, but also as an integral part of the design of the set. For *Zoo TV*, video screens of various sizes and shapes were piled on top of each other, creating the impression that the band was performing in the middle of a TV showroom; for *Popmart*, a massive video screen (roughly 150 ft by 50 ft) stretched right across the back of the stage. As these descriptions suggest, it seemed as though U2 had taken to heart the idea that post-Cold War culture was thoroughly mediatised:

> In general, [media culture] is not a system of rigid ideological indoctrination that induces consent to existing capitalist societies, but the pleasures of the media and consumer culture. Media entertainment is often highly pleasurable and uses sight, sound, and spectacle to seduce audiences into identifying with certain views, attitudes, feelings and positions. Consumer culture offers a dazzling array of goods and services that induce audiences to participate in a system of commercial gratification. Media and consumer culture work hand in hand to generate thought and behaviour that conform to existing values, institutions, beliefs and practices.[12]

It is sometimes hard to resist the image of the band, and Bono in particular, poring over texts like Kellner's in the early 1990s; and it is certainly tempting to discuss both shows as though they were exercises in practical Baudrillard for the masses – essays in the seductive, simulating power of the media. Another temptation might be to regard both tours as unconscious testimony to the power of mediatisation that Auslander describes. You don't go to these shows for the band; you go for the stage, for the images, for the video – and, for all the effort invested in the performance, U2 might as well have sent in a tape. However, once again, the performance – and the position of an authentic U2 in the middle of the technology – is rather more complex than it might first appear. This is not because of the undoubted satirical intent behind at least part of the performance. It is also not necessarily because, at certain key points in the performance, the band make a point of switching the technology off (*Zoo TV* is the first tour to make use of a B stage, on which a more intimate set is played in the middle of the audience: at certain moments during the *Popmart* tour – during performances of 'New Year's Day', for example – Bono asked for all the lights to be switched off). It is because of the place of technology in live performance, and the logic of authenticity that has formed around it.

In *Rhythm and Noise: an Aesthetics of Rock* (1996), Theodore Gracyk dismisses the idea that what we hear when we listen to rock (whether live or recorded) is a succession of real tones:

> In rock music, the musical instruments are almost always several steps removed from the audience. In live performance, speakers deliver a combination of amplified and electronic sounds. We almost never hear the 'original' sounds; when the electricity fails, the music stops.[13]

This seems commonsensical; it is impossible to ignore the technology in any live event (even the poorest groups have a backline – amps and speakers ranged across the back of the stage, usually to either side of the drums) and the bigger the event, the more unignorable the paraphernalia. In *Popmart*, for example, the PA system – painted orange – was suspended from the arch above the stage, looking for all the world like a giant pumpkin. Here, though, Gracyk's argument comes into conflict with Moore's typology; for example, The Edge's 'original sound' – the one which dominates the early singles and the first album – is generated by a Fender Stratocaster, played through an echo unit and a Vox amplifier. In Gracyk's terms, it is 'removed' from the audience – the tone signal has to be manipulated; however, according to Moore, the tonal signature that is generated is a strong assertion of first-person authenticity – only this tone, generated by this musician, guarantees the presence of the band.

We could go on. Since the mid-1980s U2 have used various types of technology – from the earliest versions of MIDI onwards – to allow them to recreate recorded sound on stage. This might seem to tip the balance too far toward mediatisation, and away from the spontaneity which is supposedly part of the rock event. However, given that this technology is so much part of contemporary performance (it has existed in various forms for the past two decades) and that it is under the control of the musician on the stage (The Edge triggers MIDI effects for each song, and has some control over the shape of these effects in performance), it becomes very hard to see the dividing line between the at least potentially authentic, although heavily treated, guitar tone he employs, and the apparently less immediate, more mediatised backing that MIDI provides. Both types of technology, regarded not as mediated sounds divorced from the 'original' notes, but as extensions of the performers, can stand as further indicators of authenticity in performance. Here, that authenticity comes from the fact that the audience knows (as far as it can know) who is responsible for the sounds: if, in the audience's eyes, it is the band, then that in itself is enough to justify the use of the technology, and to mark it as real. If, in other words, there is enough in the on-stage environment, both in terms of the performance and the technology that surrounds it, to give the audience a clear sense that the band is in control of the event, then the audience will assume that the performance, in all its gaudy splendour, is a reflection of the artistic and creative will of the performers. If a sound is created artificially, by triggering a preset, then that is acceptable if the sound itself is one composed by the musician; if the staging technology displays a clear attitude to the music produced on stage, then it is also acceptable – it stands as the visual representation of the band's or the individual's musical identity.

Gracyk, therefore, misses an important part of the way in which technology is read; he and Auslander also miss the impact that such technology has in performance. In rock music performance, stage technology is expressive and foregrounded – and the bigger the band (most of the time) the more specific the expression, and the more dramatic the foregrounding. In other types of performance, for example, technology is either integrated, and changes in lighting states (for example) are not intended to register directly on the audience; or it is fetishised, made the subject of interrogation (as in contemporary multimedia art); or it is positioned as a selling point in its own right (the obsessive marketing of stage effects in musicals, for example). In rock performance, technology has to mirror the identity of the band, and to follow the musicians as they play the music. This is what differentiates technology in rock performance from the type of technological display that Auslander describes above. For example, Auslander cites the experience of anonymous dancers working in front of a screen which overwhelms them: it is probably a safe guess that, had Auslander paid money to see a performance by a rock band, not only would he have paid more attention to the performers, but also the relation of the performers to the technology would have been different. The video screens, to take a simple example, would have shown him the band; IMAG (image magnification) technology enables even those at the back of the largest venues to convince themselves that those are the real musicians on stage far away. In rock performance, technology is defined by and expresses the performers.

In an interesting recent article, 'U2, Mythology, and Mass Mediated Survival', Fred Johnson talks convincingly of the *Zoo TV* stage of U2's evolution as a fundamental repositioning of a pre-existing mediapheme (a simplified, easily expressed identity created through the process of mediation):

> U2's image shift was more than ... savvy media-play ... Starting with the fact that Bono announced the coming image change, rather than hiding it, U2's image shift was a meta-media play that brilliantly exposed and called into question the very mechanisms and modes of operation of the mass media.[14]

This is undoubtedly true: it chimes in with the portrait of the band in Bill Flanagan's account of the *Zoo TV* tour (*U2 at the End of the World*). Johnson is also correct in noting that, on this tour (as in *Popmart*), technology carries the new, trashy, ironic U2 to the audience. However, it does more than this; it also fulfils the basic function of technology in live performance. Lighting choices and mediated images express the music, and as such demonstrate the band's agency; the multimedia effects are also (and especially in *Popmart*) crucial in creating a sense of immersion in the event – again, one of the predominating features of rock performance. Bruce Ramus, the lighting director for U2 on *Zooropa* (the second leg of the *Zoo TV* tour) and *Popmart*, describes such a moment:

> My favourite is the 'Streets' 'BANG' cue. After the stage gets plunged into darkness, and the punters' pupils are nice and wide and they're leaning forward to try to catch sight of the band, I get to hit the button that lights the entire place up, and sends the audience reeling backward like they've been struck. You can feel it. That cue, with that music, is a powerful moment. Willie [Willie Williams, the show's designer] told me when I was learning the show on *Zooropa* back in 1993, 'This is one cue you can never miss'.[15]

Even in the midst of the information overload that apparently governs both *Zoo TV* and *Popmart*, there are many such moments where technology links stage and audience by expressing the music. Johnson's article, quoted from above, falls down rather with the assertion that, post-*Zoo TV*, a 'real' U2 can no longer be discerned: leaving aside the fact that a 'real' U2 is clearly present, paradoxically, in the midst of the ironic mediatisation of the event (which is, after all, heavily authored – and flagged as such, in interview after interview), the old, authentic version of the band surfaces at such moments – when the lights flood the audience near the beginning of 'Where the Streets Have No Name', when the video screens display, not a piece of ironic text or a carefully crafted image, but the IMAG images of the musicians themselves, engaged in the creation of the music, when the screens flash up images of Martin Luther King, or when (as happened during *Zoo TV*) Sarajevo is phoned from the stage. At these moments, and at many others during these and other gigs, what is displayed is not the moment where agency disappears into mediation, but the moment where mediation reveals agency; at these points, technology does not distance – it immerses.

Conclusion

To return, once more, to *Liveness*, where the chapter began: there is a simple, dialectical elegance to Auslander's polemic. Mediation replaces liveness, or at least the ideology of liveness, and in doing so reveals the lie behind that ideology. As polemic, this might work: but as a description of the dynamic underlying rock performance, it is very badly flawed. It is far more true to the nature of the event to note that there are mediations upon mediations, at every level of the event: between the performers and the technology (both lighting and sound); the performers as individuals and as members of a band; the performers and the various personae suggested either by the music performed, or by the event; between the loose framing of the event itself, and the tighter forming imposed by the band's own performance history; between the particular performance history and style of the band, and the audience's expectations – which are based not only on that history, but on the history of performance in this context; between band, audience, venue, and the industry that drives the event; and so on, and so on.

These layers of mediation, however, do not necessarily remove, or even interfere with, the idea that the event is authentically live. It is easy to forget how deeply embedded are the processes I have described above. When discussing the performance of rock music, it is always worthwhile remembering that mediation has been there from the beginning; and, therefore, that the idea of mediation has been rountinised entirely. Mediation is everywhere in the event; but, then again, so is agency, and so is authenticity. The fact that it is difficult – in fact, probably impossible – to pin down moments of pure mediation, pure authenticity or pure agency does not mean that the real has somehow disappeared. To argue this is to forget, as Gracyk (1996) points out, how persistent, how deeply embedded, and also how useful the idea of authenticity is to those who habitually listen to rock (and, we might add, who go to gigs). Daniel Cavicchi, in *Tramps Like Us: Music and Meaning Among Springsteen Fans* (1998) comes closer than most theorists to an understanding of the complex relation that audiences have with the idea of mediation:

> For fans … authenticity is about Springsteen as a real person … In particular, while critical discussions of Springsteen's authenticity make 'Bruce Springsteen' synonymous with the production of a commodity, fans clearly see 'Bruce Springsteen' as a human being who has had to deal with commodity producing institutions.[16]

The point that Cavicchi makes about the performers' recorded personae can also, of course, be applied to the personae revealed in live performance. The real people are there, within the mood created by the layers of mediation that surround them; the event, governed by technology though it is, does not engage the audience in a false sense of community, but works – is intended to work – toward an experience of immersion, in which band and audience trade on, reactivate and develop a shared performance history.

3
Performance, Gender and Rock Music

Playing the man

Stage shows in rock, the cliché runs, are about sex; at the heart of the experience is a multiple orgasm, shared by performer and audience, so powerful that it renders them oblivious to anything other than the transcendent moment of communal ecstasy. The thrill of unbridled sexuality has, arguably, always been part of the appeal of popular music (one thinks, for example, of the bawdy versions of Burns' folk songs, and the carefully overt *double entendres* in music hall and vaudeville). However, from its inception in the mid-1950s Rock and Roll and its descendants traded in the overt performance of sexuality; those codes which remained to an extent submerged in popular music up to this point burst through into the open. Sex was no longer a by-product of the popular music experience; sex – powerfully apparent in the on-stage personae of Elvis, Little Richard, Jerry Lee Lewis, and later the Stones and (to an extent) the Beatles – was the experience's *raison d'être*.

However liberating this moment (and there are numerous accounts of the impact of a sexually charged music, embodied in a sexually charged performance, on the audiences of the 1950s), it has, for theorists of popular culture, an abiding flaw, which arguably persists to the present. Sexuality in rock is overwhelmingly male (cf. Bayton 1998; Whiteley 1997). This is not simply a question of demographics, although without doubt the paradigmatic rock performer is male (and white, and young). It is inherent, it is argued, in the nature of the event itself: the privileging of the male performer, lit while the audience is in darkness, offered up both as an object of desire and as a subject, comfortably in charge of the desire of the audience. Gender relations in rock performance, a simple reading might suggest, replicate gender relations in society as a whole. Men are in power, and exercise their power publicly; and those who lack that power, those in the dark, are forced to undergo a process of enforced feminisation. This, at least, is the main thrust of a well-known argument in popular music studies. In the late 1970s, Simon Frith and Angela McRobbie proposed and defined a particular genre that they termed 'cock-rock' (in Frith and Goodman 1998). This style was, according to their original argument, a barrier to female incorporation into the practice of the music. Its aggressive maleness was an overtly sexualised deterrent:

> In male music, cock-rock performance means an explicit, crude, 'master-ful' expression of sexuality (the approach is most obvious in the singing style that derives from Led Zeppelin's Robert Plant, in the guitar hero style that derives from Led Zeppelin's Jimmy Page). Cock-rock performers are aggressive, boastful, constantly drawing audience attention to their prowess and control. Their bodies are on display (plunging shirts and tight trousers, chest hair and genitals), mikes and guitars are phallic symbols (or else caressed like female bodies).[1]

Frith's and McRobbie's initial article (and Frith's further adoption of the term in *Sound Effects* (1983), from which the above quote comes) is one of the earliest theoretical attempts to define an intrinsically male performance style in rock. In some respects, the original thesis holds good, and developments in performance technology have made the phallus (and its numerous substitutes) even more apparent. For example, wireless technology, in use since the 1980s, has allowed performers far more freedom than was the case when Frith and McRobbie were writing. It has also allowed Mick Jagger to stuff his microphone down the front of his trousers. One does not have to be schooled in psychoanalysis to grasp the implication; this is as phallic as it gets.

Sometimes, then, in performance, the penis substitute is clearly and unambiguously a penis substitute. There is ample evidence of the overt use of guitar and microphone as phallic objects: but it should not be forgotten that these are conscious performative choices, rather than symbolically coded revelations of hidden male power. For one thing, if the guitar is already so innately phallic that it demands to be located over the crotch, why would some musicians feel the need to go further? And for another: one of the problems with such a relatively direct application of Freudian symbolism to the performance of rock music is, as Susan Fast has noted, that it does not take into account the fact that on stage, under the lights, the male body is on display – and is thus objectified (at least to an extent). The rock star is there to be looked at, and fans (male and female) are adept at constructing their own readings based on the same information, filtered through their experience of the world. There is no one version of masculinity that is unambiguously revealed when we apply a term like 'cock-rock':

> In what but the most superficial way does [Jimmy] Page's visual iconography compare to Guns n' Roses' guitarist Slash, to take an extremely contrasting example? Or how can the performance of gender by Elvis, Mick Jagger, Roger Daltrey and Plant – the four performers that Frith and McRobbie lump together – be taken as the same in anything but the most superficial of ways?[2]

Sheila Whiteley's 1997 essay on Mick Jagger ('Little Red Rooster and the Honky Tonk Woman', collected in *Sexing the Groove*) makes much the same point: in performance, Jagger's persona does not remain within an easily defined gender identity:

> Thus it is suggested that Jagger's role as singer is analogous to that of a complex character in an unfolding drama. He was, is Little Red Rooster, Jumping Jack Flash, Lucifer, the Midnight Rambler. His creation of a developing persona suggests an identity that is gendered and, at times, only ambiguously sexed.[3]

This captures the complexity of Jagger's body in performance (although I am unconvinced by Whiteley's suggestion that a performance persona is adopted, which allows Jagger to function in character: see Chapter 2 above). No one is denying that these performances are highly sexualised: however, the idea that only one type of male sexuality is on display ignores both the objectifying nature of the event (which removes at least some control from the performer) and the fact that male sexuality is itself inherently complex.

There are other objections: firstly, that to define male sexuality in performance simply as a display of gendered power leaves little room for women, either as spectators (and Fast, quoted above, is very clear on the erotic pleasure to be had from the ambiguously gendered bodies of both Page and Plant) or as performers. For example, in the 1990s the touring festival Lilith Fair was set up as an explicitly feminine alternative to the more conventionally masculine Lollapalooza; however, as Theodore Gracyk commented in 2001:

> For all its economic and media success, Lilith Fair quickly came to stand for rock's safe, non-disruptive *ecriture feminine* ... A major profile of

Tori Amos described the Lilith crowd as 'mild-mannered Pottery Barn poets,' while Amos herself worried that such festivals cannot sustain the focus and psychological intensity for her art.[4]

Another objection is that, over the past three decades, a large number of male bands and artists have set themselves up against the dominant social discourse of masculinity; and this of necessity has been reflected in the music they choose to play, and in the style of performance they have adopted. Simon Reynolds, in *Rip It Up and Start Again* (which deals with the post-punk and new pop era), notes that the thinness of the post-punk guitar sound, and the conscious avoidance of overt technical skill in much post-punk music, was a conscious attempt to emasculate (as well as to demystify) the practice of rock. Andy Bennett, in 'Plug In and Play: UK Indie Guitar Culture', links this directly to the figure of the guitarist in performance:

> [Indie] guitar players often assume a rather static on-stage posture, looking down at their fret-boards or the floor, a tendency that has resulted in the coining of the term 'shoe gazing' by music journalists ... The use of the guitar in any form of on stage posturing that even remotely resembles the thrusting movements of heavy metal players appears to be an unwritten taboo within indie guitar circles. In many ways the rejection of such masochistic and overtly sexist perform-ance traits represents a further facet of indie guitar's self-conscious manoeuvring into an anti-rock position.[5]

It is interesting to note that the upsurge in Indie music in the early 1990s presented two challenges to an apparently conventional demarcation of gender in performance, one from each gender. The shoe-gazing man was matched by the riot grrl; groups like Bikini Kill used performance to pro-mote an overtly aggressive subversion of gender categories (by, for example, demanding that female spectators move to the front of the crowd). There seems, therefore, to be pressure on the conventional image of the phallic rock god not only from without, but from within the practice of the music. As Mimi Schippers argues, this is a complex issue, which cuts squarely across conventional ideas of masculine and feminine display:

> Within the context of rock culture, adopting masculine styles makes a lot of sense. Alternative hard rockers consciously rejected the gender-bending, glam-metal bands of the 1980s, acutely aware that the same men who were wearing makeup and spandex were also the ones who

fully embraced the sexualised masculine position in relation to women. In their efforts to create something new, they not only threw out the sexual norms of glam metal, but also rejected the gender display.[6]

A well-made point, and an interesting one. For Auslander, Glam in its 1970s incarnation is the site of gender ambiguity; for Schippers, Glam-metal in the 1980s is preening, strutting cock-rock incarnate. Against this, the working man's clothes adopted by Neil Young in the 1970s as the sign of an authentic maleness now become the preferred dress code for the ambiguously gendered alternative hard rocker. In such a shifting environment, any sense of hard and fast gender categories that are always and necessarily revealed in performance melts away. We are left with an evolving argument over gender identity, in which the opposing sides' discarded clothes and styles can be picked up, used and reused.

Therefore, there is no reason why simple gender categories should be used in the analysis of rock performance; such simple categories do not exist, and arguably have never existed. However, this does not mean that rock music has managed to escape gender altogether. In what follows, I will argue that rock music in performance is predicated on a particular sexual identity. It is male – but this maleness is not homogeneous; and neither is it necessarily a comfortable fit for the performer. Rather, rock music performance is predicated on a sense of masculinity in crisis. This is what allows the codes of male behaviour and identity to be mixed and matched with such abandon: it is also what allows female performers to inhabit and contest those codes (as will be argued in Chapter 7).

Pierre Bourdieu, writing in 2001, provides a coherently argued account of the relation between gender identity and a manifestly unequal social organisation:

> The social world constructs the body as a sexually defined reality and as the depository of sexually defined principles of vision and division. The embodied social programme of perception is applied to all the things of the world and firstly to the body itself, in its biological reality. It is the programme which constructs the difference between the biological sexes in conformity with the principles of a mythic vision of the world rooted in the arbitrary relationship of domination, itself inscribed, with the division of labour, in the reality of the social order.[7]

He is clear, though, that such a division is far more deep-rooted than some postmodern theorists of gender would have it. For Bourdieu, sexual difference and gender differences are not a simple question of naming; neither can they be overcome by a simple call for the 'supersession of dualisms'.[8] They are embedded in our social organisation, in our language, in our habitual behaviour. For Bourdieu, socially enforced gender divisions actively resist subversion; simply queering gender discourse (as some theorists do) does not of itself disrupt fixed categories of male and female behaviour (cf. Bayton 1998, for a salutary, if depressing, reminder of this). However, this does not mean that gender identity is necessarily immutable. Changes in social and economic organisation lead to changes in behaviour; these changes are at their most apparent when the social formation that creates them is itself predicated on the idea of change as good in itself. John MacInnes, in *The End of Masculinity* notes that:

> Modernity produces societies which are 'transitional', in the sense that they combine the material and ideological legacy of a sexual division of labour produced by the patriarchal era which preceded this, with material and ideological forces that undermine that legacy and create the conditions for a sexually egalitarian order. Gender is the fetishistic ideology inevitably created by this transition and its contradictory social forces.[9]

In other words, gender is itself a crisis formation. It only arises when that which was invisible is made visible; male behaviour is now placed under scrutiny, because the conditions that formed it no longer apply. It is only at moments like this – when there is a seismic shift in the conditions that produce particular types of gendered behaviour – that these types of behaviour effectively go on display: their constituent elements are anatomised, their habitual modes of expression are matters for debate, and the worldview they incarnate is subject to critique. When the society is 'transitional' (that is, when change is its central dynamic), the critique described above is well-nigh constant; there is no universally agreed fixed point, no agreed mode of correct behaviour, against which it will come to rest. In the rest of the chapter, I will argue that male behaviour in rock performance is characteristically an expression of this on-going crisis; that a performance style which can embrace both a representative of the common working man and a gender-bending devil incarnate is one of the most visible examples of a deep-seated crisis in male behaviour, which shows no sign of abating.

Working men: Bruce Springsteen and the E Street Band

In the run-up to the *Born in the USA* tour, Bruce Springsteen went to the gym. Previously rather slight, at least on stage (Springsteen was never exactly waif-like: but next to the towering figure of his saxophonist Clarence Clemens, he had always appeared oddly insubstantial), he undertook the tour in prime physical condition. Images from the performances show Springsteen in T-shirts and denim waistcoats, his newly muscled arms bare. In this, he was not unique: in American popular culture, the 1980s was the decade of hyper-inflated masculinity. Springsteen's newly acquired biceps were flexed in the same cultural marketplace as Stallone's or Schwarzenegger's; superficially, it might have seemed as though, after the introspective, self-lacerating doubts of the 1970s, America was now interested in images of aggressively masculine strength – and that Springsteen fitted right in to the new dispensation. He might have expressed concerns over the co-option of *Born in the USA* by Ronald Reagan's re-election team; but even a quick glance at images from the 1984–5 tour – a muscular, bandana'd Springsteen thrashing his guitar in front of a massive Stars and Stripes – suggests that, if Reagan's election team were mistaken, it was a forgivable mistake.

There was, however, a marked contradiction between the newly inflated figure of Springsteen on stage and the figures who had come to populate his songs. It is a commonplace of writing on Springsteen (see for example both Marsh's and Sandford's biographies) that his writing moved closer and closer to direct reportage as his fame increased. The typical male figure in an 80s Springsteen song was the superfluous working man: the figure marginalised by changes in the economy, unable to reconcile himself to a world which no longer needed his skills – a stranger in his country, in his town, and (in songs like 'The River') in his home. Judging by the lyric sheet included with the album, the grease monkey on *Born in the USA*'s cover was not a proud working man; he was more likely a divorced barfly, ruefully remembering the days when there was work to do.

This contradiction, between a confident assertion of physical masculinity and an acknowledgement (at least in the lyrics) of the vulnerability of that masculinity, also worked itself out on stage. Springsteen had, in previous tours, developed a number of introductory monologues, some of which were exercises in comic mythologising (travelling through the New Jersey backwoods with Clemens, in search of the archetypal tools of rock – the guitar and the saxophone). Some, though, were more openly personal. It was an avowed part of the Springsteen persona that the singer had endured a troubled childhood: if any fan came to the gigs ignorant of this, Springsteen would enlighten them, taking them through a potted history of his life, from Asbury Park to the present. In 'Bruce Springsteen and Masculinity' (to which I am indebted for the points raised above), Gareth Palmer discusses the performative significance of these monologues:

> From the early 1980s onwards Springsteen's performance as an ordinary guy has been enhanced by long, rambling monologues in which he discusses his upbringing. The most famous of these have concerned his troubled relationship with his father, also expressed in songs such as 'Independence Day'. The monologue is a point of connection, the private man reaching out to his fans. How can we doubt such a truth when it seems so sincere?[10]

As the previous chapters have argued, though, there is a sufficiently ambiguous relation between performance and reality in rock music to allow fans to accept the presence of a performed and a real self (as noted in the previous chapter, Daniel Cavicchi's research into the attitudes of Springsteen's fans would seem to bear this out). The contradiction is, therefore, not between an apparently sincere performance and an authentic self, but between versions of masculinity played out in performance. Palmer argues that this contradiction, on closer examination, can be resolved in conventionally masculine terms:

> It is as if the body was trying to toughen itself against a world which has bruised him. This display of muscle is itself a 'natural' display of masculinity that supports patriarchy while the singer speaks of the limitations of such a system.[11]

It is to his credit that Palmer puts scare quotes around the word natural here; such an obviously constructed physical presence betrays its artificiality, even to the casual observer. However, he is wrong to assume that, especially in the context of the times, Springsteen's muscularity (which he retains; Springsteen is a substantially bulkier performer now than he was in the 1970s, and this bulk is not simply a by-product of ageing) represents a simple appeal to natural masculinity. Firstly, at the time when Springsteen's muscles were unveiled to the world, such a display suggested the high-concept, all-action FX film star more than it did the natural man (see, for example, Tasker 2002). Secondly, a muscular display such as Springsteen's was, arguably, an inversion of patriarchal body codes; men's bodies are not supposed to be objects – and, in sculpting his body, Springsteen arguably revealed, not that he was taking refuge in a 'natural' masculinity, but that he was creating for himself a fetishised gender identity (as MacInnes notes above).

Thirdly, though – and perhaps, in performance, most importantly – Springsteen's new physique was placed in a different setting. As recently released footage of Springsteen's 1975 London shows demonstrates, some of the most striking performative moments (the singer disappearing into a gap between podia during the last verse of 'Spirits in the Night', for example) were enhanced by lighting which unambiguously identified Springsteen as the star and key focal point of the show. By the mid-1980s, the lighting had become simpler, more even and less obviously emphatic. Now, Springsteen was lit as a band member, as well as the star. This change has particular resonance in Springsteen's case; part of the mythology that had come to surround him concerned the E Street Band, and his relationship to it. The E Street Band is a crucial part of the on-stage narrative of Springsteen the performer; they are the archetypal home-town gang (even though the personnel have shifted, and even though Springsteen dispensed with their services in the early 1990s, they provide a direct link back to Springsteen's earliest days as a recording artist). Typically, their presence is invoked throughout the show (in monologues; in repeated cries of 'Steve' to Steve Van Zant, or 'Big Man' to Clarence Clemens; in dialogue exchanges; and so on). Most obviously, though, the band are lit. At the beginning of the set on the *Rising* tour (documented on *Bruce Springsteen and the E Street Band: Live in Barcelona* (2002)) Springsteen starts 'The Rising' conventionally, in a spotlight centre stage. However, he is not alone: those musicians who play on the first verse are clearly, if less emphatically, lit behind him. When the song moves to the first chorus, the lights come up generally, to provide the basic white wash (with spotlights on individual band members) that is the default lighting state for the rest of the show. The lighting plot suggests an equality, even though, in terms of dynamic performance, Springsteen is definitely the focus; we don't watch a star and his touring band – we watch a group of working musicians and their leader.

The distinction is a crucial one. It matters – it is a crucial part of the Springsteen mythology – that this group of musicians backs this artist. The E Street Band are a fixed point against which Springsteen is measured; to an extent, his perceived distance or proximity to his old band mates is a measure of his distance or proximity to his roots. However, this does not mean that the identity of the band in performance has remained the same. In the mid-1970s Springsteen's extreme scruffiness was balanced by the equally extreme smartness of Van Zandt and Clemens, his two main on-stage foils. Visually, the band defined itself against the workaday world; the E Street Band came on stage dressed for a night on the town. By the time we reach Barcleona in 2002, the reformed band are dressed for the most part sombrely, in dark brown and black (the sole exception is the violinist Soozie Tyrell, dressed in burgundy) and there is no longer a visual contrast between Springsteen's clothing and that of the rest of the band. Springsteen's enhanced physique, as noted above a hang-over from the mid-1980s, does not mark him out as an American superhero; rather, it places him on a more equal footing with the rest of the band. He isn't the biggest man on stage; but he is no longer the slightest. Visually, Spingsteen and his band are far more of a piece; and now, the costuming suggests work – or at least a less carefree attitude to play.

The working men and women of 2002 have replaced the boys on the town of 1975: this, rather than the Ramboesque musculature adopted in the mid-1980s, is the decisive change in Springsteen's and the E Street Band's performance style. However, as has been noted above, the band became working men and women (mirroring the development of Springsteen's writing) at a time when the idea of work, and especially of men in work, was undergoing a sea-change:

> The US economy is rapidly changing, moving from an industrial to a post-industrial society. Jobs that once served to secure the lives and identities of many working-class people are swiftly becoming a thing of the past.[12]

The type of identity that Springsteen has come to endorse, both in his writing and in performance, is an idealised version of a unionised white working man: in touch with his community, in touch with his heritage, but inclusive (his band has always contained at least one Black American, and from the mid-1980s onward, at least one woman). His nickname (the Boss) in performance suggests not the capitalist king of industry, but the first among equals union leader. He works alongside his band; he works up more of a sweat than they do, but the stage presentation at least implies a kind of performative democracy. However, as noted above, this portrayal is presented at a time when the conditions that shaped it no longer apply; when the working class in America (and especially the white working class) is turning in on itself. That Springsteen himself is aware of this crisis is clear. He has, after all, released an album called *The Ghost of Tom Joad*; and it does not stretch credibility too far to see Springsteen and the E Street Band, in performance, similarly trying to raise the spectre of the idealised working man.

America's most unwanted: Marilyn Manson

As argued in the previous chapter, rock performance from the 1960s onwards is largely a matter of recurring (and mutating) tropes. One of the most powerful of these tropes – in fact, arguably the first – is the trope of the sexually threatening male. This comes into rock directly through the first generation of rock and rollers, who were both defiantly male (and prone to display their sexuality in performance) and also, disturbingly female (if the male archetype of the 1950s was that of the strong silent man, then Presley and his cohorts represented the ultimate transgression; loud, immature, and prone to overt display). The cock-rockers described above are similarly ambiguous. They are male, and they engage in performative bouts of aggressive sexuality, but they are also (at least in terms of the cultural norms of their time) feminised; their hair is sculpted, or long; their clothes are carefully chosen, for visual effect rather than for utility; and, crucially, they put themselves on show. In other words, by the time that Marilyn Manson (the name refers both to the star and the group) released their first album, such androgyny – overt or covert – was not simply an accepted trope in rock performance: arguably, it was one of the signs through which the form declared its presence to the rest of the world. This undoubtedly meant that the shock value of the trope was worn out through sheer repetition; what was shockingly ambiguous in the 1970s had become the matter of mainstream pop in the 1980s. Shock exhausts itself; and anyone seeking to rediscover the original transgressive impetus behind the trope must by necessity take account both of the trope itself and the shifting context that it inhabits. Or, as Manson put it:

> nothing is ever really new. It's a reinvention of a kind, as everything is these days. Everything comes back eventually, but whatever trend is reinvented it's always with a different angle...[13]

– and any musician seeking to employ shock tactics as a conscious device has constantly to battle the cultural ennui Manson describes. And yet, during the 1990s, Manson managed just that. His impact was at its greatest in America; and his persona, both in recordings and especially on stage, is built around the destruction of American icons. Something of the adroitness with which he manages this can be gleaned from the following:

> Marilyn is on stage at the Big Day Out, Britain's biggest heavy metal event of 1999. A huge sign lights up behind him as he stalks toward the audience, leaning like a preacher in predatory mode. The sign says 'DRUGS'. 'I had a dream', the Reverend Manson announces to the assembled congregation. 'I was drowning in a sea of liquor, I was washed up on a beach made of cocaine, the sky was made of LSD, the trees were made of marijuana, and God came down from heaven. He

asked me to spell his name, and I asked him how. He said, "Give me a D, give me an R...U...G...S..." What does that spell?'[11]

It is not easy to find a way to mock the pieties of the religious right and the post-Woodstock liberal left simultaneously, but in neatly conflating a sermon with an ironic version of the Fish cheer, Manson manages to do so surprisingly neatly.

It could be said, though, that for a significant proportion of American society Manson did not need to act out either an ironic valorisation of drug culture, a satirical attack on religion, or a cynical celebration of the inherent authoritarianism of American cultural life. All he had to do was stand there. A skeletally tall man in whiteface, wearing a corset, thong, stockings and heavy boots is a sufficiently disturbing figure, invoking as it does both gender transgression and at least a passing acquaintance with fetishised sex. When the costume is combined with the name, the impact of both is heightened:

> In the name of embodying opposing extremes, Marilyn Manson highlights powerful icons of voluptuous womanhood and domineering manhood, in Marilyn Monroe and Charlie Manson. His persona combines elements of traditional masculinity – like his aggressive stage performances – with characteristics traditionally associated with femininity, such as his flamboyant dress and make-up.[15]

Manson is here laying claim to a long tradition in rock performance: a performance style that marries aggression and at least the most obvious social tokens of femininity. It is a style embraced by David Bowie, Iggy Pop and Kurt Cobain (amongst many others); and as such, one might think, there is no extremity left in it. A sense that maleness can be displayed is now such a part of music culture that it does not need further noting. Why, then, was Manson such a shock? Why would he be such a convenient scapegoat on which to pin responsibility for the Columbine massacres, even though there is no evidence that either of the teenagers who committed the crime were fans? Which particular nightmare did Manson incarnate?

At least part of the answer to that question is indicated in the singer's name, which amalgamates the names of two American icons. However, it is surely a mistake to see (as Baddeley argues) Charles Manson and Marilyn Monroe as relatively unproblematic representations of American man and womanhood. Manson has yoked together these two icons for shock value, certainly (and the naming policy extends to the rest of the band – Madonna Wayne Gacy, Twiggy Ramirez, and so on); but both Manson and Monroe also register on the cultural barometer as profoundly damaged representatives of their gender, who took socially agreed notions of male and female behaviour to their destructive endpoints. Manson, a socially marginal psychopath, played out a male fantasy of control (both social and sexual) to the point of mass murder; Monroe's suicide is, in the cultural vocabulary that Manson and his audience share, the sign of a peculiarly female vulnerability.

Both Manson and Monroe are damaged examples of the gender constructions that surround them: Marilyn Manson, in picking these two icons, explicitly constructs himself as a damaged gender hybrid. There is a world of difference between calling yourself and your band Marilyn Manson, and calling it and yourself Alice Cooper, for example; Alice Cooper is an unfreighted name – it drags no cultural debris behind it, beyond the connotation of everyday white femaleness. Even the knowledge that the name originally belonged to a woman burned at the stake as a witch (and that, apparently, she revealed herself to Vincent Furnier via a ouija board) is not enough to shake this perception; the name itself does not carry any automatic cultural meaning – except that of sheer, bland ordinariness. Marilyn Manson on the other hand suggests madness, murder, suicide, cultic religion, corrupt politics, and the all-pervasive gaze of the media; it is the kind of name one might find in a cyberpunk novel, or in J.G. Ballard. It is this image – the image of the damaged gender hybrid enshrined in Manson's chosen name – that is carried forward into performance.

In *Heavy Metal: the Music and its Culture* (2000), Deena Weinstein gives a good general account of the performance style associated with Metal as a genre:

> The heavy metal performer must translate the powerful, loud and energetic music into his body movements and facial expressions. He must be acrobatically graceful enough to jump, leap, and generally bound across the stage.[16]

Not even his most dedicated fan would call Manson graceful. In fact, quite the opposite: his movements on stage are habitually awkward, unaesthetic, and sometimes dangerous. The costume he adopts makes any fast movement well-nigh impossible; props used during performance only hamper him further. During 'The Nobodies' (*Guns, God and Government* DVD), for example, he manoeuvres around the stage on elongated crutches and stilts, with his microphone attached to a metal skullcap. On the same tour, during 'Cruci-fiction in Space', a riser carries him high above the stage floor. Black material, attached to his waist, drapes down to the floor; and Manson is held in place by guardrails just above the level of his waist (which are hidden by the cloth). Not content with simply gaining height, he throws himself back and forth against the restraining harness, his upper body jerking like a puppet. On a red podium, set against Nuremberg-style hangings bearing the silhouette of the rifle-crucifix described above, Manson sings 'Antichrist Superstar' with the same characteristic jerks and puppet-like lurches. Even when unencumbered by props, Manson moves across the stage at walking pace, his shoulders hunched over; periodically, he collapses, or collides with the other musicians or the stage furniture (the accompanying documentary on the *Guns, God and Government* DVD shows the result of one such collision; a jagged wound in Manson's knee has to be stitched backstage). In part, this extreme physical ungainliness is part of the specific generic subdivision of Heavy Metal that Manson inhabits: Industrial Metal is constructed around slower beats and a monolithic, heavily chorded playing style that does not give the same musical impetus for fast, flowing stage movement as one might find in a Guns n' Roses gig (see Chapter 5). There is a strong similarity between Manson's onstage movements and those of Trent Reznor of Nine Inch Nails (see the *And All That Could Have Been* DVD, for example): the same consciously adopted gracelessness, the same sense of physical non-coordination. Reznor's onstage persona, however, doesn't carry the same gender codings as Manson's; Manson's costume – the corset, the tights, the boots – represents both a quasi-pornographic take on gender costuming, and, in its general disrepair and in his awkward attempts to remove it, a snare that he cannot escape.

In 1990, Judith Butler argued that transvestites

> can do more than simply express the difference between sex and gender, [they] challenge, at least implicitly, the distinction between appearance and reality that structures a good deal of popular thinking about gender identity.[17]

This might do as an explanation of the crisis of gender representation that was provoked by David Bowie in the early days of his fame; it might also be a good description of the implicit threat posed by Mick Jagger in the context of the early 1960s. However, it does not serve as a good description for Marilyn Manson, because Manson's performance style is built on what might be called failed transvestism. The threat posed by Ziggy Stardust was made manifest in the ease of Bowie's movements; here was a performer who could exist comfortably in an indeterminate space between male and female. Manson's performances operate in the same location, but they do so very uncomfortably indeed. The trope that shocked in the 1970s, because it feminised the male body, is shocking again in the 1990s partly because this time it emphasises, not sensuality and liberation, but constriction, alienation and pain.

Performing men

In *The Explicit Body in Performance*, Rebecca Schneider analysed contemporary feminist performance art as the

> re-enact[ment of] social dramas and traumas which have arbitrated cultural differentiations between truth and illusion, reality and dream, fact and fantasy, natural and unnatural, essential and constructed. The performers make apparent the ways in which bodies are stages for social theatrics.[18]

To link feminist performance art and Bruce Springsteen (or Marilyn Manson, for that matter) might seem to be an exercise in academic perversity; however, if I were to look for a term which adequately sums up the performances of both musicians (and which can be broadened out into a useful term to describe the performance of gender in rock generally) then 'social theatrics' is by far the most easily applicable. Performance in rock music is social in two commonsensical ways: the performer's habitual actions are heavily socially conditioned (to the extent that they form identifiable tropes), and they are played back to a socially conditioned audience (whose own behaviour is predicated on a knowledge of musician, style and cultural context; see previous chapter). At a time when, as noted above, the habitual practices of masculinity are no longer as apparently automatic as they once were, any popular form whose practitioners are overwhelmingly male (such as rock music) will find itself playing out the 'social dramas and traumas' of gender identity by default.

That this is the case can be seen from even a casual acquaintance with performers as diverse as Springsteen and Manson. Springsteen's body is constructed, certainly; in its own way (and especially in the mid-1980s) it is as consciously theatrical as Manson's make-up. However, Springsteen's persona and his relation to the rest of the E Street Band is also constructed – this time in relation to a vanished ideal of male behaviour. Manson breathes new life into an old trope of masculinity in crisis – the androgynous and/or feminised male – by playing it as Gothic bodily horror. For both, performances are shaped in the light of an absent idea of masculinity; for Springsteen, the union hero is no longer there, and for Manson, the original position of the hybrid performer – as a critique of conventional images of maleness as socially and sexually invisible – is reaffirmed in a performance which cases the hybrid male performer as traumatised victim. Both define themselves against ideas of manhood which do not perform; in Springsteen's case, the idealised union boss has no need to declare himself, because he is sure of his position, and Manson's whole persona is a calculated affront to Bible belt patriarchal authority – again, to a variety of manhood which does not make a spectacle (far less a transsexual spectacle) of itself.

Springsteen's and Manson's performances, then, are variations on a well-established theme. They are concerned with maleness, but maleness in crisis. The most obvious impact of this crisis is that men are now on display; and its most visible manifestation is the male body in popular culture, which is both subject and object, still undoubtedly male and yet open to styles of behaviour more usually thought of as feminine (from Jagger's artfully discomposed hair to Manson's mascara). This crisis is not a sign, however, of the imminent death of gender categories: I would agree with Bourdieu that these categories are deeply ingrained, and have not yet been shaken loose – the very fact that, in performance, Manson can construct a performance persona by adapting a trope from a previous stage in the crisis suggests as much. Male performers in rock music do not simply reanimate male power each time they play live; neither is the relationship between performer and audience as overtly and as conventionally sexualised as the quotes at the beginning of the chapter might suggest. Mavis Bayton (1998), Andy Bennett (2001) and Matthew Bannister (2006) have argued convincingly that the male domination of rock music is largely a question of socialisation, rather than any overt gender identity that the music itself must express; however, even that socialisation is part of the crisis – part of the social transformation that MacInnes notes above. The practice of rock music is, in far too many cases, hedged around with the kind of casual misogyny rightly deplored by Mimi Schippers, by the female journalists collected in *Girls Will Be Boys: Women Report on Rock* (ed. Liz Evans), and by the female musicians interviewed by Bayton (1998). However, the fact that there is no agreed, cross-genre style of male behaviour (and given the fact that, within genres, there is no consensus either – for example, Heavy Metal is a performance style broad enough to include both Freddie Mercury and Fred Durst) means that in practice and performance rock music is remarkably porous. It can play host to a nearly infinite variety of socialised male behaviours; what it cannot do, thankfully, is to re-establish the male figure, in the position that it used to occupy – the unacknowledged, yet all powerful, centre of society.

Part II
Performance, Authenticity and History

4
The 1960s

The evolution of a performance paradox: Elvis Presley, The Who

There are several possible dates for the birth of Rock music: the release of *Sergeant Pepper* in 1967 (or the release of *Revolver* the year before), which established the album as not only a coherent unit in itself, but as the major source of income for record companies; 'Like a Rolling Stone', the first six-minute single, which decisively expanded the aural and lyrical possibilities of the form; 'Pet Sounds', Brian Wilson's riposte to the Beatles' growing international dominance; and so on. In performance, though, the birth of rock arguably coincided with, and was spurred on by, the sudden absence of two of the new term's parents. The Beatles' growing dissatisfaction with live performance nearly led to the dissolution of the band in 1966: George Harrison, who described the prospect of the band's last US tour as '[going to] get beaten up by the Americans',[1] threatened to quit after the last gig in San Francisco. *Sergeant Pepper* confirmed that the Beatles were now a studio-based band. Bob Dylan's departure was altogether more dramatic: touring America and Europe in 1965–6, playing sets that were half acoustic and half electric, he faced nightly condemnation from those sections of his audience who were convinced that amplification (and a backing band) obviously indicated that a generational spokesman had sold out. Film of the tour, released on the *No Direction Home* DVD in 2005, shows a Dylan who is clearly exhausted – in fact, almost punch-drunk – by the tour's end. Even when responding to one of the most famous audience interventions in postwar popular music (the cry of 'Judas' – a taunt, according to C.P. Lee, claimed by two members of the audience) Dylan's response is not overtly angry; his 'I don't believe you' is weary, and his instruction to the band to 'play fucking loud' seems like nothing so much as the final rallying cry of a tired officer leading his exhausted troops over the top one more time.

However, a new style of performance does not simply spring from a sense of dissatisfaction with the way that things currently are: performance, as an explicitly social event, is a useful bell-wether for wider cultural changes – and live music is no exception. Partly, the pressure for a new performance style came from a new audience with an increasingly confident sense of its own cultural and economic importance.[2] As this new market grew, it dispersed: and bands working in the late 1960s benefited from developments earlier in the decade, which had seen various sub-genres of popular music attract specific types of audience. The Mods in Britain adopted American R&B and soul, and came to think of The Who as a house band. The emerging Hippie movement in San Francisco quickly claimed The Grateful Dead as their standard bearers. Frank Zappa's first exercise in practical ethnography occurred in the mid-1960s, when he defined and sought to shape a loose community of the socially isolated under the general category of Freaks (Slaven 2003). These emerging audiences developed a new relation to the music of their choice: it was no longer necessarily simply entertainment or escape – rather, the process of involvement with a band married enjoyment and identification in various proportions. Dave Marsh's 1983 biography of The Who begins with an almost archetypal encounter between band and fan: 'Irish' Jack Lyons, a prototypal Mod, first encountered Pete Townsend at a gig in 1962:

> [Jack's] gaze fell upon the bandstand and the guitarist at stage left, half-hidden behind a jumbo acoustic. The sight of him riveted Jack, forced him to edge nearer. 'I wanted to get a proper look', he said, 'cause it made my bloody night, it did. When I got close up to him, I could see he was wearing my true face – the face I always wanted. In him I could see me, if you know what I mean.'[3]

Jack's thinking was rather more pragmatic than the above quote might suggest (if he had a nose like Townsend's, he reasoned, people would be so busy insulting it that they would forget his Irishness); however, it does suggest the beginnings of a new relation between bands and audiences – a relation of near-equals.

This new-found equality was based initially on a shared experience of fandom. When, famously, Keith Richards and Mick Jagger met on Dartford station in 1960, Jagger was holding an armful of obscure blues and R&B albums:

> Keith was impressed. It wasn't just that Mike [Mick came later] was carrying these records. It was that anyone in England had them

at all … 'Just sitting in that train carriage in Dartford, it was almost like we made a deal without knowing it, like Robert Johnson at the crossroads…'[4]

The last comment is particularly telling: in retrospect, Richard accords the meeting the same mythical status as the *ur*-legend of Johnson selling his soul to the Devil. Cultural, social and racial divides dissolve, and the music passes, not from source to fan, but from bluesman to bluesman – and, in doing so, fulfils the fan's dreams. To ally yourself to this type of music – music that existed outside the commercial mainstream, music that had (for the committed fans who wished to express this commitment by playing the music themselves) a richer, more inherently rewarding scope and emotional range than more overtly commercialised brands – was implicitly to make a statement about your own authenticity as a potential performer. You had returned to the root of rock and roll, you had scraped away the accumulated rust of commercialisation and you had reached the authentic, true metal beneath. (Eric Clapton's relation to the blues is perhaps the paradigmatic example of this; his career path in the 1960s can be thought of as an ever-frustrated search for an authentic blues style.) Certain types of American music conferred authenticity on British performers. However, America also did something else. It provided British performers with access to the authentic past, but also with a glimpse into a culture which at the time seemed more exciting, more in tune with the future, than Britain. Brian Eno likened listening to early rock and roll to listening to sounds from an alien civilisation (cf. Tamm 1995); for Hank Marvin and the Shadows in the late 1950s, merely buying an American guitar was a means of gaining access to another world:

> The guitar arrived at a flat shared by Hank, Bruce and Cliff (Richard) in Marylebone High Street. When they opened the tweed case, saw the crushed velvet lining, smelled that smell and saw the pinky-toned Strat with birds-eye maple neck, gold-plated hardware, three pick-ups and a tremolo arm, no-one spoke. No-one touched it for a while: they just stared at it.[5]

This is rather more than simple happiness at the acquisition of a new guitar; it is irresistibly reminiscent of the encounter between ape and monolith in *2001*. It is also, in its own way, an encounter with a version of authenticity; the Strat is the authentic tone of exotic, exciting and forward-looking America.

In the US, fans were engaged in a similar quest for the authentic. For example, two of the founder members of The Grateful Dead, Jerry Garcia and Robert Hunter, found inspiration in Harry Smith's *Anthology of American Folk Music*, which appeared in the 1950s (cf. McNally 2003: 62). For American musicians like Garcia, the need to find, and to position oneself in relation to, musical forms perceived as more authentic than the mainstream was as strong as it was in Britain; however, and obviously, the music to which he and others turned would never carry the same romantically distanced charge as it would in the UK. It did, however, incarnate a different vision of American society, one which managed to root itself both in hidden histories of slavery and poverty, and in the progressive political and cultural movements that aimed to change America. However, if for some British musicians there was something authentically American (and therefore progressive) in the electric guitar, for some American musicians there was something authentically political (and therefore progressive) about the acoustic guitar:

> As a ubiquitous element of folk clubs and festivals during the folk boom, the acoustic guitar became an integral part of a 'site of resistance to the centralisation of power' (Kirschenblatt-Grimblett 1992). Folk Festivals, the best-known being the Newport Folk Festival and the Mariposa Folk Festival (Brauner 1983; Usher 1977), which included blues artists, became cultural scenes where acoustic guitars and performance were pervasive, places in which participants experienced what Jacques Attali has described as the 'jongler's return'...[6]

– that is, a return to music as inherently democratic communication rather than as spectacle.

In both the US and the UK, therefore, a significant part of the audience listening to popular music listened to it self-consciously, not because it was entertaining per se, but because it gave them access to a vision of experience that appeared to be authentic. The significance of this section of the audience was not so much in numbers as in motivation; put simply, a generation of musicians in the 1960s gained their first exposure to music as fans (as arguably had been the case for most of the century), but at a time when a particular feature of the music to which they listened – its perceived authenticity – was foregrounded to a greater extent than had been the case before. However, this authenticity wasn't simply located in the music's past; bound up in it was also an idea of the future – of the social and cultural possibilities that this music opened up. The search for an authentic style of popular music was, therefore, a rather protean undertaking: from the first, it took those engaged in it in a variety of directions – into the history of the form, into the possibilities inherent in the new technology available to bands, into the political and social transformations that seemed to be happening spontaneously in Britain and in the US. There was no one path for the music to follow: rather, at the time, a number of routes opened up – and they all, in their various ways, seemed to lead interested musicians toward at least a type of authenticity. If there was a unifying factor that characterised journeys along each one of these new routes, then it was to be found in the idea that the musician could potentially be accorded the same social status as other serious artists. After all, the reason that both Dylan and the Beatles had left the live circuit was that, for different reasons, their artistry was not recognised as such by a significant part of their audience. In both cases, the audience would not allow the artists to develop their art: if nothing else, the sudden removal of both Dylan and the Beatles from live performance seemed to prove that categories that had been more or less fixed (pop music, which should invite screams; folk music, which should invite reverent and attentive silence) had come under pressure from the musician's own need to change. Rock music, at its inception, had therefore an ambiguous relation to its audience; a band might, as noted above, grow from a particular audience, but equally the relation between band and audience might be antagonistic, or uncomprehending, or at the very least tense.

This was new. For previous generations of performers, the imperative was to capture and sustain an audience by whatever means were possible. Elvis Presley's performance style, as has been exhaustively documented, was developed with an audience in mind; playing short sets (three or four numbers at the most), as was common at the beginning of a career, a performer had to connect with their audience as quickly as possible. Impact was everything; performance techniques were adopted pragmatically:

> [Presley] could read every audience: it was, evidently, an innate skill. 'I see people all different ages and things,' he said years later, trying to explain it. 'If I do something good, they let me know it. If I don't, they let me know that, too. It's a give and take proposition in that they give me back the inspiration. I work absolutely to them.'[7]

Presley's performances (and the performances of his contemporaries: Jerry Lee Lewis, for example) were in essence designed for one overriding purpose. Performance tropes (dropping to one knee, thrashing the guitar, shaking your legs and your hips, kicking away the piano stool, playing the keyboard with your feet, and so on) were not motivated so much by the content of the material itself, but by the performer's need to sell the material and themselves to the audience. Musicians at the end of the 1960s might reject this performance style as irredeemably compromised by the pressures of commercialism; as noted at the beginning of the chapter, in the early and mid-1960s at least some bands had developed what seemed to be a closer, more organic relation to their audiences. However, the same imperative applied; Pete Townsend might claim that smashing equipment at the end of a Who gig was an exercise in pop art auto-destruction, but, once the performance gesture was established and its impact on the audience apparent, Townsend found himself caught up in the same logic that informed Presley's performance style. As Dave Marsh noted in 1983:

> But what's perhaps most curious about the Who's auto destruction ... is that the cue to keep on smashing came from the crowd, which perceived this as some sort of 'valid statement' weeks before the group did. It was the fans who gave the event meaning, by choosing to interpret Townsend's original broken instrument not just as a part of the show but as a part that could and should be repeated.[8]

An expression of an authentic emotion (in Townsend's case, the anger that he identified as the key emotion driving him on stage) becomes a trope almost as soon as it is expressed.

For a group and a musician who found themselves at the forefront of the movement from pop to rock, this presented a problem, which has already been described: the need to reconcile the apparently irreconcilable logics of expression and performance.

Townsend might say in 1965 that 'What we are trying to do in our music [is] protest against "show biz" stuff, clear the hit parade of stodge'[9] but The Who's performances, to a cynical observer, might seem as much a part of show business as P.J. Proby's famously unreliable pants; Townsend's smashed guitar, like Proby's eternally ripping trousers, was a theatrical gesture that had proved itself in front of an audience time after time. Townsend's performance style might have been learned from his audience (early accounts of Who gigs attest to the closeness of band and spectators), and his most ambitious project, *Lifehouse*, might have been predicated on the outcome of a series of concerts at the Old Vic in 1971; however, interviewed in 1966, he was rather less sanguine about the relationship between the band and its audience:

> You have to resign yourself to the fact that a large part of the audience is sort of thick, you know, and don't appreciate quality, however much you try and put it over. The fact that our group ... hasn't got any quality, it's just musical sensationalism. You do something big on the stage, and a thousand geezers sort of go, 'Ah!' It's just basic Shepherd's Bush enjoyment.[10]

It is hard to imagine Elvis Presley, in the early years of his fame, talking about his audience in these terms. The art school-trained Townsend, reflecting on his own place in a popular music tradition which was, by that time, over a decade old, feels himself licensed to express dissatisfaction with an audience that prizes entertainment over art – or, put another way, theatricality for its own sake over authentic self-expression. The paradox was, of course, that even this dissatisfaction was not enough to stop the instrumental carnage; at the end of 'Won't Get Fooled Again', recorded for *The Kids Are Alright*, and the very last time that the original four-piece band played together, Townsend was still using his Gibson to batter a cymbal across the stage. At the same time, The Who's stage show had undergone the same process as other successful bands of the era: more amplification, more lighting (including lasers during the penultimate section of 'Won't Get Fooled Again'), designed to reach larger and larger audiences.

It is fair to say that, of the long-term members of The Who, only Townsend was troubled by the paradoxical relationship between the musician as artist and the popular audience. Keith Moon turned the practice of rock drumming into an evolving clown-show; John Entwhistle cultivated an overt anonymity, his very stillness a powerful performative statement; and Roger Daltrey developed mannerisms which not only displayed his musculature (bared chest inflated, arms either extended at the apex of a punch, or framing his torso) but which extended his onstage presence, allowing him to take up more room on stage than he would otherwise do (whirling the microphone in front of him, before snapping it back into his hand for the next vocal line). It could be said that Moon, Entwhistle and Daltrey's attitude to performance marked them out as a product of their environment; each one had served an apprenticeship in popular music as entertainment, and never felt the need to agonise over their relationship to their audience in the way that Townsend did. Townsend shared this apprenticeship: but his attitude to the band, its audience, and the expression of that relationship in performance, is part of a new paradigm, one characteristic of rock music, in which the tension between art and entertainment was played out in gig after gig.

Performer and audience: The Grateful Dead, The Doors

One of the abiding images of popular music in the late 1960s is that of the crowd at Woodstock, stretching away from the small stage to the horizon in every direction. It is an image which seems to encapsulate at least a part of the ethos of the time: that a generation had come together, with a shared agenda and a shared, inherently communal spirit, to develop a new form of society in which popular music would play an integral part. In reality, of course, the large-scale grouping of young Americans at Woodstock was nowhere near as inclusive or undiscriminating as all that: the number of black faces in the Woodstock crowd is very small, and (as the film amply demonstrates) the Hippie image of the good life contained a great deal of casual misogyny (it seemed somehow to be tied up with repeated shots of naked women). However, even if the idyllic self-image of the Woodstock generation cannot and should not be taken at face value, it is still useful; it is the most visible manifestation of a new relation between bands and audiences, in which both performers and spectators were part of a unified gestalt. As Edward Macan notes, this new dispensation was not simply a matter of sloganeering; it was a crucial part of the organisation of new performance spaces:

> Around 1966 and 1967 a series of clubs opened in London, San Francisco and other major counter-cultural centres specializing in the presentation of psychedelic music. The relationship between performers and audiences at these clubs was extremely close; for instance, when the Sunday afternoon 'Spontaneous Underground' series was introduced at London's Marquee club in February 1966, there was no division between stage and audience. It was [a] type of symbiotic relationship between the audience and the band members, who were themselves products of the counter-culture.[11]

Normal society was rigid and stratified; the counterculture was organised horizontally rather than vertically; it was inclusive rather than exclusive, and it was organic, rather than mechanised. Previous generations of performers had sought to achieve a kind of unity with their audiences, if only on the shared desire to have a good time; countercultural musicians operated on the starting principle that they and their audiences were the same. This is not to say, though, that this assumption was always correct; nor was it the case that the shared experiences of bands and audiences were necessarily those of the counterculture at its most utopian. The history of The Grateful Dead, for example, might seem to be an exemplary demonstration of the ideals of the counterculture, but it was not the only set of ideals on offer.

The Dead's formation – in the Haight Ashbury district of San Francisco – exactly coincides with the moment when the remnants of the Beats of the 1950s metamorphosed into the new Hippie movement. The band were well placed to pick up on the forces that shaped this transformation; they were part of the same cultural milieu that produced, amongst other things, this all-embracing diagnosis of contemporary society's faults, offered by one of the most radical groupings in the Haight:

> [The Diggers were] a radical anarchist group that was really about authenticity and autonomy ... Because we knew the real problem was the culture. The problem wasn't capitalism. The problem wasn't communism. The problem was the culture.[12]

Viewed charitably, this is a sweeping, radical condemnation of the times; viewed uncharitably, it is almost meaningless – but it does at least point to one of the main motivating forces behind the Dead's development into a band whose most characteristic musical signature (long, flowing improvisational passages) could only be inscribed in live performance:

> [Garcia] ... So there'll be a sentence, it'll be X long, like four bars, then there'll be like the answer to that, four bars long, then there'll be like a summing-up of it that'll be like eight bars, and then there'll be an argument from the other direction, that'll be eight bars, it's kind of like that ... But as it's going along, there's also things coming in from the other band members, which sometimes say, like on bar three, 'No, no, no, this is now number one'.[13]

This description of the Dead's approach to performance strongly suggests that no one is in charge. If the problem with the world is the culture – or, as one might guess, culture imagined as hierarchical and restrictive – then the Dead, creating unrepeatable improvisations that are not governed by the will of one band member, might be said to be involved in creating a musical counterpoint to a failed social order.

This is to take the band at their own best estimate: as McNally's exhaustive biography repeatedly demonstrates, Garcia was the band's undoubted leader – and the group were frequently hamstrung by his reluctance to take decisions. It does, though, explain both the music that the band produced live, and also the relation between band and fans. The most fanatical of the band's followers – christened Deadheads – participated in performance not as spectators, but as a crucial part of the performance. They provided the ultimate justification for the band's improvisatory style:

> 'Deadheads are very patient and forgiving', Micky Hart (one of the band's two drummers) says. 'They let us do what we want musically, knowing it's not always going to be great ... and that's the best thing an audience can give me: the freedom to play what I feel. It's that way for the entire band. Our strength is in their numbers and their openness.'[14]

This attitude to the audience explains the Dead's characteristic performance style, which can be thought of as an attempt at the creation of a centreless community. When one looks at footage of the Dead playing live (for example, the closing of the Winterland Ballroom in 1978) what is most striking is that the band lacks an obvious central focus. There are three musicians (Garcia, Bob Weir, and Donna Godchaux) at the front of the stage, but none of them fulfils the role of front person: Godchaux is not on stage continually, vocal duties are shared between Weir (who makes some concessions to communicating songs to the audience; he faces forward, emphasises moments in the lyrics gesturally, looks animated) and Garcia, the band's most famous member, who is diffident while singing, looking off to the side or over the audience's heads. When the band improvise, they do so without physical emphasis – no posing, few shared moments of dynamic movement. There is no strong visual focus to hold the audience's attention: the attention of both band and audience is on the evolving textures of the music. In fact, it could be said that for the Dead and for the Deadheads, this communal, centreless involvement of both band and audience in the music is itself a defining trope.

The Grateful Dead could develop an improvisatory performance language because they evolved a strong communal relationship with their audience; however, in doing so they were exceptional. More commonly, performance techniques aimed to create a quasi-religious communal experience for both band and audience foundered, not because bands became successful and grew away from their original audiences, but because there was and is something unstable in the relationship between performer and audience, which militates against the assumption of equality. The Doors shared many features in common with The Grateful Dead: an interest in the mystical and the spiritual (Jim Morrison was interested in shamanism, and in the spiritual practices of Native American tribes; Ray Manzarek, the band's keyboard player and a practising Buddhist, used to light a joss-stick and place it on his instrument before each performance); an apprenticeship in the clubs and electric ballrooms of the west coast; and a frequently expressed dissatisfaction with the way things were. However, the history of The Doors demonstrates clearly the specificity of the new type of audience. From the beginning, the Dead could claim an authentic connection to its audiences because San Francisco itself was regarded as a more authentic location (cf. Hoskyns 2003: 144). It was easy for the Dead to maintain a sense of authentic connection with their audience, because they could trade on the existence of a supportive audience whose relation to the band formed the basis for the Deadheads – the band's own portable community. For The Doors, a more commercially successful band than the Dead, based in a location that did not offer the support of a unified underground (illusory and partial as that unity undoubtedly was), the live event was as likely to be an exercise in disillusion as it was an ecstatic communion. At the Hollywood Bowl in 1968, Morrison is nearly motionless throughout, and the audience is clearly unengaged (they can be seen walking back and forward in front of the stage as the band play): worse were the moments where his desire to provoke the audience collided with his chemical intake, as happened in 1968 at the Westbury Music Fair in Long Island:

> As the show progressed, Jim kept taunting the audience, making sexual suggestions to the girlfriends of tough-looking guys ... A fat security guard tried to restrain Jim, and was in turn grabbed and fondled by Jim while he suggested the guy lose weight. Humiliated, the guard ran up the aisle, dropping his police-type hat, which Jim seized as a trophy. Suddenly he let out a piercing scream that froze the blood of everyone in the house ... The shocked silence was deafening. Jim was twitching spastically, as if he were having an epileptic fit.[15]

Even if one subtracts some of the hyperbole from Davis's account, the image of a performer barely in control of himself and of the event is clear.

Partly, the problem was Morrison's own depressingly swift descent into alcoholism; partly, it was that a performance style honed for small clubs, and for an audience versed in the underground and perhaps more liable to accept behaviour which departed from the conventional, was transplanted on to a different type of stage. In conversation with Mick Jagger in 1968, Morrison admitted as much:

> They talked about dancing on-stage. Mick said he was embarrassed about his dancing. He said the one thing he couldn't do was dance. And he and Jim [commiserated] that it was increasingly difficult to feel comfortable and to feel smooth dancing on-stage. The larger the audiences got, the larger the working area was, and the less you could relate to it. Everything got more exaggerated.[16]

Watching footage of The Doors now, it is hard not to concur. Morrison's bouts of movement – described by his various biographers as examples of shamanic, ritual dancing (Davis 2005; Hopkins and Sugarman 1989) – are uncoordinated and arrhythmic (see *The Doors at the Hollywood Bowl*); a repeated performance trope – crouching in front of the drumkit, before executing a spinning jump to the microphone – nearly carries the flailing Morrison into the audience (see *The Doors in Europe 1968* for repeated examples of this). On a small stage, such movements might look thrillingly dangerous; on larger stages, they are inadequate, demonstrating Morrison's and the band's inability to fill the space successfully.

As a performer, Morrison's and The Doors' enduring legacy is not the liberation of the psyche through quasi-shamanic, quasi-Artaudian experiential performance. Rather, it is most clearly apparent in those moments when Morrison moves slowly across the stage; when he drapes himself around the microphone stand, his eyes closed; and when he takes advantage of a prolonged instrumental break to talk to the front rows of the audience, instead of taunting them. Here is the archetypal image of the poet in rock; the centre of attention, immersed in a self-created world; the star, sharing himself with adoring fans. One can find this trope repeated in subsequent decades; something of it shades Robert Plant's quieter performative moments; Patti Smith, Bono, Michael Stipe and Nick Cave run variations on the basic template; and Bobby Gillespie of Primal Scream adopts the model almost without alteration. Powerful though this image is, it is not the image of the shaman, the people's spiritual leader, leading his people towards transcendence; it is the image of the star, simultaneously the centre of the event, and aloof from it.

Performer and technology: Pink Floyd

Part of the impact of Dylan's tour of England in 1966 came from the sheer physical presence of the equipment that the music required. The PA system and the amplifiers were considerably more powerful than those used by British bands: Dylan and the Band were loud – in the contest between the musicians and the unruly audience the musicians would undoubtedly win, if only when they were playing. Previously, the contest had been rather more even. Audiences that came to see the Stones in the early 1960s were so vociferous that their screams could drown out the band; apparently, Brian Jones frequently took advantage of this to play 'Popeye the sailor man' while the rest of the band were playing 'Satisfaction' (Davis 2002). With an increase in available volume (and with the development of a new generation of powerful amplifiers and speakers; in particular, by Jim Marshall in London), bands were able to exploit an increased range of sonic possibilities (including feedback and distortion); increased volume also allowed bands such as The Who to create immersive musical environments, in which the sound was sufficiently loud to blank everything else out.

Alongside amplification came other technologies. In particular, lighting came to play a far greater part in performance:

> Apart from a few brief aberrations, design began in rock with the psychedelic era. Barry Melton, musician and designer with Country Joe and the Fish ... explains how the psychedelic movement in rock design – lightshows – came into being: 'The San Francisco movement, if it was about any one thing, was about ego loss, or not being egotistical and this was why the lightshow developed at that time and in that place. In a lightshow environment, musicians could not be stars. They were just part of the environment. The light was as important as the music, and the feeling that was generated was the most important thing of all: the atmosphere. It had to be a feeling of togetherness, anti-ego, communality ... Lightshows, by blurring the shapes of figures and covering everything with light and shadow and colour, created the right sort of environment for the period.'[17]

Lightshows quickly became a selling point; initially tied to specific venues (Bill Graham's Fillmore and Winterland ballrooms in the US, and the UFO club and the Round House in the UK) which were themselves associated strongly with the underground sub-cultures in both countries, and run in tandem with louder amplification, they helped to provide the illusion that venue, musicians and audience existed in a space which was qualitatively different to the world outside. If the audience were drugged, even better: but, even if this was not available, light and sound worked together to replicate the LSD experience as closely as possible.

For the groups most closely allied to the underground, lighting – and the opportunities it offered for an environment that was under the band's control – was too good a technology to pass up. Lighting and sound could be used, not simply to highlight a performer and to render the music audible in a crowded room, but as expressive environmental tools; they could express the ethos of the music, and of the particular band. For Pink Floyd – regulars at the new venues in London – experiments in light were as important as experiments in sound; new technologies, and the opportunities they offered, were eagerly embraced, even if the equipment was rudimentary and downright dangerous:

> One of [Peter Wynne Wilson, the band's lighting man's] ... creations used a movie light, pushed beyond the recommended limits to achieve maximum brightness. In front of this was mounted a coloured glass wheel spun at extremely high speed ... With two wheels the possibilities

were not just doubled but squared. By adjusting the speed of both wheels colours were produced that could only be sensed ... But the uneven temperatures, the shaking and banging, and the wildly spinning colour wheels, meant the glass had an alarming tendency to run out of control and shatter noisily, sending vicious shards of glass flying into the band at very close quarters.[18]

Even though the band risked impalement nightly, the lightshow was worthwhile. It transformed every venue at which it was used into a version of the UFO club; by extension, it allied band and audience with the cutting edge of the London underground scene. It wasn't necessary to have actually attended multi-media events like the 14-Hour Technicolour Dream (held at the Alexandra Palace as a benefit for the International Times in April 1967; in addition to performances by Pink Floyd and other underground bands like Soft Machine, the lighting towers projected films onto makeshift screens, and a helter-skelter was set up in the middle of the Palace). The Floyd's stage show recreated the ethos of such events every time they played. As the press release for the band's next major event, Games for May (held at the Queen Elizabeth Hall in May of the same year) put it, 'The Floyd intend this concert to be musical and visual exploration – not only for themselves, but for the audience too'.[19] In other words, rather than the band accommodating itself to the venue, the venue would, through the use of the band's favoured technologies, be converted into an environment suitable for both band and fans. The trend toward creating designs that can be moved from venue to venue begins with such experiments; before, the idea of bespoke design that aimed to express something of the band's music and image was technically impossible.

The new lighting show had, for Pink Floyd, another welcome side-effect: it masked the band's own inadequacy as performers. What early footage survives suggests strongly that Syd Barrett, the band's original singer and guitarist, was the only member of the band to possess any performative flair. Shots of the band playing 'Astronomy Dominie' capture Barrett, his arms stretched above his head; as he sings a descending vocal line, his arms swoop down in time with the tune. His departure left a void, which in other bands would have been filled by an equally dynamic replacement. This did not happen; footage of the band from the late 1960s onwards clearly shows a group of musicians comfortable only while concentrating on playing music. There is no difference in body language between the band's performance in an empty Roman amphitheatre (in *Live at Pompeii*) and a sold-out show at Wembley two decades later (*Pulse*). The characteristic performative tropes that have marked and defined Pink Floyd's performances are all created through technology and staging. When the band reformed in 2005 to headline Live 8, they did so against the original footage broadcast on stage during the tours for *Dark Side of the Moon*: these films performed the same performative function as Pete Townsend's wind-milling arm had done, when The Who played the same event – they signi-fied the authentic presence of the band.

Performer and race: Eric Clapton, Jimi Hendrix, Janis Joplin

In December 1968, shortly after leaving Big Brother and the Holding Company, Janis Joplin took her new backing band to Memphis, to play at the Stax/Volt Christmas party. This was an ambitious debut: the band was unprepared, and the audience was, for a number of reasons, liable to be difficult.

> Memphis, as it turned out, was a lot more like Las Vegas than San Francisco, where everyone but Bill Graham collaborated in the fiction that what they were doing wasn't showbusiness. Bay Area audiences wanted realness, not slick displays of showmanship. Janis' group realised the extent of the chasm separating them from the other acts when the reformed Bar-Kays came out wearing 'zebra-striped flannel jumpsuits' ... Stanley Booth of *Rolling Stone* looked on as Michael Bloomfield's eyes got very large and members of the new band shook their heads in disbelief. Booth observed 'It was the first sign of the cul-tural gap that was to increase as the evening progressed.'[20]

Things did not improve. For one thing, Joplin's band, schooled in the eti-quette of the Bay Area, took up the first ten minutes of their slot in decid-ing what they were going to play. To an audience used to a more tightly structured and organised performance style, this did not seem natural; rather, it seemed something of an insult (Shaar Murray 1989). Joplin's fail-ure was compounded, moreover, by the fact that the audience was mostly black; the band was rejected, as Sam Andrew (one of the musicians) made clear later, by the very community that had created the music it played:

> Janis wanted to emulate Aretha [Franklin] and Otis [Redding], but before we even had the repertoire down, we were going to play in front of one of the most demanding audiences in the country, our heroes from Stax ... It was intimidating, playing the blues for black people ... How dare we get up there and play their music?[21]

There is a complex and tense social history embedded in this quote; it speaks directly to the tense relation between a newly emerging rock music and black American musical culture at the end of the 1960s. On the one hand, as the quote suggests, there was simple hero worship (which, for some blues artists, had the welcome effect of reviving careers long since buried); on the other, hero worship coexisted uneasily with a long history of appropriation and exploitation. Moreover, black American musicians were themselves caught up in the profound social changes of the time:

> With a radical new movement being led by churchgoing blacks, the new music on the streets was influenced by the music of the church. Civil rights songs began to hit the streets, often as updated gospel tunes ... Rhythm and Blues music as 'statement' music would grow into soul music and eventually take on more explicit themes of protest, particularly after the changes promised during the civil rights movement failed to materialise.[22]

And as the racial situation in America turned to violence, with the assassinations of Martin Luther King and Malcolm X, and the wave of urban riots that followed on from the Watts riot in 1965, the relation between the cutting edges of white and black American popular music forms became even more fraught. As a generation of largely white performers developed the newly serious, self-aware musical and performative language of rock, so a generation of black musicians developed an equally serious, equally self-aware musical and performative style – Funk, which was, in the context of the time, the medium through which black performers chose to speak most directly about the position of blacks in American society. Walking into such problematic territory relatively unprepared might have been an act of the utmost foolishness; it also draws attention to the fact that, performatively as well as culturally and politically, the gap between white and black America was very wide.

This is not to argue, though, that such a gap reflects anything more essential than the political realities of the late 1960s. As Dave Headlam pointed out in 2003, to argue that the relation of white to black musicians is necessarily always that of originator and exploiter is to ignore the history of the musical forms themselves:

> The view that awards Robert Johnson the mantle of the original master of country blues and Eric Clapton a condemnation as a shallow imitator, for instance, ignores the traditional evolution of blues songs, where continual reworking of lyrics, melodies and instrumentation

into ever new styles is fundamental. In this context, Johnson and Clapton are similar, in that they took from many existing sources and reworked songs, in either close covers or more dramatic reconstructions, to create their own styles.[23]

The relation of white performers to blues artists in the late 1960s is as complex as the above quote suggests. On the one hand, and especially in Britain, blues music managed to fulfil a number of needs: it was, in tone and in content, rather more adult than the music found in the charts; it had a heritage which stretched back into the nineteenth century; it had (for British artists especially) a sheen of the exotic about it – it required the assimilation and understanding of a musical and social language that at that time had no counterpart in Britain; for white American performers, blues and folk shared the same commitment to exposing oppression in the society of the time. On the other hand, the blues as a form had by the late 1960s largely been abandoned by black Americans. By the turn of the 1960s, artists like Muddy Waters found having hits very difficult: those black artists whose music did owe a significant debt to the blues – Chuck Berry, for example – had developed a style which made their work acceptable to a younger, white audience. Blues, as white musicians encountered it, was part of a musical heritage, rather than a part of the present. It provided musicians such as Eric Clapton and Brian Jones with a pantheon of hero figures – Elmore James, Muddy Waters, B. B. King and pre-eminently Robert Johnson – who could stand comfortably as both surrogate father figures (Jones took on Elmore James's name at an early stage of his career) and cult figures, whose work was not accessible to, and therefore not tainted by, a mass audience.

When Eric Clapton approached the blues, then, he did so with a great deal of reverence. This was not any form of music: the form, tone and shape of the music guaranteed authentic art, merely by existing. It allowed the musician to express himself authentically, both on record and in performance. A solo, no matter how long, was not simply a matter of instrumental virtuosity: it was the medium through which Clapton spoke directly to an audience. As he said in 1967, 'My guitar is a medium through which I make contact with myself. It's very lonely.'[24] This statement, made just before the formation of Cream in 1967, is a useful description not only of Clapton's, but the band's performance style. The Grateful Dead, described above, might not feel the need to provide a strong central focus for the performance, but they do make eye contact with each other throughout even the longest improvisation. It is possible, in fact, to follow the changes in musical tone and pace, and it is certainly possible to trace the development of solo passages, by following the eyelines of the various members of the group. Cream on stage (as caught during their last show at the Royal Albert Hall) seem locked in their own individual worlds; most of the time, through the longer instrumental passages, Jack Bruce and Clapton have their eyes closed – a decided contrast to the unceasing watchfulness of the Dead. Of the two, Bruce is the most animated: for example, during 'Spoonful', he responds to a particularly dynamic part of the improvisation with a broad smile (but his eyes remain closed). Clapton, however, is entirely occupied with the music that he and the band are making: his closed eyes, his relatively static stage persona, and his occasional moments of truculence ('If we play "Sunshine of your Love", will that satisfy you?') mark him out as the most serious artist in a serious group.

Blues, for Clapton and for Cream, provided a platform for self-expression: although their music borrowed the idea of flowing improvisation from jazz, and lyrical ideas and the occasional chord pattern (as in 'We're Going Wrong') from psychedelia, blues was the base language that all three musicians spoke in performance. Their commitment to an idea of musical and performative purity, derived from an idea of the blues, was as responsible as the worsening relationship between Bruce and Ginger Baker for the eventual break-up of the band:

> [Every] gig was big during the first year and a half. Then it started getting silly. We'd walk on stage to a standing ovation, before we'd even played a note. And that wasn't fantastic, because we'd be doing gigs we weren't happy with, and yet we'd get this enormous wave of adulation. We'd think 'Come on, that wasn't the best stuff'. It got silly – and it got unbelievably loud.[25]

It is interesting that one of the factors that Cream (alongside The Who and Hendrix) are credited with bringing to the live event – extreme volume in performance – is cited by Bruce as a contributing factor in the increasing dissatisfaction that he and the band felt. Volume, which Bruce defends when interviewed for the Albert Hall documentary as a physical experience for the audience, becomes a problem when it stops the audience from judging the self-expressive artistry of the performance.

Cream brought to the blues the seriousness of the archivist: Jimi Hendrix's performance style was far more in tune with the performative excesses of previous Blues musicians:

> Almost twenty years before Hendrix, [Eddie 'Guitar Slim' Jones] was playing guitar behind his head, barrelling into the audience at the end of a 350-foot chord, and generally earning the title of the performin'est [sic]

blues man that ever was. Slim died at the age of 32, leaving very few recordings, but Buddy Guy was one of those who drew on his flamboyant style. Guy would slap his strings with a handkerchief or a drum stick, or begin his sets from inside the men's room.[26]

However, this did not mean that Hendrix was able to fit neatly into the performance circuits that black musicians habitually occupied. In common with many black musicians of the time, Hendrix began on the Chitlin' Circuit, a network of venues, mainly in rural areas and the Deep South, defined by the fact that the audiences were black. In these venues, a band and a musician had to make a more or less instant impact: they would be sharing the bill with a number of other performers – comics, theatre shows and pantomimes, for example. At the same time as he was honing his guitar techniques (and incidentally learning about blues music) Hendrix was also learning the performance techniques that would later make him famous; he learned the trick of playing guitar with his teeth from Alphonso Young, and playing behind his back from T-Bone Walker.[27]

However, Hendrix found that the performance style that suited his earlier live work did not fit the prevailing black musics of the time. Soul and R&B musicians tended to work through choreographed routines that framed and supported the band leader: any attempt to upstage the leader could lead to instant dismissal (as Hendrix found when he played for Little Richard). Even those groups who used Hendrix only did so in relatively short bursts, as a featured part of the performance – a short showcase, before he was expected to melt into the background (the Isley Brothers gave him a ten-minute slot in their show; ironic, as Eddie Isley later borrowed Hendrix's tone and style). The position of Hendrix in black music at the time was made even more precarious because he listened to white styles and groups: it was acceptable for a member of white society to listen to music made by blacks – but for those in a subordinate social and political position, for those subject to active discrimination, culture was something to be ring-fenced and defended:

'Black people didn't want to hear any rock'n' roll in Harlem,' Taharqa Aleem recalled. 'There was a dress code – if you didn't look, or sound, a certain way, you were shunned. Compared to the rest of the city, Harlem was like a whole other planet. We called the scene Harlem world.'[28]

Hendrix played the wrong sort of music, and he also looked wrong – too close to the emerging Hippie sub-culture to be part of the musical life of Harlem. However, when Hendrix was taken to England, he found himself in an environment where the performance style that he had learned in

another culture suddenly appeared to be, not simply a range of gim-
micks, but expressions of his essential self. (Adverts for his 1967 gigs in
England did not sell Hendrix merely on the basis of spectacle; rather,
they identified him as an ideal mixture of three artists: 'Don't miss this
man who is Dylan, Clapton and James Brown all in one'.[29]) However, as
a black American in Britain, Hendrix had other, less savoury ideas affect-
ing his reception; a newspaper tagged him 'The Wild Man of Borneo' – a
racist title in itself, and also a reminder that, for a white audience (and
particularly for an audience in a country that, up until very recently, had
had an empire) other ethnic groups were exotic, closer to nature, and
decidedly inferior. Hendrix's 'wildness' fitted: he was a popular musician,
he was associated with Hippiedom – and he was also a Negro, and therefore naturally (for a white audience, especially in Britain) inclined to spontaneity and physical display.

The problem, for Hendrix, was that, at the time he was performing,
the physical vocabulary that he employed was not one that was acceptable to black audiences, even though, to white audiences, it connoted
blackness: and, although it had elements in common with a style of guitar playing related to black musical forms, the ethos within which the
performances took place was one that was far more in tune with white
musicians' conception of authentic performance. Bobby Womack, speaking in 1986, stated Hendrix's position with rather depressing clarity:

> [Jimi Hendrix] was tryin' to fit on his side of town, but it wasn't his
> side of town. He needed to be in another place ... man, when he got
> to Europe he got with people who was like him, they was his family.
> I was glad that he found a place. And then a lotta blacks started sayin'
> how it's terrible that he had to go to the white side to make it, cause
> we treated him so bad.[30]

Womack might remember a wave of sympathy for Hendrix after he had
achieved stardom; however, according to Charles Cross, even toward the
end of his life, when Hendrix had become one of the most famous musicians of the time, black audiences still found that both his music and his
performance style did not fit. Almost three weeks after playing
Woodstock, Hendrix played the UBA festival in Harlem:

> Five thousand people had gathered for the event, which also included
> music from the Sam and Dave band, Big Maybelle, Chuck-a-luck,
> Maxine Brown, and J. D. Bryant, all playing on a tiny stage that faced
> Lenox Avenue. Before the show, Jimi spoke with a *New York Times*

reporter: 'Sometimes when I come up here, people say "He plays white rock for white people. What's he doing up here...?"' 'A lot of black people in the neighbourhood didn't even know who Jimi was,' Tunde-Ra Aleem said, 'but so many white people were in the street they became curious.'[31]

Before Hendrix began to play, missiles were thrown on to the stage; by the time he finished, only two hundred people were left in the audience. In part, this is because of the style of the music he played (rock and blues, rather than R&B, soul or funk); partly, it was because the band's only white member – Mitch Mitchell – had preceded Hendrix on to the stage. However, it was also the case that, performatively, Hendrix's physical style did not fit his audience.

Evidence for the distance between Hendrix and other black performers can be found in the film of the Woodstock festival, shot three weeks before. Sly and the Family Stone give a typically tightly controlled, choreographed reading of 'I Want To Take You Higher': it is not that the performance appears drilled – indeed, something of the elation of the show survives the act of filming (Larry Graham, the band's bassist, described the show as 'like electricity was just running all though our bodies').[32] Rather, it is that the multi-racial band have been schooled in a tradition of ensemble performance, in which individual musicians support and echo the movement of the whole group – and where there is a strict performative division between group and leader. In contrast, Hendrix, leading a band obviously far less rehearsed, more or less eschews the tropes for which he had been known (at one point he half-heartedly plucks the guitar with his teeth); he does, though, give a typical performance in other ways – he holds the guitar lightly and loosely, plays solos with his eyes closed, orchestrates feedback swoops and dives with a full sweep of his arm or with short, stabbing jabs at the Fender's tremolo arm. His movements are, characteristically, free, flowing and expressive – and, crucially, unplanned; he is also far more involved in a performative conversation with his band than is Sly Stone. One gets the sense that Stone does not need to check that the band are where they ought to be; Hendrix, however, checks constantly – nodding other musicians in, grimacing when the under-rehearsed band slips and stutters, encouraging them when the quality of the music improves. If Stone and his band give the impression that this is a show, then Hendrix gives the impression that this is him – and that his persona on stage is a necessary outcome of the music that he is playing. It affects him physically; it guides and shapes his movements; it controls him. His onstage attitude to the music that he plays has, for all the differences in performative style, a strong link to Clapton's: both are lost in the creation of the music, both conspicuously position themselves as artists first, and as entertainers second – and both use a common improvisatory musical vocabulary, grounded in the blues, to declare their artistic status.

5
The 1970s

During the 1970s, the practices which began in the previous decade were professionalised. In both Britain and the United States, networks of touring venues opened up to accommodate rock bands: at the same time, the larger bands began to carry their own backstage crews. For example, the Stones, touring America in the early 1970s, employed a lighting designer – E. Beresford, or Chip, Monck – to create a lighting design that could be carried from venue to venue. At the same time, in the early part of the decade, stage sets tended to become more elaborate (see below), and sound technology also improved; a band that had the money could now be reasonably certain that a show could be reproduced in each venue, no matter what the particular constraints of that venue might be. For these reasons, it could be said that performers in the 1970s found themselves exploring rock performance as theatre; in fact, as I shall argue below, even those performers who eschewed overtly theatrical sets and lighting found themselves involved in a theatricalised performance environment by default.

Playing theatre

At the Isle of Wight festival in 1970, a small number of enraged fans tore down sections of the wall that surrounded the site. Their reasons for doing so were almost stereotypically countercultural – a festival, like Woodstock and Monterey in 1967, should be free to all, and should refuse, as a matter of principle, anything which remotely suggested the profit motive. At the decade's end, one of the bands most closely associated with the late 60s counterculture, Pink Floyd, expended a great deal of time and energy (and a considerable amount of manpower) erecting a wall between the band and their audience. Between the demolitions of

1970 and the blank, towering wall of 1979–80, there is, of course, a vast distance; and it is very tempting to read the traversing of that distance as a journey from spontaneous and explicitly political authenticity to empty, spectacular theatricality. The tour undertaken in support of *The Wall* might be taken to demonstrate a lot of things: the technical advances of the decade, which by the turn of the 1980s had made a large-scale, complex multimedia stadium show feasible; or as the last gasp of the grandiose rock ethos of the early 1970s (when the industry was undergoing an unprecedented boom) in the straitened circumstances of the later 1970s. What it seemed to demonstrate, most obviously, was the fact that the relation between band and audience was (at least in some cases) built on the principle of *noli me tangere*. The band were separate; the band were special; the band existed in a different world to that occupied by the audience. *The Wall* played on that distance from the first:

> With all the bombast of a rock show – fireworks and special effects – the show would open with a band who appeared to be us rising from below the stage. In fact, this was a look-alike group known as the 'surrogate' band ... each equipped with life masks ... As the pyrotechnics and effects headed towards a climax, the first group of musicians froze, and the lights revealed the real band behind them. The surrogates would later appear on stage as auxiliary musicians, without their life masks – in this incarnation they were known as the 'shadow' band. All their instruments and costumes were grey, as opposed to the black we were wearing.[1]

In part, this was an overtly ironic comment on the band's facelessness and performative inadequacy (see the previous chapter); it also played on a pervasive sense of alienation, experienced by the band in general and by the bassist (and chief songwriter) Roger Waters in particular. After the success of *The Dark Side of the Moon* in the mid-1970s, Waters felt that audiences no longer listened to the music; rather, they attended the spectacle – seeing Pink Floyd, having been there, was far more important than paying attention to what the band were playing. They no longer came for the music; they came for the show.

The Wall stands both as a comment on, and an exemplar of, a trend in performance during the 1970s which firmly established the idea that a certain amount of overt theatricality was permissible in live performance. For example, the recently released footage of a Led Zeppelin 1970 gig at the Royal Albert Hall shows the band conforming rather closely to the late 1960s notion of the engaged heavy blues band (Robert Plant's head-shaking, clenched fists, and in particular his habit of finishing a vocal phrase with a sharp, abrupt twisting turn of the head irresistibly recalls Janis Joplin at Monterey in 1967). Movements are loose, free and (apparently) unplanned; it is fair to say that, performatively at least, if the band had slotted on to the bill at Woodstock (after Canned Heat, perhaps) they would not have looked out of place. Filmed at Madison Square Garden in 1973, Bonham and Jones have retained the same performance style (although, even here, their stage clothes are noticeably more decorative). Page and Plant, though, have changed markedly; they are now far more stylised – Plant emphasises the lyrics with very precise hand gestures, and the cross-stage wanderings that accompanied solos in 1970 have been replaced by a default stance (hips forward, head tilted slightly back, microphone held straight and away from the torso, cord stretched across the lower stomach, body rocking back and forth) to which he returns during the instrumental passages. Page has also adopted the full range of habitual tropes that have been anatomised at length and with great acuity by Susan Fast. It is not that these gestures are any more or less authentic than the performance language adopted in 1970; however, it is clear that, in the three extremely successful years since the Albert Hall, the band have evolved a particular performative language which marks them as different. Both Plant's overtly camp hand gestures, and Page's ritualised blessing of the audience, are the habitual performance tropes of people who have grown used to, and grown comfortable with, the idea of being watched. Moreover, they are comfortable with the idea that the mystique of the performer – that which removes the performer from the everyday – can be re-enforced in performance through a process of stylisation. Even before the band employ anything more than lighting to mark the performance space (before the lasers, and the giant video screens – whose use Zeppelin pioneered) they have already established, gesturally, the fact of their difference theatrically. They are not the spontaneous Woodstock generation bluesmen of the Albert Hall; they are stars, and they behave – they perform – accordingly.

However, as I have already indicated, we should be very wary about any assumption that an easy line between the theatrical and the real can be drawn; it is not necessarily the case that performances which seem to declare themselves as theatrical are necessarily any less authentic than those which trade in overt displays of the real – far less, that authenticity is necessarily undermined by theatricality. It is, arguably, important to bear this in mind when examining the musical landscape of the early to mid-1970s, when competing versions of the theatrical in rock music seemed to mark out more than the differences between bands; arguably, at this point in the history of the form, theatricality was the vehicle through which the authentic self was projected to the audience.

On the surface, there seems to be a vast distance between the kind of staging adopted by Yes in 1974 –

> Martyn Dean produced a finned shell that formed a pavilion for Alan White to sit inside with his drum kit ... At the climax of 'Ritual' [the last track on *Tales from Topographic Oceans*, the album the band were touring at the time] the shell opened out to release a cloud of fire and smoke. Roger [Dean, who also designed the band's album covers] contributed a series of illuminated islands that covered the stage and there was a series of organ pipes in undulating, shifting colours that were intended to be an extension of Rick Wakeman's keyboard set-up. Behind it all was a screen for lighting effects and slide projections[2]

– and the equally theatrical set for David Bowie's *Diamond Dogs* tour in the same year –

> The designer Jules Fisher was hired to create a set midway between [the album's] nightmare of urban decay and the stark, robotic world of *Metropolis*. Fisher's colleague Mark Ravitz compiled a list of props suggested by Bowie: 'tanks, turbines, smokestacks ... fluorescent lighting, alleyways, cages, watchtowers, girders, beams, Albert Speer'. A young dancer called Toni Basil choreographed the whole two hour performance. Bowie himself supervised every effect. He even conquered his fear of heights to sing 'Space Oddity' while perched on a hydraulic boom that rose to a height of seventy feet above the stage and hovered over the auditorium.[3]

It is the distance, at least as the conventional account of rock history has it, between the overtly mystical, pretentious and self-aggrandising world of progressive rock, and the rather more decadent (and therefore, perhaps, more authentic) world of Bowie, which mixed glam theatrics and sci-fi trappings with the credibility inherited from his close association with Iggy Pop and Lou Reed. As the quotes above partly suggest, the divide could be thought of as running between those who employed theatre to create a visual correlative for the content of the music (the mystic environment of Yes's stage serving as the embodiment of the other-worldliness of much of their material), and those who were interested in foregrounding the theatricality of the event. Bowie's brief mention of Albert Speer is troublingly indicative; it does display a fascination with the power relations inherent in the performance event – an interest also apparent in his choice of Nazi-style hangings and symbols for the *Ziggy Stardust* tour in 1973. Progressive rockers embraced theatre as art (or as a reflection of the art inherent in their music); performers like Bowie and Roxy Music embraced theatre as theatre, or as showbusiness, as Brian Eno pointed out in 1997:

> What was different about Roxy Music was that we were quite ironic, and this was new at the time … we came out of a context where the accepted mode for pop musicians – and most artists, actually – was to be apparently sincere, committed to one's art and immersed within it. We, on the other hand, wanted to do something that had as much to do with showbiz as with the seriousness with which rock had come to regard itself.[4]

However, it could be argued that the distinction was in practice by no means as clear cut. Take the matter of onstage costuming; it is true that early Roxy Music marked themselves as different from what Eno describes above as an over-serious musical environment by adopting costumes which mixed, in varying degrees, Hollywood glamour and the ornate futurism of 1950s SF; however, this self-conscious, ironic nod to showbiz was not that different from the stage costumes adopted by Keith Emerson at roughly the same time. Indeed, it is possible to imagine Emerson and Andy MacKay swapping costumes; they both seem addicted to skin-tight, glittering jackets and art deco shoulder pads. It is possible to draw the same link between the black leotard worn by Peter Gabriel in Genesis's early performances, and the almost identical black outfit worn by David Bowie during the encores, at the end of Ziggy Stardust's farewell gig at the Rainbow in 1973. Bowie's is see-through, but Gabriel's has a zip that runs from neck to crotch; both are spare and simple, in contrast to other costumes worn during the gig (Bowie has a number of gaudy, figure-hugging and revealing outfits; Gabriel has masks and capes) – but both have an undeniably erotic charge.

Similar links could be made between performance tropes. Eno's onstage flamboyance (positioned on one side of the stage with the rather more stiff and mannered Ferry on the other, the overtly camp Eno was perhaps the strongest visual focus that the early Roxy had) is no more nor less theatrical than Emerson's antics with revolving pianos and partially demolished Hammond organs (Emerson's assaults on a Hammond B3 – which involved stabbing the keyboard with knives and wrestling the instrument to the floor – had been a feature of the stage show of his previous group, the Nice; the act was incorporated directly into the ELP stage show from the beginning). Bowie's performance work throughout the 70s relied on the formation of a number of performance personae (Ziggy Stardust, Aladdin Sane, the Thin White Duke et al.); his delivery of songs in performance was to an extent refracted through these personae – erotically teasing as Ziggy Stardust in 1973, stylised, stiff and distant as the Thin White Duke in 1976. Gabriel, though, was at least as adept at incorporating personae; at the end of *The Musical Box*, a lustful old man; during 'I Know What I Like', a stereotypical yokel; and so on. Bowie occupied a persona (this is probably the best way of phrasing the relationship between Bowie and Ziggy: the characterisation of Ziggy is never exact enough to be described as an exercise in acting) for the course of an entire performance; Gabriel did exactly the same during performances of *The Lamb Lies Down on Broadway* – the performance followed the loose narrative of the album, but during the course of the performance the line between Rael (the central character of the album) and Gabriel was blurred. Musically, and ideologically, the worlds occupied by prog rockers and glam rockers might be very different (for example, when the emerging punk rock movement in the late 1970s was casting around for musical forebears, they found them in glam, and prog was rejected); but in terms of the worlds created in performance, there were many significant similarities. The discourse of progressive rock stressed the seriousness, the art, of the performer; however, so did the discourse established by a certain kind of glam performer. Bowie's work was supersaturated with references to the history of Western culture – and in some respects tried to presage its (apparently) inevitable decline; and Roxy Music's performances were an arch yet heartfelt rebuke to the previous generation of performers. As Ferry put it 'That whole 60s presentation of rock music, and the implied honesty that went with it, was kind of bizarre and was always alien to me.'[5] For Ferry, 60s honesty was itself inauthentic; the truth of the music was best expressed through the flash and glitter of a Roxy show. On their first US tour, Ferry responded to a heckler who wanted the band to 'play some rock 'n' roll' with the bald assertion, 'We are rock 'n' roll'.[6]

Some performers who employed theatrical devices in their performances were not so obviously doing so in the service either of the music or of their art. Kiss, for example, utilised the same kind of *mise-en-scène* for one of their tours that Bowie used for the *Diamond Dogs* shows: however, it couldn't be said to be an artistic statement about the decline of the West:

> The Kiss stage featured a painted cyclorama as a backdrop, evoking the look of a destroyed city's smoking ruins ... A Broadway designer,

Julius Fisher, had created the sprawling stage set. The city appeared to have been devastated by some sort of apocalyptic conflagration. A wall of amplifiers stretched across the stage and above them were platforms, catwalks, and stairways that the Kiss members tore up and down during the show.[7]

This playpark apocalypse was populated by cartoon characters; famously, the four band members wore elaborate black and white make-up and costumes, supposed to indicate a particular persona (Gene Simmons, the bass player, was costumed to suggest a bat, for example) and they were never photographed out of costume. Alice Cooper (like Marylin Manson, the name covers both the band and the central performer) created an equally elaborate stage set; for Cooper, the inspiration was Grand Guignol and Hollywood horror rather than Marvel Comics:

> 'We'd sit up all night talking about Dwight Frye,' Alice recalls, 'This guy who played in all those old horror movies but never got the recognition ...' Playing the role of a misunderstood character actor on the brink of insanity, and quite possibly still dangerously at large, appealed to Cooper's highly developed sense of the macabre. At the suggestion of the theatrically attuned Ezrin [Bob Ezrin, his producer], method man Alice donned a straitjacket during the recording ... 'It was easy to go on stage and become Dwight Frye,' Cooper says.[8]

A stage show that, at various times, incorporated axe killings, guillotining, electrocution, giant spiders, skeletons, a Cyclops, and a magic screen (a projection screen cut into strips, so that Cooper could run through it and – apparently – become part of a film), and a central performance persona modelled on Frye and on Bette Davis in *Whatever Happened to Baby Jane?*, seemed to mark Cooper as part of showbusiness, rather than as part of rock.

However, Cooper, and Kiss, cannot be so easily dismissed; in both cases, the personae adopted in performance have become defining characteristics, which cannot be escaped. In some cases, once a performance persona is adopted, it then, paradoxically, becomes the authentic mark of the performer's presence: when Kiss, in an attempt to revive a flagging career in the 1980s, performed without make-up, the gesture only hastened their decline. Why see Kiss, after all, if they didn't look like Kiss? In the 1990s, the make-up went back on, and all the pyrotechnics returned; the overstated performance style which had nearly bankrupted the group at the end of the 1970s was their way back to success.[9]

Alice Cooper still tours a show that incorporates horror elements; however, he is now identified as one of the founding fathers of heavy metal performance (see the next chapter) – a status humorously celebrated by Wayne and Garth in *Wayne's World 2*. Indeed, it could be said that the reincorporation of both Cooper and Kiss into the narrative of Heavy Metal (cf. Christie) is a prime example of second-person authentication, as described by Moore: and that it bequeathed the emerging metal genre an interesting relation to theatricality (see next chapter).

Perhaps the real division amongst those who employed theatrical devices in the early 1970s was not between those who thought of theatre as theatre, and those who thought of it as art; but between those who used theatricality as a comment on the world or on the music, and those who used theatricality to comment on the processes of rock performance. Neil Young toured *Tonight's the Night* in 1975:

'Welcome to Miami Beach, ladies and gentlemen. Everything is cheaper than it looks.' This is the cryptic introduction Young would customarily use to open *Tonight's the Night* shows – after banging through the title song, a number the audience had never heard but would get to know painfully well before the evening was over. 'Put a little light on that Palm Tree, BJ,' he'd call out, and roadie Willie 'Baby John' Hinds – resplendent in Hawaiian shirt and beach baggies and looking like the tackiest Florida tourist – would pull the chain on a bare forty-watt bulb to illuminate a sad, sickly specimen with about four fronds.[10]

This exercise in anti-theatricality extended to the band's general appearance (apparently, for much of the tour, washing was an optional extra); to the other accoutrements onstage (the denuded palm tree was joined by a cigar store Indian, with a Gibson round its neck, and the grand piano used on the tour was festooned with glittering platform boots); and, most disturbingly for a performance style which usually serves to magnify and fetishise the star, to Young himself. Early on in the tour, Young borrowed a second-hand, black-and-white seersucker jacket from his guitarist Nils Lofgren: he wore the coat throughout the tour – a detail which, taken in conjunction with his unkempt hair and beard, and the elaborate sunglasses he also wore, irresistibly reminded some audience members of Charles Manson.[11] At the gig's end, Young took to introducing the last song with the line 'Here's one you've heard before', only to reprise 'Tonight's the Night' for perhaps the third time. The song, album and tour were undoubtedly (and avowedly) an exercise in catharsis, based as they were on Young's reaction to the heroin-related deaths of guitarist Danny Whitten and roadie Bruce Berry, who features in the album's title song. Lofgren later commented:

> Even today, people come up to me and go 'Oh man, that heavy, horrible *Tonight's the Night* thing ...' I'm like, 'Hey man, we had a party. We were releasin' all that dark stuff – on a nightly basis'.[12]

The tour has become notorious; and that notoriety derives, as much as anything else, from its relation to an idea of theatrical rock that had, by the mid-1970s, become commonplace. A star puts on a show: the show is either artistic, decadent or overtly theatrical, but it should look as though it is the result of a great deal of planning, and the careful allocation of considerable resources. To mount a performance that wallowed in its own cheapness (as though the budget for a more elaborate show had been blown on the drugs that killed Whitten and Berry) was to mount an explicit attack on the idea of rock as theatre – an attack which used the idea of rock as theatre against itself.

At the end of the decade, a tidier and noticeably healthier Young returned to the same theme in the shows and concert film *Rust Never Sleeps*. Here, the presentation of the event is more obviously considered. The stage is a child's-eye view of the conventional rock gig, with oversize mock amplifiers masking the PA system, a gigantic microphone, and cowled roadies (rechristened Road-Eyes for the show) with glowing eyes. The gig (which has a strongly marked narrative structure) seems to tell a conventional story of early idealism corrupted by the world. At the beginning of the gig, Young wakes up and climbs down from one of the amplifiers to sing 'Sugar Mountain' and 'I am a Child', both songs about the process of growing up. At the gig's end, Young and Crazy Horse play 'Tonight's the Night' – a song which, as noted above, laments early death. The structure of the gig is, however, complicated through the repeated use of iconic stage announcements from the Woodstock festival; in particular, the famous chant of 'No rain' is countered by a solo acoustic version of 'The Needle and the Damage Done'. At the end of the 1970s, in other words, Young creates the antithetical version of one of the founding events of rock; a version of Woodstock which asserts, not that band and audience are one, but that (as one of the bits of stage business attempts to prove, by requiring the audience to put on 3D glasses, better to observe the inescapable process of artistic decay) 'all bands rust'.[13]

This principle – that the idealism of the late 1960s should be subjected to ironic scrutiny – had already found performative expression in the stage shows mounted by Frank Zappa and the various incarnations of the Mothers of Invention in the late 1960s. Zappa's early shows were marked by the scatological surrealism that was a feature of his live work throughout his career (an early show featured a toy giraffe which fired shaving foam from its anus); they also featured the peculiar mix of serious musicianship and musical dumbness that could still be heard on the final tour in 1988. They also featured moments of direct (and uncomfortable) satire; during one show at the Garrick theatre in New York, also in 1967, he invited some US marines onstage, and asked them to dismember a doll; Zappa then displayed the broken doll to the audience. At the turn of the new decade, however, Zappa's and the Mothers' performances seemed to turn inwards; raw material for the shows no longer came from events in the wider world, but from the bizarre social microclimate that forms in and around a touring rock band. Routines would be based on the band members' insatiable desire for sex; the ubiquity of bad room service; the day-to-day boredom of road life; the chance remarks and encounters that filled the time when the band was not actually performing; throw-away comments that were enshrined in songs and onstage routines (Terry Bozzio, the drummer in Zappa's band, expressed momentary interest in a carefully posed photograph of Punky Meadows, the guitarist with the now forgotten band Angel; this momentary interest was turned by Zappa into the song and routine 'Punky's Whips'). At the time, critics like Charles Shaar Murray took this change in subject matter as a sure sign that Zappa had retreated from satirical commentary to crowd-pleasingly offensive comedy. However, in practice, Zappa's newly found interest in the life of his various bands seems a particularly apposite comment on the whole decade. The communal engine of the late 1960s was rock music; the band (as noted above) was in some ways an ideal social formation, either because it represented community, or because it articulated the tensions and aspirations of the time. Zappa's bands, as revealed in the onstage routines performed night after night on tour after tour, were as stupid, as venal and as self-obsessed as the characters in the songs they performed. During one of the annual New York Halloween shows, Zappa asked the audience:

> How many of you people feel that rock has got entirely too preposterous? ... Some of you believe that rock is real. I can see from here that about 20% of the audience have had it up to here (places hand well over head) and the rest of you still believe in that shit.[14]

Zappa's stage shows of the 1970s can be thought of as a simultaneous invocation and exorcism of the ingrained preposterousness of rock as a form (at least, as Zappa conceived of it), and, by implication, of the ingrained stupidity of the culture that created and supported it. The audience were not exempt from this process; they were intimately involved in it – in the various contests and moments of audience participation (memorably described by Zappa during one performance of 'Don't Eat the Yellow Snow' as 'enforced recreation'[15]) that were built in to the concerts. The only figure who remained at least partially exempt from the process was Zappa himself; conducting both the music and the on-stage events; stepping forward to deliver an ironic monologue or to play a solo; or sometimes simply sitting by the side of the stage, smoking – Uncle Frank, the only adult in a world full of greedy children, watching the show.

Playing reality

In 1976, the Band (a group of musicians whose place in performance mythology was already secure; they had served as Dylan's backing band in 1965/6) staged a farewell performance at the Winterland Ballroom in San Francisco. They invited a number of guests to the farewell party (Dylan himself, Muddy Waters, Van Morrison, Joni Mitchell, Neil Young, Ron Wood, Ringo Starr et al.). In an interview during the film, the Band's leader, Robbie Robertson, described the guest-list as 'some old friends who showed up to help us take it home'; pushed further by Scorsese, he assigned a more specific significance to the choice:

> They're more than just friends ... I feel they're probably some of the greatest influences on music on [sic] a whole generation.[16]

This is, of course, a partial and biased statement; but it is interesting because, in sharp distinction to the bands and performers described above, the artists in *The Last Waltz* are at pains to prove themselves 'real'. In other words, Robertson is identifying (and implicitly placing himself within) a tradition of rock music performance which has its roots in the kind of environment described in the previous chapter – the environment that nourished groups like The Grateful Dead. It might be termed the Woodstock ethos – a commitment to the idea of the performer as representative artist, integrated into the traditions that shaped his or her music and the audience that supported it; an artist as untainted as possible by the pressures of commerciality. In performance, this meant that rough-hewn, untheatrical (in the sense of apparently spontaneous and unrehearsed) or apparently revealing performances were mandatory: the idea, enthusiastically embraced by Gabriel, Cooper or Bowie, that the performer should know their marks and hit them at the same time each night was anathema.

The impetus behind this came from a variety of sources: the melding of psychedelia and country music in the late 1960s (in the work of the Dead and the Byrds, for example); the turn towards folk music, either as a means of connecting oneself with tradition or as a means of self-expression (in the work of the Band itself, and the music of Young, James Taylor, Joni Mitchell et al.); and a continued commitment to the idea of spontaneous authenticity enshrined, at least as the mythology of the time had it, in black American musical styles. In part, too, it was a return to basics, after the perceived indulgences of the late 1960s – an attempt to return from the outer reaches of space, and to recover a kind of honesty, both on record and in performance. Even when the performance contains moments which might be described as unprofessional, it is still legitimate; as in Lester Bangs's description of Van Morrison at the Fillmore East in 1970:

> He drives the song ['Cyprus Avenue'], the band and himself to a finish. With consummate dynamics that allow him to snap from indescribably eccentric throwaway phrasing to sheer passion in the very next breath he brings the music surging up through crescendo after crescendo, stopping and starting the song again and again, imposing long maniacal silences like giant question marks between the stops and starts and ruling the room through sheer tension, building to a surge of 'It's too late to stop now!', and just when you think it's all going to surge over the top, he cuts it off stone cold dead, the hollow of a murdered explosion, throws the microphone down and stalks off the stage. It is truly one of the most perverse things I have ever seen a performer do in my life. And, of course, it is sensational: our guts are knotted up, we're crazed and clawing for more, but we damn well know we've seen and felt something.[17]

A more nakedly commercial performer would have provided the climax towards which the music had been inexorably building; Morrison, the artist, in touch with an imperative that only he can sense, an imperative rooted in the music he performs, knows better – and he has no compunction about demonstrating that knowledge. Paradoxically, the effect of this demonstration is itself far more powerful than the conventional climax. For Bangs, we haven't simply watched a set of showbiz moves, but Morrison's own spontaneous experience of the song. Morrison's performance, even when it courts absurdity, evinces petulance or (as has frequently happened during the course of his career) an apparently complete disregard for the audience, is valid and effective because his onstage persona is of a musician who is into the music. It is unsurprising that Morrison himself should choose this very phrase for the title of his 1979 album.

When watching Morrison – indeed, when watching most of the artists in this general category, male and female – it is hard to escape the thought that such performances are only accidentally physical; that, instead of serving to demonstrate the song, such physical movements as there are occur as the by-products of an engagement with the music. For example, Joni Mitchell's performances for much of the 1970s were almost private affairs. Rather than a kinetic, outer-directed stage presence, Mitchell radiates inwardness – her eyes are closed more often than not, her body more or less stationary (at most, swaying to the rhythm of the music), and her performance directed, not to the audience, but to the microphone directly in front of her. Even when there are other musicians on stage, the focus of such performances changes only slightly; the most intense relationship is still with the microphone, but the other musicians are allowed in to the singer's solitude, their relation to the music established performatively by a series of small gestures (glances, small or momentary turns of the body or the head). Dylan himself during the decade provides the best example of this type of performance. The overtly performative gestures of the mid-1960s (caught well on *No Direction Home* – the quasi-religious, testifying upraised hand, for example) were replaced in the 1970s by an intense watchfulness, with frequent glances exchanged between Dylan and his backing musicians during the performances of each song. Given Dylan's habitual and at times unpredictable reworking of his back catalogue, this is understandable; without this almost constant flow of silent communication, the performances of even the most well-known tracks would grind to a halt. There is an excellent example of this on *The Last Waltz* itself; apparently without warning, with the briefest of verbal indications, Dylan segues into 'Baby let me follow you down' from 'Forever Young'. The chord that would introduce the chord sequence of 'Forever Young's' verses is held, while Dylan and Robertson huddle; the rest of the Band are, at this moment, bystanders, until Dylan and Robertson play the opening riff to the new song; Rick Danko, playing bass, grins; and the Band slide into the new track. Paul Williams, in his multi-volume exploration of Dylan's live work, talks of the singer playing his backing band as a musical instrument; in performance, this is achieved through a radically different series of gestures to those used by Frank Zappa (whose relation to his backing musicians is closer to Dylan's than is usually recognised). Zappa, though, conducts his band in a style which seems a parodic (if very effective) version of the style of the classical conductor; precise hand gestures, but enacted with a raised eyebrow, and with a Winston cigarette dangling from his mouth. Dylan similarly triggers a specific, spontaneous performance from his band, but he does so in the tradition that, as much as anyone else, he established; a style in which the performance of music is a moment of semi-private communion between musicians, or between the musician and his or her muse.

Real theatre

> 'We were real. We were unique. We're like four unique individuals. It's a chemical thing. It's a strong chemical imbalance. Opposites attract and all that crap.'[18]

In the mythology that has grown up around the relatively brief explosion of punk – both in the States and in Britain – at the end of the 1970s, there is an inherent contradiction. On the one hand, there is the idea, given expression by Joey Ramone in the above quote, that punk and the new wave represented a return to reality after the indulgences of the earlier part of the decade. It is part of the foundational myth of punk that rock music had lost touch with ordinary (and especially working-class) life; on the other hand, punk's antagonistic relation to conventional rock discourse meant that its relation to previous ideas of authenticity was equally problematic. As Robert Garnett argues, visually and performatively, punk groups like the Sex Pistols and the artists (like Jamie Reid, who designed the band's single and album sleeves) who associated with them set out to pull the structures of popular culture to shreds:

> The most direct way in which Reid's visuals relate to the Pistols' music is in terms of their montage form, their decentred pillaging of fragments of pop-cultural detritus. The Pistols pilfered their riffs from a repository of stock rock 'n' roll prototypes, and in doing so, literally trashed them, along with any last vestiges of 'authenticity', 'competence', 'originality', 'meaning', 'artiness' and significance'.[19]

And yet both arguments are themselves easily countered: a band like The Ramones, kitted out in identikit leather jackets and ripped jeans, with pudding bowl hair and assumed names, might lay claim to many things, but reality isn't necessarily the most obvious one; and the idea that the Pistols trashed 'authenticity' does not sit well with Johnny Rotten's quickly assumed role of spokesman for the newly disaffected young.

Built in to the fabric of punk, therefore, is a tension between the overt creation of art, and the roughness and rawness of unmediated experience. When punk musicians came to identify a tradition that fed the music that they produced, it is unsurprising that they placed most emphasis on those groups and performers whose work had demonstrated a similar tension. British groups picked The Who, The Kinks, Alice Cooper, Bowie, Roxy Music and the glam movement; American groups picked The Who, The Rolling Stones, Alice Cooper, Glam, The MC5 and 60s garage pop and rock. For both sides of the emergent movement, however, the most influential – and the most obsessively referenced – performers were Lou Reed, Iggy Pop and the New York Dolls: musicians whose performances seemed both the perfect examples of a certain type of self-revelatory theatre, in which the self-destruction of the performer was an ever-present threat.

When Lou Reed had played with the Velvet Underground in the late 1960s, he was static, a fixed presence in the midst of the flickering films and lightshows created by Andy Warhol; from the 1980s onwards, his status as a serious rock artist assured, he stopped moving once more. In the 1970s, though, Reed was undoubtedly a theatrical performer, presenting shows which mixed stand-up comedy (the album *Live-Take No Prisoners* could almost pass as an updated version of Lenny Bruce set to music) and Artaudian immolation. In both modes, Reed used himself as raw material, even when to do so was to risk a great deal. In the mid-1970s, and experiencing a level of commercial success that had previously eluded him, Reed was on the point of complete collapse. The journalist Nick Kent encountered the singer, unexpectedly, at Max's Kansas City:

> [Reed's] hair was shaved as close to the head as possible, like Charles Manson's when he was graced with a prison cut, and went one step further, but mutilated even way beyond that by what appeared to be large patches of diseased albino colouring. It was only when I got closer that I noticed these areas on the sides of the head were specifically shaped like Nazi iron crosses. Then there was the face which possessed not only the most uniquely grey and decayed fleshy pallor I've yet to witness on any human visage but also a fixed, glazed look to the eyes like several hundred watts of electricity were being fired through his central nervous system. The body was skinny and emaciated almost beyond belief.[20]

There seemed little to choose between the versions of himself Reed presented on and offstage; his performances in the early to mid-70s were exercises in the theatre of self-destruction. Whereas other performers might have been careful to mask the effects of drugs or alcohol, Reed's live work placed his drug problems in the spotlight. The stage was black; his backing band were only faintly lit; and Reed was the clear focus of the audience's attention. His appearance – in whiteface, with black hair, eyes, lips and costume – was a theatricalised version of the wasted death's head of the terminal junkie; in a trope that played off the idea of his imminent self-destruction, during 'Heroin' Reed wrapped the microphone cable around his arm and mimed injecting himself. Musically, the work that Reed did with the Velvet Underground might be his most influential. In terms of performance, though, the Reed of 1973 – touring at a time when the generation who would form New Wave bands were first attending gigs – provided a template that proved irresistible; performances that took known facts about the performer's life and transformed them into what seemed a nakedly revelatory type of theatre. Bowie, given credit for reviving Reed's career, performed shows which were about aliens, America and apocalypse; Reed performed himself – and audiences responded.

He was not alone. Iggy Pop and The New York Dolls occupied the same uncomfortable territory. The Dolls, formed in the early 1970s, combined the Stones, glam rock and a love of 60s girl groups, with a visual style that could be described as trash transvestism:

> The primary image of the early Dolls' collective image was cheap glamour ... [The] impoverished trio of Johnny [Thunders], Arthur [Kane] and David [Johansen] were generally dependent on their imaginations and ready access to a number of thrift shops, which were common on the lower East Side. Anything gaudy, camp or kitsch was fine. Frocks were even better. The Dolls were *A Rock Band* and aimed for a cartoon-like distillation of their chosen medium's primal essence. They wanted to thrill the kids, shock the squares and, above all, to look totally unlike the hippies.[21]

As I argued in Chapter 3, the idea of heterosexual male transvestism has been part of the visual coding of rock since the late 1960s: paradoxically, the more make-up the Dolls applied, and the more elaborate their costumes became, the more they signified the 'primal essence' of the form. They might have offered their audiences a set of performative tropes which bordered on the parodic (David Johansen's default performance style was that of a wide-eyed ingénue playing at being Mick Jagger) but, as argued in Chapter 1, the idea of rock as performance does not invalidate the idea of rock as authentic expression. This certainly was the case for the Dolls. They might have been dismissed famously by Bob Harris, the doyenne of serious rock broadcasting in the 1970s, as mock rock; but it was equally valid to argue (as Michael Watts did, in a review for *Melody Maker*, that '... The Dolls, with their crude musicality and exaggerated posturings, are the new children of pop mimicking their elders ... that make you feel sixteen again...'[22] There was, though, another reason for the Dolls' notoriety; at the point where they seemed poised for an early breakthrough, Billy Murcia, their first drummer, died from a combination of drink and drugs. Murcia's death, referenced by David Bowie in the song 'Time', helped to establish the Dolls' reputation as drug-fuelled and self-destructive; the band's adoption of the Swastika, their predilection for Nazi salutes, the barely hidden addictions which occasionally made a shambles of their live shows, fuelled the idea that the Dolls' audience were watching (as another *Melody Maker* reviewer put it) 'the story of the last Rock and Roll band. The New York Dolls. There won't be another...' at what might conceivably be the point of their final disappearance.[23] The Dolls, in other words, would play out the performative paradox at the heart of rock (that a show is both a show and an authentic revelation) to the point of its, and their, destruction.

Reed's and the Dolls' self-destructive performances took place in front of an audience; Iggy Pop's occasionally enlisted the audience:

> Eggs kept flying up on the stage, and as the set went on I was getting really sick of it. So I said 'OK, stop the show right now!' I'm calling the fucker down ... So everybody clears out and here's this guy about six foot three, like 300 pounds, with a knuckle glove on up to his elbow, with little studs on it. So I said, 'Well, what the fuck.' I might as well get it over with. So I put down my mike and stepped out. And it was just like seeing a train coming. Bam! He just got me, but he didn't deck me. He couldn't knock me down ... Finally, the blood got too much for him so he just stopped and said, 'OK, you're cool.' I didn't feel so cool. But we went back on and played 'Louie Louie'.[24]

This moment of extremity would, for other performers, be a relatively isolated moment either on the way up to stardom or the way down; for Pop, it was yet another illustration of the guiding principle of his live work. Live performance, for Pop, was a ritual which exorcised suburban boredom (the target of many of the Stooges' songs) and provided as graphic a demonstration of the performer's authentic self as possible. This would involve a testing of Pop's own limits of physical tolerance: he would drip hot candle-wax over his naked torso, expose himself to his audience, or cut himself:

> *After Dark* reported that, in the middle of his set during the second evening at Max's [Max's Kansas City, in 1973] the singer could be seen standing stage centre with blood gushing out of a number of wounds on his face and body. 'Insiders,' the magazine confided, 'reported that Iggy, distressed about his attachment to a local beauty ... announced "my heart is broken," and went to work with some broken glass.'[25]

Pop's performances, from the very first, have shown an absolute disregard for physical safety, both his own, and that of the musicians who perform with him (who might find themselves ducking out of the way when Pop swings a guitar around his neck, for example). The aim of these performances is neatly summed up by Pop himself, in comments to the crowd during a 1991 gig in Paris: he introduces 'Lust for Life' with 'Hey mothers! I want to be up there with you, getting fucked and getting fucked up',[26] and 'I Wanna be Your Dog' is introduced with the self-deflating statement 'I would rather be a real dog than a fucking scumbag rock star'.[27] To reach the audience, Pop is willing to perform tropes which theatricalise his own destruction: the title of the Paris DVD (*Lick my Blood* – an instruction that Pop gives to the audience in Paris; an instruction that some audience members gleefully obey) echoes an earlier performance in Cincinatti in 1970, where Pop smeared himself in peanut butter and dived into the crowd. The cameras filming the event have trouble picking him up, because he is at points completely immersed. In the clearest possible way, Pop invites the audience to complete the logic of the performance style that he has chosen; he invites them to consume him.

The visual template established by Reed, the Dolls and Pop was variously applied by Punk and New Wave performers. There were some direct steals; Sid Vicious engaged in onstage self-mutilation in the style of Iggy Pop, and the Sex Pistols' Steve Jones admitted to borrowing Johnny Thunder's stage persona wholesale. However, the main lesson learned by the nascent punk movement was performance was simultaneously a useful mask and a means of passionate revelation. When John Lydon came to forge the Johnny Rotten persona he admitted to borrowing from a number of (more or less unlikely) sources:

> I die of nerves before I go on stage, because I don't know what I'm going to do; and because of that, I have to just pull things out from

down deep inside ... Look, there's Arthur Askey in there: there's Ken Dodd ... There's even (mimes Norman Wisdom) 'There's nothing wrong with me' ... What England didn't understand about the Sex Pistols is that we were Music Hall.[28]

Taken altogether, these comments strongly suggest a persona formed around the idea of oddness – of failed or comic masculinity, of ugliness; the outsider, forced to construct a persona which negates his status as a physical and social outsider. Interestingly, though, Lydon suggests that this persona was not pre-planned; it was forged in the heat of performance – and it emerged from the depths of his own consciousness (just before the comment quoted above, Lydon has described himself as 'one ugly fucker').[29] The performance, it seems, is both Rotten being himself – fetishising his own ugliness – and Rotten acting out, adopting a ready-made comic style which allowed him to overcome the terror of self-exposure. This contradiction is clearly apparent in footage of the band, particularly in the early days; Rotten transmits passion, and at the same time seems to watch himself doing so. An apparently unguarded moment (a blank-eyed, furious sneer) is followed by oddly contorted moments of self-parody (hanging down from the microphone stand, his body bent over, with an equally blank-eyed grin). Rotten is not entirely overtaken by the event; like Pop, and like Reed, he has placed himself in the midst of the maelstrom, and, even at the last, at the Winterland in 1978, carefully monitors its effect on him, on the band, and on the audience.

Like Lydon, bands like The Ramones could establish themselves as both comic and deadly serious; identikit costumes, identikit names, nearly identikit songs and a stage performance that remained resolutely static (with its own catchphrases – 'Hey Ho, Let's Go' and 'Gabba Gabba Hey') managed to appear both knowingly camp and aggressively confrontational. The leather jackets and ripped drainpipe jeans placed The Ramones in the same performative universe as The New York Dolls (if the Dolls were the Shangri-La's, the Ramones were the Leaders of the Pack); and yet, the long pudding-bowl hair and the sheer physical unlikeliness of the band (the lanky, big-nosed Joey, the unsmiling, thuggish Johnny, the monkeyish Dee Dee) played against the ostentatious 50s themed coolness of their outfits. At the heart of The Ramones' stage image, therefore, was the same contradiction that existed at the heart of the Rotten persona; the outsider placed centre stage, the geek given the chance to assemble a performance that, at least momentarily, enabled him to be both cool and a commentary on the fact that cool is socially

constructed. Even the most ungainly physical type can become an ideal –
if the clothes are right, and if the pose is shaped precisely enough.

Other performers used different means to create a theatre of the self.
Patti Smith experienced a moment of epiphany at a Stones gig at Madison
Square Garden:

> Jagger was so tired that he needed the energy of the audience. He was
> not a rock & roller that Tuesday night. He was closer to a poet than
> he ever has been, because he was so tired, he could hardly sing. I love
> the music of the Rolling Stones, but what was foremost was not the
> music but the performance. It was his naked performance, his rhythm,
> his movement, his talk.[30]

For a young aspiring poet who had come to believe in the power of performance, the idea that music could enable and support a kind of naked
performance was a very enticing one. Songs in performance were constructed in such a way as to allow Smith access to this state; most
famously, 'Gloria' (by Them) was rebuilt as a gradual exercise in loss of
control, from the slow piano beginning – over which Smith intoned her
own poetry – to the release of the original chorus toward the song's end.
In her early performances, Smith dressed as she did on the front cover of
Horses, her debut album, in a man's white shirt and trousers; the costume
suggesting a *tabula rasa* form of masculinity, not connoting any particular identity other than that of an ambiguous maleness. From a static
beginning, standing at the microphone, her hands by her sides, Smith
would build gradually to the end – finally spinning around and around
on stage as the song built to a climax. The echoes in this of trance performance were entirely intentional:

> *James Grauerholtz*: Patti told me that she considered every perform-
> ance to be a life or death encounter with ecstasy. She had a 'whirling
> dervish' philosophy with her performance, and felt that her obliga-
> tion to the audience was to put herself into a trance.[31]

This style might have been less inherently risky than Iggy Pop's, but it
carried its own dangers; during a 'whirling dervish' moment in Tampa in
1979, Smith whirled herself off the end of the stage, putting an end to
the early part of her live career.

Smith wanted to engage the audience in a naked performance of the
self; The Clash, on the other hand, were interested in a naked performance

of the truth. For Joe Strummer, the Notting Hill riots were as much of an epiphany as the Rolling Stones were for Smith:

> For Joe, who'd had to observe the evenements of 1968 from afar, it was the opportunity he'd been waiting for to unleash his deeply felt anti-establishment brio ... Having spent several years busking and squatting, always being hassled, forever watching the police pushing racial minorities around, he relished the opportunity to get his own back.[32]

The Clash's onstage personae derived from the 'anti-establishment brio' Gilbert identifies. As Paul Simonon, the group's bassist, put it, 'we all realised that we needed a unified look on stage' (*Westway* DVD); this, though, could be said for most punk/New Wave groups, who were keen to establish a visual identity that marked them out from previous visual styles. However, after an initial flirtation with DIY painted costumes in the style of Jackson Pollock, The Clash adopted stage clothes which brought a Mod aesthetic (neat, exact clothing that gave the band a very sharp silhouette) to clothes that were described by the journalist Nick Kent as 'pop-star army fatigues'.[33] Given the overt social commentary in the lyrics, the visual impact of the clothing was obvious; The Clash were dressing for the coming class war. The group on stage moved as a unit, the three guitarists executing the same tropes (moving back and forward in short, quick bursts from the mike to the back of the stage, then back to the mike); the chopped chords of the songs were executed in abrupt, sharp movements; and songs were presented, physically and vocally, as aggressively as possible, with none of the obvious, music hall irony espoused by the Pistols. Most of The Clash's songs were intended as telegrams from the front line of the anti-capitalist struggle; the band's performances were honed so that the audience would be confronted by the band's passion – even if the finer details of the message were lost in the heat of performance. The band's image was, of course, a lie. At the time, the fact that Mick Jones and Simonon had been art school students, and that not only had Strummer's father been a career diplomat, but he himself had attended a minor public school, were potential sources of embarrassment for a band that saw itself as on the front line of the anti-capitalist war. However, it was a necessary lie, because on record and in performance it allowed the band to put forward what they saw as a deeper political truth.

By the end of the decade, the idea that performance could be employed as part of an investigation of the authentic nature of the performer or of the world had been fully assimilated into rock music culture. Given the imprimatur of punk (a stable reference point for performers, *pace* Gilbert above; the discourse of punk is used to guarantee a type of authenticity – one in which the performer is aware of the process of mediation, but remains unfazed by it) the idea of authentic self-performance remains strong; it can be traced in U2, REM, the Sub Pop bands, Rage Against The Machine, The Pixies, The Stone Roses, Oasis, Radiohead, The White Stripes and The Arctic Monkeys. It also gave a new spin to the romantic-ally disturbing myth of the young rock star, dying at the height of his or her powers. Morrison's, Hendrix's, Joplin's and Brian Jones's deaths estab-lished one mythical framework: the star whose weakness or over-indul-gence blighted and destroyed first their talent and then their lives. The kind of performances described here helped to establish another, equally romantic, and equally pernicious mythology: that of the rock performer who found ultimate expression in the self-immolation that their songs and their performances had seemed to promise.

At the end of the 1970s, the singer Ian Curtis of Joy Division committed suicide. He had a history of mental heath disorders, and was depressed over the state of his personal life, but he was also under an increasing strain, brought on by recurrent epileptic seizures:

> I saw three attacks and it was always two-thirds of the way through a set. And it came to the point where, in the last year, you'd watch the group and suddenly you'd feel Ian was dancing great and suddenly he's dancing really great. Hooky [*Peter Hook, bassist*] and Barney [*Bernard Sumner, guitarist*] would be looking nervously at the stage and you could see what was going through their minds. So I always presumed that it wasn't because he was taking the tablets, but that he wasn't taking enough. For something was happening within a set, doing what he did, that actually took him to that point, that actually over-came the drugs and made him have the attack.[34]

Curtis's seizures were made more shockingly powerful by the fact that the band as a whole performed with an undemonstrative intensity; they dressed with the sober smartness more usually associated with Kraftwerk, and (aside from Curtis) were physically undemonstrative. This ceded the central position to Curtis almost by default; even when not in the grip of an epileptic attack, he occupied this position uncom-fortably – the dances that Wilson describes were robotically awkward, and mirrored the uncontrollable physical twitches and jerks of a *grand mal* episode uncomfortably closely. When Curtis's illness came to dom-inate his performances, its impact had already been prepared; it was the final sign that the barely controllable fragility that Curtis performed on stage was a true indication of the man. No wonder that, as his widow dryly noted, '[it] was allowed to become an expected part of Joy Division's act and the more sick he became, the more the band's popularity grew'.[35] Iggy Pop, Reed and the surviving members of the Dolls might be famous now for evading the destruction their performances seemed to threaten. Rather depressingly, Ian Curtis, Sid Vicious and others (Kurt Cobain being the most obvious example) are famous, because they did not; because the damaged selves each of them seemed to reveal in performance were finally confirmed as authentic by the manner of their deaths.

6
The 1980s

The New Wave movement at the end of the 1970s had seemed, at least on the surface, to move rock performance away from the more elaborate trappings of theatrical presentation towards a simpler, more direct performance of the self. However, at the beginning of the new decade, the influence of MTV pushed rock performance in the opposite direction – toward a style of presentation which had the visual impact of a video. To this end, stage designs became more flexible (wireless technology, gradually introduced through the decade meant that microphones and instruments did not have to have leads; the vari*lite, first used by Genesis on a 1981 tour, enabled lighting designers to programme and move light sources during the performance), and, as I argue below, the design of the stage was ever more closely bound to the other images which helped to shape the audience's perception of the band. At the same time, the whole process of touring became more overtly commercialised. The practice of touring sponsorship began around about this time (for example, The Who tour in 1983 was sponsored by Miller Beer).

The MTV generation

In 1987, David Bowie embarked on the kind of elaborate, closely choreographed tour that had helped to establish him as one of the key performers of the previous decade. The tour was given the title *Glass Spider*, after a track on the album *Never Let Me Down*: as with the tour which supported *Diamond Dogs*, Bowie constructed an event which used the available technology in as elaborate and striking a way as possible:

> For his entrance, Bowie was lowered on to the stage from inside a translucent spider's belly; a troupe of dancers abseiled down from

the scaffolding, leading one cynic to wonder if he was witnessing a rock concert or an SAS-type storming of an embassy: films were shown; each song was choreographed. In a final gimmick, Bowie emerged atop a radio tower sporting wings and then shimmied down for the encore.[1]

The tour was undoubtedly spectacular; however, it was not a success. Ticket sales were variable, and the shows were panned, one critic commenting:

> Bowie has simply smashed his blond head into the wall of the pretentious end of a cul-de-sac. If this is the way rock music is going to get back its meaning, the answer is no.[2]

The tour failed for a number of reasons, some of which could have been easily predicted, perhaps even before the opening show. Bowie was not news any more; the sexually and politically ambiguous chameleon of the 1970s had become the comfortably successful Live Aid performer of the 1980s. The album he was touring was not a strong one; moreover, it was the second weak album in a row – *Tonight* had failed to match the success of its predecessor, *Let's Dance*. Bowie, whose early performances had traded on sexual ambiguity, was on this tour (as he had been throughout the decade) definitely heterosexual; the performances lacked the sense of *louche*, decadent risk that had defined the Bowie persona in the mid-1970s. The choice of touring personnel was rather idiosyncratic; for his lead guitarist, Bowie chose Peter Frampton – a 70s superstar whose AOR-inflected hard rock had fallen out of favour in the 80s. On tour with Bowie, Frampton (dressed, like a conventional rock star, in jeans and T-shirt, and with long, curling blond hair) looked simply out of place; as Bowie and the dancers acted out each song, Frampton stood downstage right, looking for all the world as though he had strayed in from the stadium next door.

However, considered as a performance, the choreographing of the *Glass Spider* tour is very similar to that used by Bowie over ten years before; the NBC special *The 1980 Floor Show* had united Bowie, dancers and musicians in much the same manner. However, in the 1980s, the visual discourse of popular music had changed. In 1981 the video channel MTV went on air; within a few years, aided by the phenomenal success of showcase videos like those for the Michael Jackson album *Thriller* (especially the videos for 'Beat It', and the epic constructed for the album's title track) the video had become the industry's marketing tool of choice. For some commentators, the fact that a performer's visual identity was apparently no longer predicated on the idea of direct engagement with the audience decisively robbed live performance of those few shards of authenticity left to it. Video mass-produced performance; in Benjaminian terms, the live performance was quintessentially 'auratic' – spontaneous, never to be repeated – and the video was mechanical, locking performance into an endlessly recycled set of fixed tropes:

> Within the emerging languages of these formations [Grossberg has already discussed MTV and the youth cinema of the 1980s] authenticity is no better or no worse than the most ironically constructed signs of inauthenticity. The notion of authenticity is constantly reduced to a signifier of the performer's place within the rock culture: that is, it increasingly serves to mark the generic investment of the performer, to affirm their commitment to particular apparatuses within the rock culture. Or else it serves to problematically reinscribe the codes of performance (e.g. direct address) which have become little more than the signs of a decreasingly powerful appeal to authenticity.[3]

For Grossberg in 1993, one suspects, a tour like *Glass Spider* was simply not cynical enough to survive in the new visual dispensation; it relied too heavily on the auratic power of Bowie's presence (the god-like descent at the gig's beginning, the reincarnation at the end). Neither Bowie nor his supporting team had noticed that the tropes of rock performance had been debased through mechanised repetition; a style that looked thrillingly theatrical in the 1970s was now part of the visual mainstream. A carefully worked out moment of direct contact during the show, where Bowie apparently pulled a member of the audience (in reality, one of the dancers) on stage with him, would no longer surprise; Bruce Springsteen, in the video for 'Dancing in the Dark', had done exactly the same thing – and he did it over and over again, on channel after channel after channel, night after night after night.

Older musicians like Springsteen (and Bowie, with the *Let's Dance* album and the *Serious Moonlight* tour) might have been able to come to an accommodation with the new video age; Bowie had, after all, pioneered the use of promotional clips in the 70s. However, MTV seemed to be force-breeding a new generation of performers (or, alternatively, fast-tracking performers from a previous generation) whose work could achieve 'synergy'; this term, much used in the marketing discourses of the 80s, was used to describe the happy condition of the performer whose work crossed previously impermeable boundaries, and whose image could be coined anew in a number of media:

> [*Purple Rain*] opened in 917 theatres across the US. Another 100 theatres were added the second week. The press reviews were mostly

favourable ... Remarkably, it went on to become the 10th biggest film of 1984, grossing almost $70 million. The amazing success of the album and film had a great deal to do with a closely co-ordinated cross-media marketing campaign. Warner Bros spent $3.5 million buying ads on MTV, local and national television, while MTV ran footage from the celebrity-packed premiere party, which was their first live broadcast of a film-oriented event. A powerful synergy was created because the album functioned as an advertisement for the film, which in turn sold the album, while the video clips of the singles, aired on MTV, promoted both the film and album.[4]

Purple Rain made Prince a star; a musician who had been attempting the difficult task of crossing over (shifting his fan base from a predominantly black audience to one more racially mixed) since the late 1970s, his initial successes were partly due to the fact that MTV had latched on to the first singles from his previous album ('Little Red Corvette' and '1999', from the album *1999*). *Purple Rain*, which was one of the greatest successes of the 1980s (in addition to the money generated by the film, the album went on to sell 15 million copies), managed to combine successfully those forces identified by Grossberg in 1993 (the video and the youth film) as the main culprits in 'problematically reinscribing the codes of performance'. As if to add further fuel to Grossberg's argument, the *Purple Rain* tour restaged performance moments from the film (which had themselves received an airing on MTV).

Prince's success was rather surprising; at the time, the number of black artists whose work received the widespread coverage that MTV could offer was very small. His presence on the video channel was partly due to the fact that his music combined an extremely eclectic number of influences, from both white and black musical traditions (James Brown, Jimi Hendrix, Joni Mitchell, Sly Stone, Bowie, Santana, the Beatles, Punk and New Wave, Stevie Wonder, Kraftwerk et al.); partly, though, it was due to the fact that his visual image blended an equally diverse range of influences – the closely co-ordinated choreography of Stone, James Brown's dance moves, the gender ambiguity of Bowie, the overt sexuality of Mick Jagger, the sartorial display of the New Romantics, and the heroic style of guitar-playing first established by Hendrix. Even his band, which mixed races and genders, had acceptable antecedents; he seemed to be the leader of a Family Stone for the 1980s. There was more than enough here to appeal to a very wide audience; Prince seemed to fit the age – a talented magpie, both musically and visually, whose work could be marketed across all the outlets now available to record companies. There was nothing that was new in this; youth films had been in existence since the 1950s, and the promo video had existed in various forms since the 1960s. However, in the new age, a number of disparate forms of dissemination were unified; the video mirrored the album cover, the live set mirrored the video, the film (for some performers) borrowed the visual vocabulary employed on video and in performance. In the midst of this visual overload, the idea that live performance engaged the audience in a way that no other form could was (it was argued) no longer sustainable; we had entered the over-determined visual universe of the postmodern, and live performance – which seemed to hold out the promise of communication (if not communion) – now stood revealed as just another set of hollowed-out images.

Those images, though, did not appear fully formed from nowhere. As noted in previous chapters, the live performance of rock music has always traded on the fact that bands and styles of music are already bound up in a network of images; when the presence of MTV elevated the music video from an optional extra to a necessary part of the dissemination process, there was a ready-made catalogue of tropes on which to draw. For example, the idea that the performer might change his or her appearance was already an accepted part of the performance process for certain types of artist; video merely extended this logic into a new medium:

> The ability to rewrite the body is a rearticulation of the case of live performance in which artists used costumes. Peter Gabriel, for example, used costume changes to illustrate the complex, fairy-tale world of early Genesis compositions. Gabriel himself illustrates this rearticulation in his video 'Sedgehammer' by morphing himself into forms not possible outside of the video medium. Aerosmith's 'Pink' and Busta Rhymes' 'Gimme Some More' are other examples of this heightened sense of persona, and the ability to quickly code and recode the body.[5]

In other words, the articulation of a persona in video observes much the same logic as it does in performance; a body is coded and recoded because the framework that surrounds it makes such a coding possible. Video, one might say, provides another example of the type of framing that Schechner describes above: as Carol Vernallis, in an excellent recent monograph on music video, points out, there is an established style of performance in music video which foregrounds the idea of direct communication:

> Music video performance differs markedly from acting styles in film and television. For a number of reasons, the genre brings to the foreground

candour, self-disclosure, and direct address ... In addition, the setting often seems organic, as if it were the projection of the performer's own psyche.[6]

Candour, self-disclosure and direct address, in a framework which seems both aimed at the audience while still appearing to be a 'projection of the performer's own psyche', at least as determined by the music. In other words, music video and live performance can be thought of as partaking of the same performative logic: one which prizes the performance of the artist's self, in a manner that is designed to appear candid and truthful – or, in other words, authentic. The match is, of course, not exact; but the sense that both stage and video are projections of the performer's psyche (as manifested in the music, which is an important qualification to add to Vernallis' argument) is, it seems to me, a better way of thinking about the impact of video than the argument put forward by Grossberg in 1993. The existence of video as an integral part of the musician's image-bank has, in practice, meant that old discussions about authenticity, authentication and authorship have been played out in another medium; it has not meant that such arguments have become redundant.

In 1987, Prince toured the album *Sign O' The Times* in Europe. The tour was designed by Roy Bennett, who had worked with Prince on previous tours; by his account, the design discussion was rather short ('Basically, Prince gave me a picture of the album cover and said, "Make it look like this".'[7] The set which emerged was, to say the least, elaborate:

Echoing the cover of *Sign O' The Times*, the set resembled a seedy downtown bar district, complete with neon signs flashing 'Girls, Girls, Girls', 'Bar & Grill', 'Funk Corner', and 'Uptown'. Prince was on the stage level with Levi Seacer Jr, Cat, Greg Brooks, and Wally Safford. Much like on the album cover, prominently displayed at the centre was the front end of a Pontiac bearing a Minnesota licence plate. Shelia E. was elevated above the frontline performers, nearly buried within her drum-set. On the second tier, high above the stage, stood horn players Eric Leeds and Matt Blistan, and the keyboardists, Matt Fink and Boni Boyer. The concert posters and tickets requested the audience to 'wear something peach or black', in keeping with the colour scheme of Prince's clothing.[8]

On one level, this set might seem like the performative incarnation of the MTV age: album cover begets design, which is used both as a live set and as a video location (the promo clip for 'U Got the Look' was filmed on the *Sign O' The Times* set). The audience are even included in the dressing of the set; Prince would prefer it if they wear clothing that will not clash with the star. However, this reading, although it does contain some truth (performers are sold as musicians and as images, and those images will be replicated and developed each time the performer and the audience meet), does not invalidate another reading, one which is perhaps of equal or greater importance for Prince and for his audience. To take one example: a neon sign flashes the word 'Uptown'; at first glance this might seem an insignificant design detail – but it is also the name Prince gave to the Minneapolis music scene in the 1970s. This scene not only provided the young Prince with an early introduction to performance; it also represented an ideal environment. One of the young Prince's compatriots remembered Uptown as 'cool ... We'd throw dances and everybody would come and party'.[9] The final, extended encore of the tour, 'It's Gonna Be a Beautiful Night', uses the full resources of performers and set to restage an Uptown party; this serves both as an effective performance moment (one of those characteristic moments at the end of an elaborately staged gig when everything gets in on the act; even the lighting rig, which contains hexagonal lighting panels which can be raised and lowered hydraulically, moves in time to the music) and as a recoding of the performers' bodies. The gig becomes a street party, to which the audience are invited; and, for those who know, for his fans, Prince has re-created a private memory (or at least given clues for the *ex post facto* authentication of the event), on a set which, in certain crucial ways, can stand as a 'projection of his own psyche' – as much of a projection as the album cover, or the video.

Really heavy authentic Metal

> In the beginning there was just a shadowy expanse of night sky and unknown. There in disquieting oblivion whirled the unanswered secrets of history, animated by forces as ancient as civilisation itself – everything smoking, silvery, religious, and dark. These strong currents often lay forgotten and docile, until the opportunities of war, crisis, and anguish called forth their awful powers. They had no sound or definition of their own until trapped and subjugated by the epiphany of Black Sabbath – the originators of Heavy Metal.[10]

It is oddly fitting that the beginning of a history of Heavy Metal should read like the opening paragraph of a lost H. P. Lovecroft novel. Fitting, because the eldritch, doomy atmosphere of Lovecroft's work is one that many metal bands, from Black Sabbath to Slipknot, would endorse; and fitting also, because Lovecroft's work, like Heavy Metal, is routinely despised. Robert Duncan's catalogue of clichéd dismissals, assembled for *The Noise: Notes from a Rock 'n' Roll Era* in 1984, remains as good a place to begin as any:

> Heavy Metal: pimply, prole, putrid, unchic, unsophisticated, anti-intellectual (but impossibly pretentious), dismal, abysmal, terrible, horrible, and stupid music, barely music at all ...[11]

The list is exaggerated for comic effect, but not greatly; the idea that Heavy Metal, especially in the 1980s, represented little more than a monolithic, debased sub-division of popular music was, and is, very deeply entrenched (see Walser 1993, Weinstein 2000). It even tempers apparently reasonable judgements, like the one delivered by Stuessey and Lipscomb, in a purportedly objective reader on popular music history:

> What have changed over the years [in Heavy Metal] are the lyrics and the extramusical factors (e.g., image and theatrics). The antihero mentality, combined with the post-Alice Cooper shock trend, have created an escalating situation in which every band must be louder, grosser, more rebellious, and more shocking than its predecessors.[12]

Heavy Metal is fixed; it does not develop musically. The only way in which the form could be said to grow is along the lines of an equally despised generic form – the gross-out horror flick. The *Halloween* and *Friday the 13th* franchises pile death upon death, each film in the series trying to outdo its predecessor; each new Metal act is caught in a similar logic – it has to outdo the bands that came before it, by simply extending the logic of the genre. Excess – sonic, lyric, performative – is hard-wired into the form; and excess can only be trumped by even more excess.

Needless to say, this is a very simplified view of the genre; Heavy Metal is no more monolithic than any other musical style – as with any genre, there are boundaries to the definition which fans, press and musicians rigorously police, but these boundaries are not fixed (see Kärjä 2006 for an interesting discussion on the process of canon formation in popular music). It does betray, though, a profound anxiety about this particular style, an anxiety which (it could be argued) is at least partly rooted in an aspect of Heavy Metal that its fans prize, and its detractors find impossible to ignore. Heavy Metal foregrounds performance; Metal musicians put on a show. Deena Weinstein's argument, that the Metal concert is an epiphany, '...the event which epitomizes the cultural form and brings it to fulfilment',[13] is an argument that could be made of any live event that brings band and fan together. The problem, though, is the kind of epiphany Metal achieved, which was, in essence, a theatrical epiphany.

As noted in the previous chapter, other bands and artists employed overtly theatrical devices in the 1970s; but some forms of theatre were at the time deemed more authentic than others. The theatrical tradition that evolved around the nascent Heavy Metal genre – the one associated with Kiss and Alice Cooper – had by the end of the 1970s already been dismissed as showbusiness rather than art. New Metal bands (for example, the bands who constituted the New Wave of British Heavy Metal at the turn of the 1980s) employed a performance language which was, at least at the time, regarded as debased. When Iron Maiden, for example, had their particular epiphany, it was not one which would endear them to the majority of rock critics:

> We had smoke machines, bubble machines, all home made – bung a bit of dry ice in a kettle, that sort of thing. Then a singer we had, Dennis Wilcock, started us thinking. He had this stunt where he waved this sword about, then slashed the blade across his mouth and blood would come pouring out. Of course, it wasn't real, but a couple of girls did faint right in from of him.[14]

The singer did not last; but the idea did – and it gave rise to the band's longest lasting visual symbol:

> Eddie was this 'orrible mask which stood at the back of the stage. We rigged up this pump we got out of a fish-tank and at a given moment it would spit buckets of blood over the drummer.[15]

From this relatively small-scale beginning, Eddie – a long-haired, skeletal, emaciated version of the archetypal Metal fan – grew: he appeared on the band's album and single covers, in various guises, and began to take a larger role in the band's live work. At first, a roadie wearing an Eddie mask would lumber on stage; later, as the band's stage presentations became more and more elaborate, Eddie changed. A mechanised version of the character was employed at various stages of the band's development; and, when Eddie appeared, he did so in a manner which chimed with the visual theme of that year's album and tour. For example, the *Powerslave* tour in 1985 used a stage set which, like the album cover, was based around the architecture and art of ancient Egypt; Eddie, predictably, appeared as a mummy. The visual image provided by the band's mascot proved remarkably long-lasting. In 1992, the band's vocalist, Bruce Dickinson, thought that 'Eddie's run his course. It would be nice to put him to sleep';[16] however, when Dickinson himself left the band in the same year, Eddie was still in place.

On the face of it, Eddie's persistence might seem to confirm the view of the form given above. Each time the band's mascot appears, he does so in accordance with an accelerating logic of static progression; he must be the same – he must conform to the visual style already established – but he should also be more than he was the last time the audience saw him. The genre's logic, in other words, requires that the same tropes be recast in progressively larger moulds. However, perhaps it is more truthful to say that the same complex arguments over authenticity in rock music as a whole also figure in Heavy Metal; the only difference is that the acceptable level of theatricality that the form can sustain is greater than it is in other genres. For example, to a non-sympathetic critic, the onstage flamboyance of an Iron Maiden gig might confirm the genre's essential non-seriousness; looked at by a fan, and indeed looked at by the band themselves, the stage shows are the visible expression of the music – even Eddie is not an iconic prop, but simultaneously a band member and the image of the ultimate Metal fan. Heavy Metal shows in the 1980s were built on the foundations established by Black Sabbath, Kiss, Led Zeppelin, Judas Priest and Alice Cooper in the 1970s. Each one of these bands had come to be identified with onstage theatricality: elaborate visual presentations, flamboyant performance styles and iconic, theatrical clothing. The form was predicated on performative excess, whether it was Kiss' pyrotechnics and make-up, Zeppelin's lasers and video screen (first used at Earl's Court in 1975), or Judas Priest's leathers, studs and bikes (the band's lead vocalist, Rob Halford, used to make his first entrance on a motorbike). The excesses of the set were echoed in a performance style that was equally flamboyant; in contrast to the studied non-theatricality of a band like the Eagles, Heavy Metal musicians accepted that musical instruments were both tools and props:

[Angus Young, the lead guitarist and founder member of AC/DC] told *Rip* magazine that his spasmodic, seemingly out of control onstage body language has always come naturally. 'For some unknown reason, whatever I'm playing, it's like, being a little guy, where most people bend a note on the guitar, my whole body bends. Then when I hit a chord on the bottom of the guitar, I just follow it. Other guys let their fingers do the walking. With me, the body does the walking.'[17]

In the 1960s, Jimi Hendrix's intensely physical style of guitar playing, abstracted from the culture that had shaped it, was taken as a template for expressive performance; Heavy Metal musicians, it is fair to say, accepted this template as a given, and over the following decades produced a number of variations on it.

Iron Maiden, and other Heavy Metal bands of the early 1980s, managed to become successful not because they simply provided ever greater theatrical and musical thrills for their audience; they also managed to establish and develop a fan base which conformed to Deena Weinstein's argument that the Metal community had taken on the status of 'Proud Pariahs'; that principled outsiderdom was part of the self-image of Metal culture. The band established their fan base through touring; the theatrical image that it projected had been developed in performance – that is, had been developed as part of a dialogue with a growing community of like-minded fans. This was, at least, the way in which Dickinson envisaged the band's live work:

> You're building yourself up all day and then just letting it go during that two hours. You have to visualise what is happening ... I shut my eyes and think of the audience and it's like a huge sea and the waves come rolling over you and you're part of this huge great thing. You can call me an old fucking hippy, it's like a meditation and when I'm singing and there are no distractions, there's a little voice that you become aware of that's singing along with you and you're aware of the crowd. Shit, I'm making it sound fucking religious, like it's a way through to God.[18]

It is hard to imagine Johnny Rotten speaking of the live event in such terms; and it is very easy indeed to imagine the satirical fun that, say, Frank Zappa would have with Dickinson's statement. It is an expression of a shared mythology of authenticity that surrounds live performance (it is an expression of the ethos behind Woodstock, for example; it also covers the relation between band and audience mapped out in the Talking Heads' *Stop Making Sense* tour and film); however, it represents that mythology taken to an extreme. This is no longer a show; it is an apotheosis – a meeting without barriers between band and audience. It is closer, perhaps, to the average fan's view of the event than the clichéd notion of the jaundiced rock star, playing his way from one gig to the next. There is undoubtedly a little self-aggrandisement in Dickinson's description of the ideal gig; to make the performance work, Dickinson and the rest of the band could not afford to lose themselves so completely in the moment. But it is interesting that the stages Dickinson describes – building oneself up to the gig, pre-visualising the event, and then using the music and the atmosphere as a means of attaining complete release – echo the stages through which a Metal fan will pass before and during the gig, as described by Weinstein.[19] The shared sense of community between band and fans, in this genre, can include even the most ornate type of theatrical device (Ronnie Dio battling a dragon; or, to pick a more recent example, a drum solo during a Slipknot gig that ends with the drummer on a platform tipped until it is at 90 degrees to the stage – and with a pentagram, picked out in red neon, clearly visible on the platform's floor). Such apparently excessive stage devices are an acknowledged part of the show. Indeed, they make the performance possible, precisely because they fulfil the same function as Pink Floyd's lightshow in the late 1960s; they shift both band and audience into a conducive visual environment.

This is not to say, though, that all types of theatricality proved equally acceptable. During the 1980s a style of generic performance, equally theatrical, equally ornate, proved much more difficult for the fans of the genre to accept. The style was variously named glam metal or hair metal; it took the visual trappings of glam rock – the make-up, the teased hair, the ornate, declarative costuming – and married them to an anthemic, and in some cases a softened, version of Metal riffs and powerchords. For a while, its influence was all-pervasive:

> Dirtbag rockers dyed, bleached, and teased their hair into synthetic floral displays, then spent their last pennies on platform boots, vinyl pants, ripped T-shirts, and extra-strength mascara.[20]

It is not difficult to discern which side of the divide Christie occupies; it is no wonder that, on the next page, he quotes Rob Halford approvingly: 'Those bands, in their style and approach, that's what I call tits-and-ass metal ... Nothing wrong with that – I wouldn't expect anything else to come out of Hollywood'.[21] From these descriptions, it would seem that glam metal proved problematic for some members of the Metal community for a simple, well-rehearsed reason: it simply made too many concessions to show business. However, such an argument does not sit well with Weinstein's point, already quoted in Chapter 3, that Heavy Metal is fundamentally a performance art – after all, in most versions of the articulation of this particular trope, it is the act of performance which is itself the problem. A genre which, at least to some of its adherents, claims a line of performative descent from Kiss and Iron Maiden might be considered already infected by the virus of entertainment. Nor does it sit well with another potential objection that some bands affiliated with the genre encountered in the 1980s. Robert Walser, for example, cites the case of Bon Jovi:

> once a standard leather/chains/eyeliner heavy metal band, with lots of tragic, macho songs about running, shooting and falling down, the band sought to capture a wider audience for *Slippery When Wet* ... But by not wearing makeup any more and by wearing jeans, not leather or spandex, Bon Jovi abandoned much of heavy metal's fantastic dimension in favour of signs of rock 'authenticity'.[22]

As Walser notes, this shift ensured that the band managed to broaden its appeal successfully; interestingly, though, there is the suggestion in the above comment that the authenticity of metal as a genre resides somewhere in the 'fantastic dimension' that Bon Jovi abandoned.

There is (as Walser has noted) something of a generalised, homophobic anxiety about the practice of androgyny in this, at least on the part of some fans (and especially those affiliated with the emerging thrash and death metal scenes); Walser quotes a sticker which the band MX Machine placed on their *Manic Panic* album: 'No Glam Fags! All Metal! No Makeup!'[23] Given the reputations of some glam metal bands (Motley Crue in particular), and the reaction of indie musicians noted by Mimi Schippers in Chapter 3, the sticker's slogan seems misplaced; but it does give an indication as to why, for some fans and bands, some performances were permissible, and some were not. However, it is not the only reason; another problem, hinted at above, is the suggestion that the performance styles adopted by glam metal bands were not aimed primarily at a Metal audience. Part of the reason for Metal's popularity in the 1980s was precisely because it was a genre which relied on visual impact as much as on a clearly defined musical style; this made it ideal for MTV. But, for some styles and bands, MTV was a poisoned chalice; it necessarily meant that image was elevated over music:

> 'It's fair to say that even Judas Priest was influenced by the opportunities that existed only in America through radio and through TV,' says Rob Halford. 'If you look and sound a certain way, it can open up to a potentially bigger audience. The way that Priest handled that is first and foremost we said that we would never be a sell-out band. We were never in this for the money. There's a way of handling it and developing it while still remaining true to the beliefs of what your

music is about, while hoping that you're making something that can reach more people. It's a fine balance, really.'[24]

Instructive though Halford's comments are, they contain a rather glaring contradiction. It would be possible to look at the visual style that Priest established in their stage work and to argue that their shows were simply MTV videos waiting for the camera (and the prevalence of performance footage in Metal videos would seem to suggest as much). Perhaps an answer to this apparent performative conundrum is offered by Weinstein's contention, quoted above, that Metal fans (and the Metal community in general) regard themselves as 'proud pariahs'; as outsiders whose status as outsiders is almost a matter of honour. Perhaps, then, we should be looking, not at the struggle between image and content in 80s Metal, but at the struggle between images; images which are co-opted into the mainstream, and images which declare the band's distance from the mainstream.

In some ways Guns n' Roses are an archetypal Glam Metal band; in early publicity photographs they are as posed and as preened as any of the other LA groups, and their lyrics, like other glam metal acts, stress the decadence of urban America (with the ever-present possibility of romantic love as an escape). Even when the band tried to distance themselves from the LA scene, their denials seemed rather rote. Slash, the band's guitarist, might say that:

We just didn't want to get lumped in with the LA scene. We were dying to get away from that. The Who, the Stones, Aerosmith ... that's what we grew up with. The decadent 70s shit.[25]

But this does not sound too different from the denial issued by Nikki Six of Motley Crue:

We were the real deal. It was doom, gloom destruction, girls, twenty-four hours a day, the fastest cars, the loudest guitars. It was all the shit that makes Spinal Tap wonderful ... To be honest, I don't see that in these other [hair metal] bands. I see them as being a fabricated version.[26]

And yet there is evidence (Christie 2004; McIver 2006) that Guns n' Roses, unlike Motley Crue, managed to negotiate the tension between image and music successfully – or at least successfully enough so as not to disqualify themselves entirely from the core Metal audience. Musically, this was for a variety of factors; the subject matter of the songs, which tended to deal with urban sleaze more directly than the other LA bands; Axl Rose's vocals, which tended to be harsh – giving even the band's more tender songs like 'Sweet Child o' Mine' a rougher edge; the production on the band's first album, which emphasised the bottom end of the tonal picture (and, in doing so, allied Guns n' Roses loosely to the kind of production style more commonly favoured by the thrash metal bands of the period). In performance, it is fair to say, the band sent out mixed messages. Axl Rose might dress to emphasise his physical attractiveness, in tight shorts and cut-off T-shirts, and he might change costume frequently during the show, but his choices of costuming would not always be MTV friendly. On the *Use Your Illusion* tour, for example, he chose a variety of tops – one with Christ's head crowned with thorns, one with the face of Charles Manson etched in black and white. Rose's stage moves might seem as posed as any glam metal lead vocalist; but they play against the performance persona adopted by Slash. Rose, in a characteristic gesture, tosses his head so that his hair flies away from his face; Slash allows his hair to fall down, sometimes obscuring his face entirely. Rose habitually pauses, legs together, body leaning to the left, right arm extended, in a careful pose which suggests momentarily suspended action; Slash's characteristic pose suggests a far slower bodily rhythm – cigarette drooping from the mouth, guitar slung low, even by the standard of other Metal guitarists. It is not that Slash is incapable of speedier movements, and more dynamic poses; it is that, characteristically, he and Rose seem to inhabit different performative universes – the visual images suggested by the band's two most prominent performers do not add up to a carefully maintained illusion of unity. It is as though the process of mutation that Christie describes above – dirt bag rocker into glam metal star – is being played out in reverse on stage; Rose's stage persona might make an incomplete gesture toward MTV, but the gesture is heavily qualified – and Slash seems concerned to appear the very antithesis of the carefully coiffured lead guitar virtuoso. Even the band's stage intro is a defiant assertion that they will not live up to expectations; it knowingly parodies Kiss' intro ('You wanted the best! You got the best!'), twisting it into 'You wanted the best! Well, they didn't fucking make it so here's what you get!'[27]

On the other hand, a band like Metallica set themselves, musically and performatively, against the glam metal mainstream; rather than spandex and leather, they adopted first jeans and T-shirts, and then simple outfits in basic black. In performance, tropes connoting spontaneous investment, passion and energy replaced the more theatrical props and costumes used by other bands. In doing so, they supplied a performative correlative to the music they produced – a harder, faster, less immediately melodic version of Metal which came to be known as thrash metal. However, in doing so the band necessarily constructed onstage personae; these personae had, again necessarily, to reinforce the fact that the band existed at the opposite performative pole to glam metal:

> Metallica appeared on stage [at the 1985 Monsters of Rock festival at Castle Donnington] between two glam-metal acts, Ratt and Bon Jovi. This highly inappropriate placing escaped neither the band nor their fans, and was highlighted when [James Hetfield, singer and guitarist] uttered the immortal (and much quoted) words at the start of the set: 'If you came here to see spandex, eye make-up, and the words "Oh baby" in every fuckin' song, this ain't the fuckin' band!'[28]

It could be said, though, that Hetfield's own performance persona is as tightly constrained as the glam rockers he rejected. Characteristically, Hetfield sings into a mike that is significantly lower than his mouth, so that he has to hunch his shoulders and bend his knees; when he moves with the guitar, he tends not to straighten up. The overall impression, when facial expression and delivery are added, is of a snarling intensity – a pose described by the photographer Ross Halfirn as 'very metal'. It is an image, but an image which plays directly to the 'proud pariah' culture that shapes and supports the band. Guns n' Roses' performances contain enough references to the idea that true Metal bands are outsiders to pass muster when the question of authenticity is raised (as it frequently is, in Metal as elsewhere); Metallica, at least in the 1980s, were proud pariahs first and foremost. For these bands, as with the genre as a whole, discussions of authenticity were not about the relative balance that bands struck between the music and the image; rather, they depended heavily on the image itself. Glam metal seemed to make too many visual concessions to the mainstream; the bands seemed to have adopted too many of the visual conventions which were used to sell Metal on MTV. However, if bands presented an image which could be incorporated into the dominant defining feature of the culture – its and the fans' 'proud pariah' status – then the band would be allowed into the culture as a true representative of its underlying ethos.

Genderfucking

In 2006, Channel Four invited critics to give their nominations for the best gig ever; beating U2's career defining performance at Red Rocks, Radiohead playing Glastonbury in 1997 and Pink Floyd's (near) career-ending *Wall* tour was a performance which lasted roughly twenty minutes: Queen, playing a medley of their greatest hits during Live Aid. Or rather, it was not Queen's performance; it was Freddie Mercury's. His bandmates, talking after Mercury's death in 1991, agreed that the singer always seemed more comfortable playing large venues (*Queen at Wembley* DVD), and Live Aid gave him the largest possible platform on which to employ a full range of well-honed performative tricks – leading the crowd in quasi-operatic sing-alongs and chants, using his trademark cut-off microphone stand as a combination of swagger-stick and ersatz guitar, moving back and forth across the stage in a manner entirely peculiar to himself (a kind of syncopated, strutting march).

Mercury was without doubt the main focus of a Queen performance; the repeated elements that marked Queen stage sets from the early days (blocks of coloured lights which, from the late 1970s onwards, were lifted into place at the gig's beginning; Brian May's long, curled hair and trademark home-made guitar; the grand piano, placed stage left) never managed to attain the iconic status of Mercury's body language. When the band's songs were used as the basis of a West End musical, the producers effectively chose Mercury as the show's logo; and a giant golden statue of the singer, legs spread, fist upraised, adorned the front of the theatre.

Mercury's performances, then, might seem to bear out Deena Weinstein's (2004) argument that the singer is a stranger at the heart of the band; if we are looking for a visible incarnation of the singer as stranger, in the group but not fully part of it, then Mercury's relation to the rest of the band is so appropriate as to be paradigmatic. John Deacon, the bassist, is a workman, focused on his instrument or on the other musicians; Roger Taylor, the drummer, has some of Mercury's exuberance, but the constraints of his instrument and the music he has to play means that an energetic performance is of necessity largely hidden from the audience. Brian May is the thoughtful virtuoso; he has a range of excessive performative gestures, but neither his face nor his body displays the kind of ecstatic loss of control that is so characteristic of, say, Angus Young. The rest of the band, in other words, clear the space for Mercury to overperform; but this over-performance frequently topples over into irony – the most ornate gesture is delivered with a wide, deflating grin.

The well-worn word that best describes Mercury's performance is camp (defined in the *OED* as 'exaggerated and theatrical in style, typically for humorous effect'.[29] However, as the *OED* also notes, campness carries with it the strong suggestion of effeminacy – a culturally loaded word which might seem to lock Mercury, as a gay man, into a performative universe inhabited by the most limiting of stereotypes: that of the homosexual whose sexuality is purely theatrical, carries no taint of the erotic, and which can therefore be recuperated unproblematically into mainstream culture. Such a reading might be reinforced by the status of Mercury's sexuality; his gayness was an open secret, but it was only at the end of his life – a few days before he died of an AIDS-related illness – that the singer came close to acknowledging what was already widely known. Mercury's relation to his sexuality echoed that of other prom resistant attitude to their gayness – George Michael masking it behind a well-groomed heterosexuality, and Boy George famously declaring that, when it came to sex, he preferred a nice cup of tea. Other performers in other genres (Rob Halford, the lead singer of Judas Priest during the years of their greatest success) remained firmly closeted; the number of gay musicians whose sexuality was, if not foregrounded, then at least not seriously in question (the Pet Shop Boys; Marc Almond) was relatively small. However, Mercury's performance, although it is related to a sexuality that the singer was careful to keep private, carries more than a taint of the erotic; Mercury's onstage sexuality blended both overt, macho display with equally overt social signifiers of gayness (painted fingernails in the early days; the haircut and moustache of the archetypal San Francisco gay man at the end of his performative life). Mercury's performances were, it could be said, undeniably sexually charged – but the motor of that sexuality was never made entirely clear, at least not by Mercury himself.

Mercury, then, is part of a group of performers, whose relation to sexuality might be described as elusive. It is worthwhile making a distinction between this term and the more familiar idea of the closeted gay performer; sexual orientation is, in this case, not denied – but it is not entirely admitted. In the early 1970s, David Bowie might be keen to admit his bisexuality; in the 1980s, a number of performers seemed to operate on a principle that could be defined, in the words of REM's singer Michael Stipe, as genderfucking:

> [Stipe] showed a tendency to conflate elusive sexuality with gender deviance, at one point answering the question 'Do you like your sexuality being indecipherable?' by saying 'Yeah. I kind of like genderfucking' ... Genderfuck, stylized gender deviance, does not always involve queer sexuality, but often it does, and ... for Stipe the issues are close enough that he sometimes seems to have trouble distinguishing them. Stipe's public departures from normative masculinity, and their consequences for the general effect of R.E.M., are not sharply distinct from expression of queerness.[30]

For Stipe it is not a matter of denying sexuality; it is rather a question of escaping the constraints of 'normative masculinity' – an interesting phrase, given that I have argued above that gendered male behaviour in rock performance has the same dynamic. There is, though, rather more at stake for performers whose rejection of normative masculinity is not part of a rebellious heterosexuality; the idea of performance – and especially the performance of music – could hold a special significance for those whose sexual identity is less socially acceptable:

> To gay children, who often experience a shutdown of all feeling as the result of sensing their parents' and society's disapproval of a basic part of their sentient life, music appears as a veritable lifeline.[31]

And the physical manifestation of music in performance can be a chance for the gay musician to express his or her identity – both because music offers a framework for that expression, and because the performative culture that surrounds that music can support (and embrace) behavioural styles that are self-consciously 'decadent' or 'deviant'.

However, as I have argued above, gender identity is not as fluid as some performance theorists might have it; gender behaviour is adaptive, but it is adaptive within a structure that can accommodate a wide range of behaviours:

> If stereotypes reflect the social structure, then, surely, as social roles change so ought the stereotypes. Yet research shows that rather than altering the general stereotypes of men and women, exceptions and social changes are accommodated through a proliferation of subtypes.[32]

There are enough examples in the history of rock of what we might term a 'genderfucking' sub-type; however, these examples tend to be performers whose orientation is heterosexual, and is openly acknowledged. Such an open acknowledgement is far more problematic for a gay performer; music might be a perfect vehicle for the expression of emotion, but the public expression of that emotion takes place in a society that does not fully accept its validity. The gay rock performer, then, finds him- or herself in a rather ambiguous position; there is a sub-type available for the genderfucking rock performer, but it is a sub-type already marked out as heterosexual; an open avowal of gayness runs the risk of violating the rules of the sub-type – and there are other, rather more confining sub-types ready for the gay performer (for example, the camp sub-type described above). Rock at least offers a framework in which 'stylised gender deviance' is possible, because, as noted above, the idea of gender deviance is hardwired into the form; in the terms used above, it constitutes a valid sub-type.

However, the stylised gender deviance displayed by Mercury is not simply a matter of the overt display of an erotically charged, if unacknowledged, gayness; it is a sexuality expressed in a framework which is homosocial. The archetypal band is a gang, and a gang of men; they are bound by the shared exercise of creating and performing music, but also they operate in an atmosphere where the romantic myth of the male-bonded gang operates strongly. The repeated trope – that such and such a band are the last Rock and Rollers, or the last gang in town – connotes strongly the sense that such a band are romantic outsiders, heroically posed against conformity. The mythology that surrounds the formation and life of a rock band is one that can, and does, support the expression of emotions that come close to the direct avowal of love:

> Johnny [Marr] had grasped the thread of all that was relevant and yet he was – and remains – a very happy-go-lucky, optimistic person who was interested in doing it now. Not tomorrow, but right now! Also, he appeared at a time when I was deeper than the depths, if you like. And he provided me with this massive energy boost. I could feel Johnny's energy just seething inside me.[33]

Interestingly, Simpson does not regard statements like this as a direct expression of desire; rather, he incorporates it into a set of standard romantic rock tropes – the outsider finding other outsiders. Somewhere in the construction of the iconic rock performer, therefore, there are elements which can figure both as homosocial and as homosexual; sexuality does not have to be overtly acknowledged, because the construction of the group already enables the coded expression of the stylised gender deviance noted above. A singer's performative language, as Weinstein argues, will be different from the rest of the band, because his or her role in the performance is different:

> Most importantly, the position of the singer in a rock band stands out from the others because he has two separate roles: singer and frontman ...
>
> The problem with these two roles is that the requirements of a frontman decisively separate the singer from the other band members. Exuding personality, showing 'attitude' ... and representing a group's

personality compressed into one person all serve to distinguish the singer … The singer's structural position conflicts with the egalitarian ethos of the rock band.[34]

This is undoubtedly true; the singer, in many forms of musical performance, has to act as the hyperbolic exemplar of the band; and, in many instances (as Weinstein notes), this has led to a performative tension between singer and band. However, there is another way in which singer and band can interact in performance, one which stresses and makes a performative virtue out of the distance between them. Matthew Bannister, in *White Boys, White Noise* (2006), argues that both the Smiths and REM exercise a typically male form of collective group behaviour:

It seems possible that one reason why R.E.M. and The Smiths are both relatively successful is that they display a version of [the] classic rock partnership, a singer who is the star and acts as a point of audience identification and a guitarist who confirms the rock authenticity of the group.[35]

However, this underestimates the extent to which, in performance, the other musicians in both bands melt into the background, leaving the stage free for Morrissey and Stipe; it means that, in performance, both bands are closer to Queen than they are to other indie groups. The stylised gender deviance of Mercury, Stipe and Morrissey would not be so effective if it were not played against musicians whose performance styles are part of the heterosexual but homosocial discourse of rock. So, Mercury's campness is set against the performances of three musicians who themselves incarnate and inhabit standard rock performance positions – the workman bassist, the energetic drummer and the thoughtful virtuoso guitarist. Mercury's radically different performance style can fit, because he is the singer – and the singer is meant to be different.

The same performative gap is apparent in the relation between Morrissey and The Smiths (and the other bands that have backed him in performance), and between Michael Stipe and the other members of REM. Morrissey's performance style has been well described by Simpson, and by David Bret:

Morrissey certainly liked exploiting his own body, regularly whipping open his shirt to expose his finely toned torso as often as not inscribed with some potent message, or occasionally he would shrug the garment back over his shoulder to titillate, while always staying within the bounds of Catholic decency.[36]

Other frequently employed performance tropes include: using the microphone cable as a bullwhip; wearing a hearing aid; carrying flowers, either in his hand or in the back pocket of his trousers; reclining on the stage floor or across the monitors; and so on. However, when one sees footage of Morrissey and The Smiths performing (or when one sees performances from Morrissey's solo career) what is immediately striking is that these tricks – in fact, everything about Morrissey's performance – take place at a far slower pace than that of the rest of the band. The Smiths conform to the same performance tropes as Queen; Morrissey, though, delivers the songs in a markedly more languorous style – as though both the words and the music have a narcotic, rather than an energising effect on him. The rest of the musicians simply play the music – Morrissey is drugged by it, as intoxicated as any fan. When, as happened frequently in the 1980s, his performances were interrupted by stage invasions, Morrissey was able to attribute their frequency to desire ('It's *always* passion, never *ever* violence...')[37] The desire, though, is not to contact a performer who is in energetic control of the event; rather, it is to unite with a singer whose response to the performance is as prostrated, as swooning, as the fan's.

Michael Stipe's performance as the frontman of REM is far more energised than Morrissey's; it is also far more vulnerable. The other musicians again conform to a standard set of performance tropes; here, though, the drummer is the workman, and both bassist (Mike Mills) and guitarist (Peter Buck) produce performances that are energetic and engaged, rather than those of virtuosi. Stipe uses some of the same performance tricks as Morrissey and Mercury – disrobing, baring the torso – but whereas both Mercury and Morrissey seem entirely in control of their performances, Stipe manages to be simultaneously poised and oddly private, if not actually shy. For example, during the performance of 'Country Feedback' on the tour supporting *Monster*, he turns the microphone around and sings the song with his back turned to the majority of the audience; the song is directed at the images projected on the gauze hanging behind the band. When dancing to the music, he is loose-limbed and (almost) uncoordinated; his onstage clothes look like thrift-store cast-offs; when he wears make-up, it is applied in broad stripes of colour, as though it were poster paint; and, frequently, when he faces the audience he does so with his legs together and his hands clasped behind his back. Much of the early attention that the band attracted centred on Stipe as an enigmatic front man, whose lyrics, like his sexuality, tended toward the indistinct. In performance, the enigma is manifested in a performance which tends to emphasise Stipe's almost childish powerlessness – as though he is exposed on stage, rather than in control.

In performance, Mercury, Morrissey and Stipe are able to present an identity which allows their homosexuality to be partially incorporated in the homosociality of the band. However, there are other ways to engage in stylised gender deviance. When Talking Heads first began to attract attention in the late 1970s, they did not seem to fit into the New York punk scene at all – the band barely rates a mention in McNeil's and McCain's oral history of punk. Early photographs show the band on stage wearing T-shirts and slacks; the lead singer, David Byrne, wrote songs in praise of civil servants ('Don't Worry About the Government') and management theory ('The Good Thing'). Far from being romantically at odds with conventional heterosexual social organisation, the group seemed to regard the practices of everyday America with a rather distanced, amused affection. As the band's career progressed, Byrne came to inhabit the onstage persona of the amicable, respectable American rather more closely; during the band's last tour (filmed as the concert movie *Stop Making Sense*) he wore a linen suit, with a white shirt buttoned up to the neck – a costume which made the gawky Byrne look very much like a younger Jimmy Stewart. However, the associations called up by this piece of clothing run counter to other aspects of Byrne's performance: its angularity, its awkwardness, the sense he gives of being overmastered by the music the band is producing. The concert begins with Byrne walking on to an empty stage with a beatbox and a guitar. He plays 'Psycho Killer' as the beatbox provides a rhythm track; near the song's end, the rhythm track stutters – and it seems to blow Byrne sideways, causing him to stagger across the stage before picking up the beat. The concert is peppered with such moments; the microphone collapsing during 'Life During Wartime'; the sudden, doubled-over trembling near the end of 'Burning Down the House'; the eruption of glossolalia in 'Once in a Lifetime', and so on. Even those parts of the performance that are timed and choreographed are awkward – running around the musicians at the end of 'Life During Wartime', Byrne is all elbows and knees, his gait flat-footed. The normal man in performance finds his body uninhabitable; everyone else on stage – black and white, male and female – moves fluidly and unselfconsciously to the music, making Byrne's precisely rendered physical discomfort even more apparent. And for the last two numbers of the gig proper, Byrne wears an overpoweringly large version of the original costume; he appears on stage as a hyperbolic, absurd, deviant version of the most clichéd signifier of supposedly normal heterosexual masculinity, a version of the male that rock performers usually try to efface – the man in the suit.

7
The 1990s

Partly as a reaction to the perceived victory of MTV in the 1980s, bands and audiences in the 1990s found a variety of means through which their authenticity could be proclaimed in performance; either directly (as with Nirvana or Oasis) or ironically (as with U2). However, this return to authenticity was played out against a stage environment which was becoming ever more controllable; film projections (a part of rock performance since the 1970s) had yielded to digital projection and to the large-scale video screen; lighting and sound programmes were now fully computerised; and, more importantly, these technologies could be integrated in performance, rather than existing as separate elements in the show (compare Pink Floyd in the 1970s, who had to use a click track to synchronise the music to the projections, to the Floyd of the 1990s, who were able to rely on digital technology to mesh all the elements of the show). It is rather ironic that a decade which, to an extent, is marked by the recovery of authenticity in performance should also be the decade in which all the theatrical technologies employed in performance are successfully unified.

The authentic audience

In Dallas, on October 19th, Kurt went into meltdown mode again, this time onstage. The show was doomed from the start because it was oversold and the audience spilled onto the stage. Frustrated, Kurt destroyed a monitor console by whacking his guitar against it. When a few minutes later he dived into the crowd, a bouncer attempted to help him back on stage, which Kurt mistakenly read as an aggressive act. He responded by smashing the butt end of his guitar on the bouncer's head, drawing blood. It was a blow that might have killed a smaller man, but it only stunned the bouncer, who punched Kurt in the head, and kicked him as the singer fled.[1]

Footage of this incident (on the video *Nirvana: Live Tonight Sold Out*, and uploaded numerous times to the Youtube website) captures a moment of performative chaos; the dive, during the track 'Love Buzz' from the band's first album, is preceded by a chaotic, flailing guitar solo, after which Cobain tries to hurl himself, backwards, into the crowd. The venue is so packed that he barely succeeds; almost as soon as he leaves the stage, his body is caught by the fans and by the bouncers, who play tug-of-war with it for a moment. The moments of violence – Cobain twice hitting the bouncer, and the bouncer punching Cobain (when the singer had been hoisted safely back on to the stage and was walking away) – are shockingly abrupt.

The shock that the footage undoubtedly generates comes from a variety of sources: the knowledge of Cobain's life and early death, and the place that it now occupies in the mythology of 90s rock; the constricting proximity of band, bouncers and audience; the sense of a performer losing control over every aspect of the performance; and from the fact that, as Cross notes, the incident did not end there (when the band left the venue after the gig, the bouncer smashed the windows of their taxi with his fist). Over and above all of these, though, is the sense that a boundary has been breached; that, in diving from the stage to the audience, Cobain has chosen an especially risky way of effacing his growing stardom – risky both because the closely packed fans might harm him, and because the bouncers placed between the stage and the audience are paid not to let him go. He is doing what a large number of fans would habitually do at Nirvana gigs: when the layout of the venue permitted, fans would climb on stage, dance triumphantly for a second, and then dive back into the waiting arms of the audience before the security guards could eject them. Cobain attempts the same journey, but in the other direction – stage/audience/stage, rather than audience/stage/audience. Both routes are dangerous, but for different reasons; the audience member might find either that he or she is not quick enough to evade the bouncers, or that the welcoming arms that should be outstretched in support have suddenly vanished. The star might find (as did Courtney Love, stage diving at the London Astoria in 1991) that his or her stardom is no protection; in fact, that it actually legitimates assault. In doing something which by its nature is risky, but which is part of the accepted behaviour of a fan signalling his or her identification with the band, Cobain is making a statement; in fact, he is virtually espousing an ideology – that there is no difference between performer and audience, and that the audience's preferred mode of behaviour is perhaps the truest expression of the authenticity of the event.

Acknowledging the audience has always been part of the star's onstage duty (so much so that it can acceptably be mocked – as in the projected titles at the beginning of REM's *Green* tour; one caption read: 'It's great to be in (insert the name of your town here)'.[2] The kind of behaviour evinced by Nirvana and their fans in Dallas, however, is different, and reflects the emergence into the mainstream of a number of behaviours which had previously been most closely associated with underground, alternative genres such as punk, grindcore, the emerging emo movement and the kind of rock/rap fusion promoted by the Red Hot Chili Peppers, and which had drawn its ultimate inspiration from the first generation of punk rockers and their influences (chief amongst them Iggy Pop). These behaviours were given the collective title of moshing:

> Moshing is a combination of three main factors. Crowd surfing, stage diving, and the slam dancing of the original punks taken to a new level of violence. It usually takes place in a semicircular space right in front of the stage, the heaviest and most violent moshing happening in front of the lead singer, but a little back from the security barriers. There are certain acts like Limp Bizkit, Kid Rock and Slipknot, where the mosh pit extends to the entire auditorium or field where they are playing.[3]

Moshing (the term comes from 'Milano Mosh'; a single by SOD – a side-project of the speed-metal band Anthrax) soon became notorious; during the 90s, there were a number of well-publicised incidents associated with mosh pits – perhaps the most infamous being the large-scale destruction which attended the 30-year anniversary Woodstock festival in 1999:

> During the Limp Bizkit set a 24-year-old woman was stripped, pulled down from the crowd, raped, and then surfed to security. Police later said: 'Due to the congestion of the crowd she felt that if she yelled for help or fought, she feared she was going to be beaten.'[4]

Anthony Keidis of the Chili Peppers had to ask the crowd to let the local fire trucks through to the fires that had been lit around the festival ground on the Sunday night; looking out from the stage, he commented 'It's like Apocalypse Now out there' (footage available on the Youtube website). According to Ambrose, the violence which marred the event was caused, at least in part, by an overtly provocative set by Limp Bizkit on the festival's second day, during which the lead vocalist, Fred Durst, encouraged the crowd to 'smash stuff'.[5] It was not, though, that the Limp Bizkit front man simply instructed the audience to unleash themselves on the festival site and on each other; Durst's invocations were rather more ambiguous than that:

> It's time to reach down and bring some positive energy to this mother-fucker. It's time to let yourself go right now, 'cause there are no moth-erfucking rules out there. No matter what's going on in your life that's bad, when that shit goes away, you're always going to be the same, there aint nothing gonna change y'all. Y'gotta remember that. It's time to let it all out. You fucking feel me or not? We'll see if you feel me. The whole world is watchin' us right now, the whole world is watchin you. Let's put out some positive vibes in this motherfucker an have a bigass party.[6]

A cynic, comparing Durst's assertion that 'there aint nothing gonna change' with the world-transforming ethos of the original event, might type this as nothing more than a typically unfocused rant from the spokesman of an unfocused, apolitical generation; but it is rather more interesting than that. Durst seems to be supporting both overwhelming transformation ('there are no motherfucking rules out there') and absolute stasis ('you're always going to be the same'); he pushes the audience towards action, by promising that, no matter what happens, they will recieve a positive energy that will leave them curiously untouched.

This paradox bears closer examination; it speaks of what might be termed an active helplessness, a recasting both of the band and the audi-ence as curiously impotent. The best they can hope for is survival; but this does not mean that they should be passive. Rather, they can and should act, if only to 'let it all out'. At these moments, band and audience form a tight, collective front; the music coming from the stage provides an enveloping aural environment within which the audience can both share an experience with the band and also express themselves fully, in the only place that allows such an expression. This sense of collectivity buffers band and audience from the world outside the gig; it also separates them from those who do not participate. Joey Jordison, Slipknot's drummer (described by Ambrose as looking 'exactly like a lot of the tough little runts you come across in the pit')[7] is keenly aware of this division:

> I went to the SnoCore tour which had System of a Down, Mr Bungle, Incubus. I had backstage passes. Fuck that. I'm watching from out front. That's the way a band is playing – out to *that*. They're putting energy out that way, and that's the way it's being received.[8]

Interestingly, this star is keen to eschew the profits of stardom; he wishes to experience the gig as a fan experiences it; wrapped up in the music and the energy coming from the stage. This is an attitude that has a long provenance in rock; we have encountered it before – when Iggy Pop threw himself from the stage into the audience, for example. However, when Pop did it, he did so very much as the rock star transgressing on to the audience's territory; the quotes given in Chapter 5 can be seen as a self-conscious declaration of difference and distance; I wish I was with you, I wish I was you, but I'm not. This is not the tenor either of Durst's or of Jordison's comments. Here the identification is much closer; in this environment, conceivably, we could swap places – I could join you, and you could join me.

It is no wonder that such an attitude becomes mainstream at the turn of the 90s; after the initial impact of MTV had faded, and in light of hip-hop's rise to market prominence (see above and below), it is unsurprising that the idea of an authentic connection with the audience should recur. It is oddly fitting that the impact of this new form of audience behaviour should be re-enforced in an epoch-marking video, for Nirvana's 'Smells Like Teen Spirit'. The video, it is not too fanciful to suggest, captures the 1980s morphing into the 1990s. The clean-cut students of innumerable 80s youth films who would normally populate a high-school gym have been replaced by the moshing social outcasts of the 1990s, crowd-surfing while Cobain butts the camera. Placed on heavy rotation as the single sold in massive quantities, the video is both exemplar of and impetus for a paradigm shift; what was underground behaviour has now become mainstream. In Cobain this new type of behaviour found its perfect vehicle. Cobain's appeal was very much grounded in the idea of active helplessness; one of the iconic moments of Nirvana's live performances occurred at the Reading Festival in 1992, when the apparently worn-out Cobain was wheeled onstage wearing a medical smock and a white wig. After words of support from Krist Novoselic, Cobain tried to reach the microphone, but collapsed on the stage floor, only to leap up and begin the performance. This vacillation – between stasis and energised action – characterised Cobain's performative life: Gina Arnold, reviewing a gig at San Francisco's Cow Palace on 31 December 1991, described both the crowd's and Cobain's responses:

> By the time Nirvana threw in its hit 'Smells like Teen Spirit' in midset, the crowd had risen up, rolling forward in a relentless wave of motion. The atmosphere was so infectious that even members of the band's own entourage, standing in the comparative safety of the stage wings, periodically lost their heads and leapt off the rim into the boiling crowd below ... Singer Kurt Cobain, his hair dyed purple for the occasion,

vacillated onstage between nearly cataleptic detachment and unnerving inner intensity.[9]

The crowd go wild; but Cobain, the centre of the maelstrom, is periodically curiously detached from it – as though the activities in the audience, activities which involve the band's support team, are not sufficiently powerful to reach him. Footage of the band in performance bears this out: Novoselic is a perennially active presence, but Cobain alternates between intensity and detachment, alternately invested in and unimpressed by the event.

At the turn of the 90s, then, audiences and bands, at least in some genres, invested in a collective idea of authentic behaviour: a style of behaviour that went beyond the ritualised tropes of band–audience interaction that had characterised much of the past two and a half decades. The emphasis of the performance partly switched, from the performers onstage to the audience; the boundary between stage and auditorium became (at least where physically possible) more porous; and, ideally, both band and audience came to view the venue as the only place in which authentic social interaction could take place, free from the 'motherfucking rules out there'. However, the sense of freedom in such an environment is limited and partial; it does not stretch beyond the auditorium, and it legitimises (at least for some participants, both on and off stage) a kind of performative freedom that does not baulk at violence. The energy of the audience turns inward; a form of behaviour which seems to challenge an implicit hierarchy (star on stage, audience in auditorium) in fact creates another hierarchy – the band and audience as already defeated outsiders, hunkering down together against a cruel world. Such a worldview is, at base, passive rather than active; and it serves, in some instances, as a romantic cloak for behaviour which reproduces the worst aspects of rock ideology – misogyny, violence and wilful destructiveness.

'Hips. Tits. Lips. Power'

Writing at the end of the decade, Sheila Whiteley argued that, for women musicians, the 1990s had been a time when two types of musical style came together:

> *Musically* the period is discursively constructed by two distinguishing practices (each with its own assumptions, values and premises) and these are contextualised by the cultural space or context from and through which [women] artists 'speak' or represent themselves. The

first relates to folk (and the singer/songwriter tradition) in its emphasis on authenticity, 'truthfulness' to personal experience, and community; the second is concerned with artifice, and is largely governed by the imperatives of commercial success.[10]

The drive towards authenticity at the turn of the decade (Whiteley identifies the period 1991–4 as the time when these two trends came into their own) is shared with a number of musical genres of the period. As noted above and below, grunge, nu-metal and hip-hop all declare themselves as newly authentic genres, in opposition to what were regarded as the overly commercialised genres of the previous decade. The place of women performers in this general return to the authentic is interesting; and it is interesting because of the way in which the second trend that Whiteley identifies – the pressure of commercialism – works in relation to women. As argued in Chapter 3, the greater part of the received discourse of performance in popular music is derived from a peculiarly male crisis – where male performers place themselves in relation or opposition to a socially derived idea of invisible maleness in mainstream society; part of the result of this is that, in performative terms, most gender positions have at some point been covered by male performers. This has effectively closed out, or at the least severely limited, the ability of women performers to establish themselves as the authentic creators of new musical or performative genres.[11] Even the most individual female performer can be incorporated into the mainstream history of the form through the influence that she has had on male, rather than female, musicians; for example, Patti Smith's most famous descendant is Michael Stipe.

In rock music women are reduced; regarded as individual artists rather than as part of a tradition; and within this restriction, another restriction operates. Mavis Bayton argues, in *Frock Rock,* that:

> women's singing is seen in contrast with the learnt skills of playing an instrument, a kind of direct female emotional expression, rather than a set of refined techniques … It is the only 'instrument' possessed solely by women.[12]

There is a long-standing tradition in Western art and culture which allies woman with nature and with the body; therefore, it is unsurprising (if rather depressing) to find that, even within a form whose gender boundaries are flexible – at least if you are a man – the same demarcations operate. Even when a woman musician is regarded as more than a voice, the description of her musicianship is itself problematic, as Anna Feigenbaum has argued in an astute article on Ani DiFranco:

> When praise for DiFranco frames her as a *female* guitarist, the anomalistic component of this type of complement also comes at the expense of other women.[13]

Maleness, as socially created, is bound up in notions of craft competence and technical ability; femaleness is not. In popular music, a woman can be reduced, like Echo, purely to a voice. The body – and what the body does, and the competences the body displays – are secondary; the body is important because it can be adorned, not because it can run through scales with ease and facility.

When, in 1994, Q *Magazine* gathered Tori Amos, Bjork and PJ Harvey together for an interview, it bore predictable testimony to Bayton's and Fiegenbaum's arguments. For example, the article identified the key defining features of the three women's music; it started, unsurprisingly, with their voices:

> But what sets these women apart from the mainstream soft soul of Mariah Carey and Dina Caroll is their extraordinary singing voices. Bjork's is a heavenly hiccuping thing that almost defies terrestrial description; Polly's is as if opera diva had eaten a drum kit – swooping and percussive, and Tori's is a finely tutored instrument that manages to simultaneously preach, purr and plead.[14]

No mention of the fact that Bjork and Amos have received classical training; no indication that Harvey, although she favours guitar, can turn her hand to a large number of musical instruments. The woman is the voice; her distinctive sound provides a point of access to her essential self. The implication of this quote is that Carey and Carroll have swung far too far towards the kind of commercially palatable sound that Whiteley identifies above as artificial; the marketplace has shaped them so much that even their voices – the guarantee of their essential female selves – have been rendered inauthentic. In contrast, Amos', Bjork's and Harvey's voices are the source of their performative power, and the imprimatur of their identities. Their voices render them formidable; for, in the blurb that accompanies the article, and in its title, we are left in no doubt that these three are the equal of any men:

> Well, would you spill their pint? In the last 18 months, Polly Harvey, Bjork, and Tori Amos have rogered the charts with their special brew of

spooky, left-field weirdness and oestrogen-marinated musings. Q invites the gleesome threesome over for a tupperware party with attitude.[15]

It is hard to think of a paragraph more unintentionally revealing than this. The interview is supposed to be a celebration of the efficacy of these performers (they have the hips, they have the tits, they have the lips, but they also have the power); but the magazine seems entirely unsure as to what kind of power they should have. They are male; and not only male, they are blokes (ready to deck anyone who spills their pint; out to roger the charts). On the other hand, they are women; in fact, they are simultaneously uncontrollably hormonal and decorously polite. Even as an example of the hyperbolic humour that characterises much rock reporting, this is profoundly uneasy. One gets the sense that, even though the magazine wishes to celebrate them, it does not know how to deal with them.

There is ample evidence of such a bias in the reporting of rock: as Helen Davis points out (and as I have argued above), the contradictory typing of Amos, Bjork and Harvey is of a piece with the homosocial nature of rock culture:

> subcultures do not generally welcome women, and those that have tend to accept them only in very limited roles. This coupled with the association of femininity with the mainstream, means that female artists can rarely hope to gain the sense of excitement, rebellion and therefore credibility which comes from an association with a sub-culture.[16]

However, what is particularly interesting about the three performers is that their work resists such incorporation; that musically, and performatively, they have not allowed themselves to make the move that Davis describes. They manage, in their various ways, to balance the tension described by Whiteley, between the competing pressures of authenticity and artifice; and they do so by feeding back gender positions already occupied by male performers, back into the discourses of rock performance.

Whiteley notes that, in performance, Tori Amos' persona is strongly sexualised:

> Amos' open-legged stance at the piano, her reverence toward masturbation, her independence, would certainly have allied her with the out of control carnal lust that historically characterised witches.[17]

True as this undoubtedly is, there is another way to read Amos' performances; the attacking piano style, the arms bearing down on the keyboard, and the constantly agitating body suggest, perhaps, not a lack of control but performative power and confidence. Performing 'Raspberry Swirl' at Glastonbury in 1998, Amos balances moments in which the self is apparently lost (the eyes closed, the vocal line moving toward glossolalia) with performative tropes which display power and control. There are the typical, quick glances to the rest of the musicians on stage, as Amos conducts them through the song; and midway through the performance, Amos stops playing piano for a second, and turns directly toward the audience, her arms above her head, crossed at the wrist. This is the most overt example of a type of gesture that Amos employs; others are the turn of the upper body toward the audience, or the knowing look, focused on specific areas of the audience (or, as Amos' fans would have it, focused on specific audience members – fan reviews of Amos' gigs are full of descriptions of what seems like a purely personal link between performer and fan).

Taken together, these gestures serve to connect her directly with the audience. The extreme inner-directedness which typifies the singer-songwriter is here inverted; the song is not a communion between Amos and her inner self, so much as a performed communication between Amos and the audience. Amos always seems very well aware that she is engaged in something which is in some sense artificial; that the song has to be performed; but she is also invested enough in the performance to allow it to be read as authentic. Indeed, her authenticity and her knowingness are opposite sides of the same coin; even when performing a song as disturbingly personal as 'Me and a Gun' (on *Later with Jules Holland* in 1992), spot-lit on a stool as the camera tracks in to her face, she retains control over the song's narrative primarily by meeting the camera's gaze directly, or by directing the song at the audience on either side of the lens.

Bjork's performance persona, it seems, is for most critics and commentators inextricably bound up with the state of her mental health, and with the state of her clothing. However, it is hard not to ask oneself what is so particularly bizarre about Bjork's choice of outfits; after all, other male performers are equally oddly costumed (one thinks of the layers of thrift-store clothing worn – and then removed – by Michael Stipe on the *Monster* tour). Eccentricity which would at best receive a passing mention in a male performer (or which would, in the case of Brian Eno in the 1970s, attract largely positive attention for its transgressive effectiveness) is here the visible sign of Bjork's strangeness. As with Amos' wide-legged stance at the piano, it can be used as a way of containing Bjork within a fixed set of readings; this woman is kooky, instinctive, fey, naïve, and not entirely in charge of her life or her music. Bjork herself, however, gives this character description short shrift:

> Yeah, but I don't know how many times I've had this conversation with people where, they've met me four or five times, got to know me a bit, they say, You know, I thought you were this sort of pixie-type person, but you're actually one of the toughest people I've ever met.[18]

Wearing a red dress with a ballooning skirt of dyed ostrich feathers (on the tour supporting the *Vespertine* album in 2002) might seem to confirm the critical consensus; it is an overtly performative dress – not only because of the design, but also because it emphasises movement (and particularly the movement of the lower torso). However, the dress in performance serves to draw attention to the fact that Bjork's movements are as far removed as possible from the 'pixie-type person' of the popular imagination. Characteristically, there is something almost pugilistic about her movements; her feet are firmly planted, and her body moves in a series of short, abrupt steps. Her characteristic performance style owes more to the strongly angular, rooted choreography developed by Martha Graham – a choreographic approach designed to counteract the construction of female identity in dance as necessarily light and ethereal. Furthermore, the dress she wears shifts the visual centre of gravity down to her hips and thighs – further anchoring her to the ground.

PJ Harvey's persona is equally contradictory:

> In PJ Harvey, British pop has produced its most prominent female icon in a decade, a wistfully thin, stridently bluesy chanteuse who sings, screams sometimes, of her sexuality. Yet there is a problem. An idea, Polly Jean Harvey undoubtedly is, but an idea of what no one knows for sure.[19]

Famously, one of the ideas that Harvey does not endorse – and which contributes to her unreadability (at least in gender-political terms) – is feminism. In the interview quoted above, she comments, 'Feminism is just something I really haven't come up against', and there are elements of her performance style which hark back to a female persona whose relation to feminism is rather ambiguous. The rock chick is a woman who works within the constraints of the male world of rock performance. As Whiteley notes, in relation to Janis Joplin (the rock chick archetype), this places the female performer in an unenviable position:

> Joplin's aggressiveness marked her as uncontrollable, unnaturally active, and earthy and, as such, lying outside the dominant symbolic

order. Thus, while her performing career suggests both a challenge and a compliance with the masculine codes of power, dominance, hierarchy and competition inherent in rock, it is suggested that her physicality ... was interpreted, at the time, as either imitative or confrontational.[20]

No wonder that subsequent rock chicks – Stevie Nicks, Pat Benatar et al. – chose to emphasise glamour as well as assertiveness; to do so provided them with a way of deflecting the kind of misogyny that Joplin used to attract. Harvey, similarly, adopts the trappings of glamour in performance; she wears high heels, short skirts, and, famously, during the *To Bring You My Love* tour, a pink cat-suit and bright red lipstick (equally famously, she was at the time seriously anorexic, and on the verge of a breakdown). However, the rock chick (as with the male androgene) most usually inhabits both the male and female elements of her persona equally comfortably; Harvey, notably, does not, and does not attempt to:

> 'I don't want to do anything that's just straight glamorous,' she's said, 'like "Oh, Polly Harvey's suddenly becoming a woman." It has to have some element of uneasiness or humor.'[21]

To this we might add that Harvey does nothing which is straight male. In her performances, both the signifiers of maleness (the characteristic address to the microphone – in particular pulling the stand down until it is at 45 degrees to the stage floor; the iconic guitar – in this case a Gibson Explorer) and the signifiers of femaleness (the heels, the dress) simply do not fit with each other: the uneasiness, and the humour, comes from the fact that Harvey seems to have constructed her onstage self from elements which are usually not allowed to operate in the same performative universe. In effect, it is not that Harvey's act does not 'envision ways of transcending a long-standing system of gender stereotypes', as Mark Mazullo argues.[22] Rather, her act explodes those stereotypes by placing them next to each other, and allowing the fact that they are incommensurate to register throughout the performance.

Harvey's ambivalence toward feminism was shared by other women performers at the time (it was frequently repeated by Riot Grrl musicians, as Mimi Schippers' interviews attest). However, this does not mean that a critique of gender relations is not played out in her performance; it manifestly is – as, indeed, it is in Amos' performances, and as it is in Bjork's. Amos takes the internalised, confessional singer/songwriter trope, and turns it outward – both in terms of the dynamism of her performance and the element of direct, controlled address that it contains; Bjork takes the stereotype of the spiritual, and eccentrically unworldly woman artist, roots it firmly to the ground, and imbues it with a distinctly non-ethereal strength; and Harvey takes the tropes of the rock chick and turns them into an exercise in imposture. No wonder the Q interview is couched in such uneasy terms; the threat posed to male ideas of performative identity by each of these performers is very great, because none of them is pre-pared fully to inhabit the spaces prepared for them in the homosocial world of rock.

The great British male

Blur finished off 1994 with a gig at Alexandra Palace. Suitably, for a group who had laboriously rediscovered their home culture, Alexandra Palace was an iconically English location; the original home of the BBC, it was a good place to finish a year in which the group had, it seemed, been the main orchestrators of a long celebration of the fine details of English life. During 'There's No Other Way', the band's first top ten single, Damon Albarn launched himself into the audience, and crowd-surfed back into the bouncers' arms. When Kurt Cobain attempted a similar thing in Dallas in 1991, the incident ended in violence (as described above); in London, Albarn's dive provoked nothing more devastating than a mild touch of irony. Graham Coxon, the band's guitarist, swapped the chorus line of the song for the plea, 'Please don't kill our singer/ Please don't kill our singer ...'[23]

It was a moment of archetypal Englishness; such an overt display of enthusiasm couldn't pass without its own small, accompanying moment of deflation. And the bigger the moment (and the more extravagant the claims made for it), the more necessary the irony; when Oasis capped their years of initial success by playing two consecutive gigs at Knebworth Park in front of a combined audience of 250 000, Noel Gallagher was profoundly moved:

> 'This is history!' yelped Noel, with no little gravitas. 'Right here, right now, this is history!' Finding the opportunity to burst his bubble too good to pass up, Liam provided the punchline. 'Really?' he shot back, 'I thought it was Knebworth.'[24]

If there is one thing that reliably separates American bands and British bands in the mid-90s, it is this. American bands (and Nirvana are a prime example) might respond to the world with angry cynicism; they might satirise the image that the media had created for them; but the under-cutting of the band's image by the band themselves was a peculiarly British – or English – habit. If nothing else, it brought bands back down to the quotidian: a place where a significant number of British groups and singers felt most at home. Interviewed in 1992, Jarvis Cocker of Pulp spoke of 'The sense of the romantic in the everyday. Ray Davies finding the poetic in the sun going down over Waterloo station.'[25] British bands, in other words, made both ironic and romantic capital from straitened circumstances and narrow horizons; British – or, once again, more prop-erly English – life was an amalgamation of small details, just waiting to be puffed up into significance by the aspiring musician.

However, this is not to say that there was an accepted image of Britishness to which bands and singers could refer. The 1990s were a curi-ous moment in recent British history. The removal of Margaret Thatcher in 1990 might have seemed like the signal for vast and over-reaching change; but what the country got was the strange interregnum of the Major government – seven years in which the central dynamic that had shaped Thatcherism atrophied. When the Conservatives were at last voted out of power in 1997, the party had already collapsed from within, weighed down by scandals and policy divisions; they were replaced, however, by a Labour party that had agreed to operate within and ame-liorate the Thatcherite model. With the argument over the composition of a modern economy out of bounds, political differences were largely expressed in symbolic national terms. Labour, in the run up to the 1997 election, positioned themselves as a new party for a new Britain; in con-trast, Major's vision of an eternal Britain (for which, once again, we should read an eternal England) was straight out of Orwell in the 1940s – warm beer, spinsters cycling to evensong, and so on. Kenneth Lunn noted in 1996:

> [It] seems remarkable that, at the end of the twentieth century, and following an intense period of radical political and economic change instituted by successive Conservative governments, the image of Englishness evoked remains significantly rural and replicates the hierarchical values of previous societies.[26]

This point can be extended beyond the eternal verities of Conservative rhetoric; it also calls into question the rootedness of Labour's version of a new, young country waiting to be born in the wake of a Tory defeat. After all, if the default symbolic condition of England had remained unchanged since the early part of the century, it would not be amenable to the kind of purely rhetorical newness proposed by Labour. It could be said, that the only thing that was new about the decade was that Britain became England; both Scotland and to a lesser extent Wales used the decade to assert an identity which ran against the idea of a unified British identity; England was no longer an easy synonym for the United Kingdom – but England seemed to lack a secure idea of itself as a country and as a society.

It is sometimes easy to assume that the title 'Britpop', given to the slew of bands who dominated British music from 1994 to 1997, is as nostalgic as Major's hypothesised England; and, as such, is a misleading symbol of cultural health:

> It is one of the profound failures of New Labour that its symbolic rep-resentations of 'Cool Britannia' have tended to stress the more nostalgic, monocultural Britpop at the expense of ... genuinely new terms.[27]

This is simply wrong, for two reasons. Firstly, it suggests that Britpop was a single, cohesive genre, based on pre-existing musical forms; this is, to say the least, inaccurate. Secondly, it suggests that there is a single idea of British culture that all Britpop bands reflect; as I have just argued, dur-ing the 1990s no such idea was available. Rather, it makes more sense to see Britpop, in all its divisive incoherence, as a response to the kind of social and cultural uncertainty that seemed to typify British life in the 1990s. It is hard to think of many Britpop songs which unambiguously embrace Englishness (Oasis' 'Round Are Way' is the only one which springs to mind). Most of the time, Britpop anthems describe a country in crisis: the trapped, disregarded poor in Pulp's 'Common People'; the suburban escapees who populate Suede's songs; the various stereotypes, acting out an Englishness without meaning, in Blur's *Modern Life is Rubbish, Parklife,* and *The Great Escape.* There is no general nostalgia for a lost Britishness in Britpop; what there is, is the notion that the behaviours which seem to mark out British life have been drained of meaning, and should be escaped.

In performance, this ambiguous attitude to British culture coincides with another set of uncertainties, this time related to masculinity. In popular cultural discourse, the 1990s marked the time when the 'new man' of the 1980s (who had accepted the chief tenets of feminism, and was willing to eschew the conventional trappings of male behaviour) was replaced by the new lad; the new lad, in contrast, was unafraid of his masculinity, and saw nothing wrong in indulging in overt displays of macho hedonism. Many accounts of the 'new lad' see the phenomenon as part of a generalised backlash against feminism; Imelda Whelan, in 2000, described new laddism as 'a nostalgic revival of old patriarchy; a direct challenge to feminism's call for social transformation, by reaffirming – albeit ironically – the unchanging nature of gender relations and sexual roles'.[28] However, other commentators see the creation of the figure of the new lad as more than an attempt to restore male hegemony. For example, as Rosalind Gill points out, the hedonistic new lad is a reaction against traditional images of the responsible family man; and he is also a reaction against the new man of the 80s. Gill looked at a number of 'obituaries' for the new man, published in newspapers in the US, Britain and Australia in the 90s:

> New man is condemned as inauthentic. In these accounts, in a somewhat strange ontological move, the final nail in his coffin is that he never existed at all! He was, alternately, a media fabrication or marketing strategy or a calculating pose by ordinary men in order to get a woman (or women) to sleep with them.[29]

And at this point, presumably, thoroughly trounced, the new man evaporates into the media aether. Gill is careful (and correct) to note that the new lad is as much of a construction as the new man; and she also notes how all-pervasive the new lad was – he populated the new men's magazines that sprang up during the decade; he was anatomised in newspaper articles and commentaries; and, it might seem, he stalked the stage every time a Britpop band played, his unreconstructed maleness bedecked and enhanced by some clear token of his Englishness. All new lads aspired to the condition of Noel Gallagher – playing a gig at Maine Road (the home ground of Manchester City – thus neatly conflating music and football, two key new lad leisure pursuits), with a Union Jack guitar around his neck.

In the discourse which soon grew up around Britpop (and which still conditions discussions of the music of the mid-90s), new laddishness and Englishness are conflated; but, interestingly, both in terms of the music bands produced and the personae adopted in video and in performance, neither term is employed entirely unironically. This irony manifests itself in various forms: one of the most overt is in the performance style of Jarvis Cocker, the lead singer and chief songwriter of Pulp. It is impossible to watch Cocker performing – particularly during the period of the group's peak success in 1994–5 – without gaining the sense that each gesture has been placed in quotation marks; that Cocker is a hyperconscious performer, who in some ways finds the whole process faintly absurd. In interview, Cocker has commented on his uneasy awareness of the reality of mediation, as a major structuring principle in contemporary behaviour:

> But I also believe that people nowadays are so used to the mediated version of things that when the real thing comes along it doesn't seem as real, and that's always been a bugbear of mine.[30]

This, however, does not mean that he is entirely subsumed behind the processes that he describes. He escapes the process of mediation, first of all, by demonstrating an ironic awareness of it; and, in doing so, he arguably manages to create a communal awareness, shared by both the performer and the audience, that such processes can be observed from the outside. When the band played Brixton Academy in 1995, it was at the end of a very successful year, in which Cocker's image had become ubiquitous – as ubiquitous as that of the Gallaghers. Cut-out images of Cocker and the rest of the band were placed on a catwalk behind the drums; Cocker had been photographed in a characteristically angular pose, looking upward, his arms folded, his long fingers splayed (these images also formed part of the packaging for the *Different Class* album). Before the performance of 'I Spy', Cocker posed beside his image, adopting exactly the same pose, in an unmistakable ironisation of the iconic nature of the image (as though he were saying, 'Look at me: I'm playing at Jarvis Cocker'). This does not mean that, at other points, he is not invested in the performance; but it is a comment on the mediation process that he and the band have undergone. It re-enforces the band's and Cocker's outsider status; and removes him both from the idea that his performances are direct celebrations of Englishness, or of the figure of the new lad. Cocker's characteristic performance style – the emphasis he places on the thinness and narrowness of his body, the stylised poses and deadpan face – serve to confirm his status as passionately ironic outsider; discussing the country, and discussing male behaviour, without buying in to the mythology that supposedly surrounds them.

Cocker in performance establishes a considerable distance between himself and the then-current manifestation of English maleness, and ensures that his and the band's work cannot be seen as a simple endorsement either of his country or his gender; and in this he is, arguably, typical of his time. Rupa Huq, in an excellent recent study (*Beyond Subculture*, 2005), has rightly drawn attention to the relatively large number of female performers in Britpop:

> Britpop's ranks have included a number of high profile strong female role models, including Elastica's Justine Frischmann, Sleeper's Louise

Weiner and Echobelly's Sonia Madan – the latter also being Asian. This has strong parallels with riot grrl. This liberated feminism, exhibited by both styles, is unlike old-style 'women's lib', or at least the negative associations with which it was tainted in the 1990s, for it substitutes hedonism in the face of austerity ...[31]

– and as such, it bears an interesting resemblance to the relation between the new man and the new lad. The point can be taken further; successful female Britpop performers, like their riot grrl counterparts in the States (see Schippers 2002) provided a performative template for male performers as well. For example, Suede's accommodation with the three-minute Britpop single (on the album *Coming Up*) was accompanied by a performative transformation. Brett Anderson swapped an overt performance of sexualised ambiguity (whipping his bottom with the microphone, executing snake-like contortions which served to emphasise the slimness of his hips) with another form of androgyny; visually, if not performatively, his androgynous role model was now provided by Justine Frischmann of Elastica (herself a former member of Suede). Even those bands – like Blur – who had seemed to adopt the values of English new laddishness, reveal in performance elements of ambiguity which remove them from an exclusively male environment; the Alexandra Palace gig mentioned above might feature the band kitted out in the kind of casual dress that defined the stereotypical new lad (trainers, T-shirt, jeans); but the performance takes place in a set that contains symbols of the type of feminised environment that the new lad was supposed to escape (large, fringed light-fittings hang from the ceiling; the evening is introduced by a game of bingo). In performance, then, amongst the most celebrated of the Britpop bands, the idea that the form enshrines a particularly celebratory evocation either of the new lad or of the country that shaped him is very hard to maintain.

What, though, of the most visible incarnations of English new laddishness, Oasis? After all, they provided the archetypal images of the period; given both the Gallagher brothers' extremely high profile during Britpop's peak period, it is hard to think of the mid-90s in British culture generally, without thinking of them first. Liam Gallagher, in performance, might seem the new lad incarnate; he is the only mobile member of the band, prowling and swaggering around the stage, a can of lager (especially in the mid-90s) an indispensable prop. Noel Gallagher, on the other hand, stressed his allegiance to the canon of British popular music in as obvious a way as possible, by playing a hollow-body guitar on which was painted a Union Jack. Even here, though, the performance of that identity is rather more ambiguous. Firstly, the Gallaghers are not new lads together, united against the world; in an interview for the DVD ... *There and Then*, Noel is asked if he has any strong memories of performances after they are over: he replies 'It's trying to get our kid to shut up rambling complete and utter gibberish between songs...'[32] The answer, with its strong suggestion of a father exasperated by the uncontrollability of a problem son, is a revealing one, because it helps to describe the dynamic that the band play out on stage; Liam might be the new lad, but Noel is the authority figure – the professional whose job it is to keep the new lad in check. New laddishness is not given its head; it is subject to control. It is not simply celebrated – it is indulged, but the level to which this is allowed accounts for the curious atmosphere of a mid-90s Oasis gig. During the band's 1995 gig at Maine Road stadium, Liam begins to introduce 'Wonderwall' – but he is cut off by Noel, who gets his introduction in first. Liam's retort – an angry, inquiring 'Oh Yeah?' – might in other circumstances serve as the prelude to a fight; it has that sense of aggressiveness held in momentary check until the situation clarifies itself. The band go straight into the song; but the tension, notably, is not diffused or reconciled.

In a 2005 interview, Noel Gallagher talks about the experience of growing up in Manchester:

> Standing in a room with grown men who were supposed to be your role models, who were just gone, absolutely shot to bits – no hope, fuck all, nothing. And the place where you live is falling down, and the gang culture is just starting. And you tell people from good backgrounds and they think it's all Alan Bleasdale and all that, but believe me. The real life of it is no fucking good.[33]

This is as far removed from an endorsement of one's culture as it is possible to get; there is no celebration of a mythic England here; in its place, and in Britpop as a whole, there are anthems which talk either about living within or about escaping a Britain which traps the individual. Neither is there in Britpop a simple celebration of hedonism; the new lad is presented – but he is also contained, and the expression of contemporary maleness in Britain ironised – revealed as a mediation by those who are themselves uncomfortably aware of their own mediation. If Britpop, as some commentators asserted, was a movement in which the twin discourses of Englishness and the new lad combined, then they did so in a context which did not allow the simple celebration of either. Both discourses, in practice and in performance, were deflated and circumscribed.

Dealing with the real: rock/hip-hop

As noted in the previous chapter, Heavy Metal managed to reconstitute itself at the end of the 1980s through a recourse to a well-established strategy which had the support of both the genre's bands and its audiences – the 'proud pariah' strategy, or the willing adoption of the role of the social outsider. At the end of the 1990s, it is arguable that the same kind of change occurred: Metal, which had lost the market position that it occupied in the 1980s with the advent of grunge, managed to claw back some of that lost territory through an alignment with a musical style which occupied something of the same ideological territory, albeit in a radically different form. Rap had survived a number of obituaries, read out over the genre's supposed corpse during the 80s; by the beginning of the 90s, it had established itself as a commercial genre whose potential audience crossed some apparently impermeable boundaries. Previously, acts like Michael Jackson and Prince had managed to gain a cross-over audience (one which had an impact on both black and white American music markets) by producing tracks which were generically hybrid – which borrowed from funk, soul, mainstream pop and rock. Rap exhibited a similar hybridity; musical history could be sampled and reshaped to provide an appropriate musical environment for the rapper; but the form as a whole did not concede much to the mainstream. Rap operated by co-opting musical forms (electronica, soul, disco and, as the decade progressed, rock and metal); it did so in the service of a developing idea of authenticity, which was in its expression at least as complex as the authenticity espoused by earlier generations of rock musicians.

Rap had grown up, in New York in the early and mid-1970s, as an adjunct of an emerging culture which found expression in a number of media: graffiti, break-dancing, mixing and manipulating recorded music, and so on. When it began to move out of its original location at the end of the decade, it did so with all the accoutrements of the culture that had formed it; rap, unlike rock in the late 1960s, did not have to lay claim to previously existing musical forms to provide it with the necessary grounding in authenticity – it carried an authenticating culture and set of behaviours with it into the mainstream. As Foreman suggests,[34] that sense of authenticity was rooted in the social exclusion and outright discrimination which was part of the lives of generations of black Americans; it was and is a reaction to social constraint. Rather than masking or evading black urban experience, many rap artists foregrounded it; indeed, as Tricia Rose has argued, the form of the music itself, and that of the culture that surrounds it, might be seen as a direct reflection of and reaction to the regimes of surveillance described by Foreman; a deliberately hermetic series of codes, designed to establish a counterculture that either refuses or countermands an oppressive social system:

> Developing a style nobody can deal with – a style that cannot be easily understood or erased, a style which has the reflexivity to create counter-dominant narratives against a mobile and shifting enemy – may be one of the most effective ways to fortify communities of resistance and *simultaneously* reserve the right to communal pleasure.[35]

Musically, rap was very well placed to act as the set of counter-narratives that Rose describes. Given that much of rap's output built on pre-existing musics, it could legitimately orient itself within the history of popular musical forms; however, given the fact that rap relied increasingly on complex sampling technologies, and that the lyrics could take as their starting point a version of contemporary black experience, rap could function simultaneously as a connection with black musical traditions, and as an appropriation of musical forms that (as some rappers argued) had been appropriated from black musicians by white society. At the same time, lyrically, rappers asserted their authenticity in rhetoric which was increasingly specific in terms of character and locale (see Forman 2002). Rap authenticity was and is a matter of the past, the present and the future of the form: It is not (as Keir Keighley suggests for rock) split between the music and the artist; it is positioned both as a reanimation of history and an entirely contemporary – in fact, a state of the art – intervention in that history.

By the mid-90s, rap had firmly established itself as a commercial presence in both black and white markets. David Samuels ('The Rap on Rap' (1992) collected in Forman and Neal 2004) noticed a paradox in this: the commercial mainstreaming of rap did not coincide with a dilution of the perceived 'blackness' of the form; in fact, it was quite the opposite – after the temporary success of MC Hammer and Vanilla Ice, the baton passed to Public Enemy and NWA. In the essay 'Black Empires, White Desires' (collected in Forman and Neal 2004), Davarian L. Baldwin argued persuasively that such a presence was not simply a matter of the appropriation of the music of a subordinate culture by a dominant one. Somewhere in the reception of the music, a complex dialectic was playing itself out around the figure of the nigga – a figure imagined as enshrining a localised resistance to the powers of an oppressive society. The nigga was inherently dangerous, but, as Baldwin argues, as an image of the outsider he was irresistible for black and white listeners alike. Rap, after all, had gained a reputation as an inherently dangerous form by the early 90s, especially in live performance; this reputation was undeserved, and said more about the moral panic that the form had sparked in American society (a panic which could not help but repeat persistently racist tropes, deeply embedded in the culture). As Mark Anthony Neal argued:

> [In] the eyes of many suburban whites, hip-hop concerts in places like Long Island's Nassau Coliseum represented a typical threat to the day-to-day stability of white suburban life. The historic policing of public spaces where blacks congregated often had a profound impact on the ability of African-Americans to build and maintain community, and such was the case when young African-Americans congregated at the local clubs and concert venues where the core values of the 'hip-hop' generation were distributed and critiqued.[36]

Although this did not stop live performance in the genre, it did limit it. At the point where the discourses of rap changed – when it became either more directly political (with Public Enemy) or more overtly about the violent Ghetto (with NWA) – the genre moved from novelty to threat.

Paradoxically, as Baldwin notes, this sense of threat made the genre even more appealing to a white audience – and to a generation of American rock musicians. Some groups – like the mixed race Rage Against the Machine – were drawn to the form because of the political content of some of the material. Other groups seem to have been drawn to rap because it chimed in with established rock tropes – especially those that had clustered around the ideas of authenticity and male display. In particular, the idea that rap was frequently an exercise in male bonding seemed to resonate with many bands. Summarising previous discussions of the posse in hip hop culture, Murray Forman concludes:

> Each expression ... isolates the posse as the fundamental social unit binding a rap act and its production crew together. It creates a relatively coherent or unified group identity that is rooted in place and within which the creative process is supported.[37]

In essence, the posse provides more than musical support; it provides rappers with a way of dealing with a hostile environment, while at the same time remaining true to it. Forman argues that, as the form develops, the idea of the 'hood' (the specific location to which a rapper declares his allegiance) becomes increasingly important. The posse gives musical and personal support to the rapper; but the posse also recreates the 'hood' and gives the rapper a visible sign of a continued link with his roots – with all the authenticating power that such a link suggests. It is not surprising, then, that when rock musicians who have adopted rap discuss their own origins, something like the same narrative emerges. For example, here is Fred Durst, talking about the formation of Limp Bizkit:

> I just went to see every band I could and found that there was nobody serious but I'd pick one person. Like Sam stuck out of his band – he was serious and go-hard. Wes stuck out of his band and John in his. I said, 'hey, I'm really serious. I wanna do this. I wanna mix a lot of things and these are my ideas.' I already had some songs written and we started playing those out and it caught on. Then we all started getting the chemistry and writing together and realized it was real.[38]

And here is Slipknot, looking for a DJ:

> One night Joey and Shawn checked out a clan named 'The Sound Proof Coalition' at the Safari containing the DJs, A-Rock, Loodachris, Phase II, Rek, Sub Two, Iniversoul and Starscream. Starscream, a.k.a Sid Wilson introduced himself to them and told them they rocked at Dotfest, Shawn said they needed a DJ, Sid said he was the man. Following pestering by Sid he was allowed to view a practice and following a session of head butting it was decided he was fit to be part of the group.[39]

And Korn:

> All the members of Korn were bonded together in some way in their youth. Fieldy, for example, made the switch from guitar to bass when his buddy and future Korn guitarist, Head, mentioned on the way home from a party that he needed a guitarist for his new band. Fieldy and Davis had the additional linkage of their Dads playing together in a band.[40]

From these accounts, one can clearly see the appeal that the social structure of rap had for some white musicians; it was a way of rearticulating an old tale – that of the band as the last gang in town, a refuge for like-minded souls in a hostile world. Another part of the rap ethos, outlined above, perhaps helps to explain why in the 1990s a specific type of white musician was drawn to the style. The descriptions of rap, given above, strongly suggest that rappers are, at least in some respects, 'proud pariahs' – an idea that, as noted above, runs through the practice and reception of Heavy Metal. There are, of course, significant differences between the two genres; in Heavy Metal, the tag is a consciously adopted self-description, while in rap (as Forman suggests above) it is an inescapable condition of a prejudiced society. However, there is sufficient overlap to allow, for example, Korn to invite Ice Cube on to the first of their *Family Values* tours in 1998, without the juxtaposition seeming too incongruous.

However, in performance the genres – rap and rap-metal (or nu-metal) – diverge, and diverge markedly. It is easy for the rapper to enact the relation implied by the idea of the posse in performance because, quite simply, the floor is clear enough to allow it. Much has been made of the form's reliance on technology, and by extension its complex relation to the idea of musical authenticity; the fact that, for many rappers, the type of technology that creates the music also allows groups and artists to perform on a bare stage is perhaps too apparently commonsensical to require much comment. However, it is a crucial part of the creation of the posse on stage; when (say) the Wu Tang Clan played live at full strength, a bare stage allowed free movement, unencumbered by the need to avoid musicians who might be tied to one location on stage. It meant that the performance of a track like 'Wu Tang Clan ain't Nuthin to Fuck Wit' would have no strongly defined visual centre, because there would be no one occupying the role of the lead singer or lead musician; the flow moves from MC to MC, and the crowd's perception of the flow is not located in any one figure – it is dispersed across the stage. Even when a solo artist performed, it would be quite common to bring another posse member along; when Ice Cube joined Korn's *Family Values* tour, he performed alongside the rapper WC (another member of the Westside Connection, a three-man rap team formed in 1997). On stage, the spotlight might be on Ice Cube; but WC was also a strong visual presence, employing the same body language, rapping alongside the star, and engaging Ice Cube in conversation between and during tracks.

On the other hand, when rock bands employed rap techniques, they could not help but be set in the framework already established for rock performance; the visual impact of a shared body language and delivery style that flows across a bare stage, very much a part of the live performance of rap, simply ceases to be possible when the performers also play the music. There are, as I have argued, established tropes for the enactment of music which govern the way that instrumentalists work on stage; more than this, and quite obviously, the guitar around the performer's neck limits the performer's ability to mirror body language. A series of gestures and poses which, in performance, mark rappers out as part of a posse, serve in rap metal to isolate the lead singer. Zack de la Rocha from Rage Against the Machine, or Jonathan Davis from Korn, might adopt rap moves to a greater or lesser extent; but when they do so, those gestures form part of another dynamic – that of the engaged front man, mediating between the audience and technical expertise of the musicians. Also, the range and style of movement subtly altered; characteristically, rap performers remain within the initial performative environment, which formed in the genre's early days; rap began (as commentators like Rose have noted) as a conversation between the MC and the audience, and that sense of a conversation – of a performance always delivered out to the audience with few moments of introspection – is still integral to the form. With the notable exception of de la Rocha, rap metal vocalists tend to present themselves as a mixture of the outer-directed rapper, and the internalised, intense rock front man; for example, Fred Durst is at one moment the outer-directed rapper, and then, and especially during the typically crunching, aggressive choruses, a performing member of the authentic audience described above – bent double over the microphone, eyes closed, completely immersed in the moment. Around the front man, the other musicians (and especially the guitarists) tend to incarnate the performance tropes mapped out in hard rock or Heavy Metal; Tom Morello is the virtuoso, focused on his guitar, able to use it to replicate the scratches and noise-bursts of late-80s Public Enemy; Limp Bizkit's Wes Borland is the theatrical, extreme metal guitarist, with a look and a set of movements borrowed from the slasher film; and Slipknot recreate and update the horror aesthetic first employed by Alice Cooper in the 1970s. In performance, then, the posse ideal, inherited from rap, clashed with performance tropes already established in metal – and the metal tropes won out.

8
The 21st Century

So far this century there have been no great technological advances to equal the strides in lighting and sound design in the previous decades: rather, these advances have bedded down, and have become entirely normal parts of the performance event (and, as such, their power to disrupt the processes of authentication that Moore sees as crucial to the ascription of authenticity has lessened). However, there has been a change in the status of the touring event; as a Channel Four news report on 16 August 2006 pointed out, record companies have responded to an uncertain commercial environment (created by file-sharing technologies that they find hard to control) by putting an increased emphasis on the live event as a sure source of income. This has given an added impetus to a phenomenon already well underway by the 1990s; the megatour, spanning several continents, used to maximise the profits from a particular recording, and to garner more revenue both from ticket sales (the top price for a ticket on Madonna's *Confessions* tour, for example, was £160) and from ancillary merchandise. This has not only become a reliable source of income (the Stones' *Bigger Bang* tour (see below) grossed £400 000 000 worldwide), but it has also helped to prolong the economic lives of well-established bands like the Stones and Yes, as well as giving other bands – like The Who – a reason to re-form and tour.

The coolest guy on earth

In 2005, the Stones went out on tour again, in support of a new album. The tour was a standard Stones event; the set was, to say the least, elaborate:

> The 90 ft high, 285 ft wide steel-constructed stage, weighing in at 300,000 tons, looked like a cross between the Guggenheim and an

airport lounge and is said to be the largest and most expensive ever assembled. Giant screens showed an animated video of exploding molten rocks, depicting the original big bang. All that was missing was a commentary by Professor Stephen Hawking. There were jets of fire, fireworks and inflatables. Halfway through the show, the entire central section of the stage lurched forward like a carnival float, carrying the band 100 yards to a second stage located in the middle of 'the sacred turf' of what is normally the Red Sox baseball field.[1]

Since the 1970s, Stones tours had relied on spectacle, as much as on music; sometimes relatively restrained (the sliding IMAG screens on the stadium sets during the *Forty Licks* tour in 2002/3), sometimes verging on the ridiculous (the giant inflatable model of a feral dog which appeared to swallow Jagger on the *Steel Wheels* tour). However, this reliance had come at a price; it contributed to a narrative which had built up around the band since their touring hiatus in the mid-1980s. Each time the Stones toured, journalists would gleefully total the combined ages of the band members; and each time a performance failed, age would be cited as the overwhelming reason (the *NME*, reviewing a bad gig at the Shepherd's Bush Empire in 2003, described the band as 'Old guys desperately in need of a rest'.[2]

The Stones suffered from such comments, it could be argued, not only because they simply kept going (after all, other musicians – Bob Dylan being an obvious example – stayed on the road over the same period without attracting the same type of criticism), but because their continued existence seemed in some ways to be a betrayal of their earlier selves. The Stones had seemed the incarnation of the revolutionary, transformative power of rock music in the late 1960s. Jagger had espoused revolutionary politics; the band had sung about the coming revolution – and yet, here they still were, making more money, with the ennobled lead singer still trotting out the anthems of nearly forty years ago. One of the most vitriolic responses to the undead Stones came from John Strausbaugh:

There was something sadly metaphoric about the huge empty spaces separating them from one another. They weren't a band any more; they were the board of directors of Rolling Stones Inc., called together for their annual meeting. Not a rock band any more, but a handful of middle aged men acting like a rock band. The stages and sets and fireworks only kept getting bigger in the 90s, the show more and more soulless, less like rock – even outdoor stadium rock, a dicey proposition in the best of times – and more like a truck pull.[3]

There is something to Strausbaugh's critique; the band had become notably more corporate in the 1980s, with Jagger taking on an increased role in their management (Strausbaugh fails to mention, though, that this only happened after decades of relative exploitation). However, the critique has some rather glaring flaws. Firstly, Strausbaugh's argument is not new; it is a version of the argument Jagger himself made about large-scale gigs in the 1960s (see Chapter 4). This of itself does not entirely invalidate Strausbaugh's point; but it does qualify it – the constraints of the stadium gig had shaped the band's performances, even during their heyday.

There is another, more telling objection. Strausbaugh wishes to argue that there is something inherently ridiculous in the idea of old men playing rock; he is absolutely explicit about this – 'Rock is youth music'.[4] The Stones, in simply keeping going, are traducing the spirit of youthful rebellion. However, it could be argued that, in keeping going, the Stones are committing another transgression, this time against the fetishisation of youth:

> One particular feature of the mode of production in late capitalist society is, however, that it does not require an ascetic mode of desire; indeed, pleasures are produced by the process of commodification and elaborated by the process of consumption. The regimen of bodies is no longer based on a principle of ascetic restraint, but on hedonistic calculation and the amplification of desire. Asceticism has been transformed into the practices which promote the body in the interests of commercial sensualism. The new anti-Protestant ethic defines premature aging, obesity and unfitness as sins of the flesh.[5]

Turner's point does help to explain something of the viciousness of critiques like Strausbugh's, and the routine totting up of the Stones' collective ages: what more shocking sight can there be, in an age which promotes commercialised sensuality, than a bunch of old men making a spectacle of themselves? However, and perhaps more interestingly, it helps to explain a facet of the contemporary Stones which is most clearly seen in performance: a change in the relative importance of Mick Jagger and Keith Richards.

As has been indicated above (see Chapter 3) Mick Jagger's performance persona has come in for detailed analysis; the gender identities assumed in passing on record and in performance have excited some incisive criticism. However, by the time that the Stones reconstituted themselves as a touring band after a hiatus in the mid-1980s, the ageing Jagger no longer carried the same sense of sexual threat:

> Everyone knows that Mick is the sexually incontinent gym master, gurning and shape throwing his way to the Zimmer frame, camper than Christmas, the indefatigable rocking luvvie.[6]

In other words, Jagger's persona, carefully balanced between performative excess and dangerous ambiguity, had become routinised; it had become a performance, in the pejorative sense of the term – a series of actions executed for no other reason than habit. On the other hand, when the *Observer* marked the *Bigger Bang* tour by sending the newly successful comic Russell Brand to meet the Stones, his encounter with Richards was the centre of the article; the interview's strap-line identified Richards as rock's greatest icon; and the front cover of the paper's music magazine declared him 'the coolest man on Earth'. Richards had come to occupy a new role which had been unavailable to him in the late 1960s and 1970s – that of the archetypal survivor. It is as though he has trumped the process that Turner describes above, not by rediscovering a sense of the ascetic body, but by pushing the culture of excess as far as it can possibly go. He has travelled through the processes of commercialised sensuality; and he has emerged on the other side, with the marks of the journey etched on his face:

> It's October 31st, so Keef says 'Hallowe'en. One night for you. Every night for me!'
> Mick Jagger wears a crow mask for SFM ('Street Fighting Man') and Keef – his face a cross between Freddie Kruger and an elephant's ass – still looks scarier.[7]

In the band's current performances, Richards' persona is shaped around the fact that, after years of abuse, he isn't dead yet (a frequent onstage comment is 'it's great to be here: it's great to be anywhere'). In performance, his body is far looser than it was in the 1960s; as footage of the Hyde Park concert in 1968 demonstrates, Richard was initially a diffident performer at the time of the Stones' initial success. Now, and in contrast with Jagger (who utilises the same repertoire of stylised tropes to animate and punctuate the songs as he did in the 1960s), Richards moves fluidly, almost bonelessly, across the stage, his attention as much on the band as it is on the audience, a performative foil not for Jagger but for Ronnie Wood (whose appearance closely mirrors his) and for the other musicians. Jagger dances to the audience; Richards, in contrast, seems to move purely as the moment of performance dictates. It is as though, to use the terms that Turner employs, a man whose face clearly indicates that he is guilty of one of the new sins of the flesh, inhabits the realm of commercialised sensuality far more easily in his old age than he ever did during the 1960s; that, *pace* Strausbaugh, Richards rather than Jagger is these days the face of generational rebellion – an old man happily inhabiting a performance style which seemed an uncomfortable fit in his youth.

How to disappear completely

> Being in a band can make you feel like you're a cartoon – so just become a cartoon. Accept it.[8]

In 2002, one of the most successful bands of the early part of the century made their live debut:

> The houselights were lowered and an aerial tracking shot surveyed the venue before honing in on a darkened stage. Kick drum simulations of a heartbeat triggered the illumination of four towering screens. The silhouetted image of 2D, the aptly named animated frontman of 'virtual' band Gorillaz, emerged out of the primal matter of television static in a manner resembling a key scene in the classic suspense film *Poltergeist*. Three additional figures materialized on separate screens before the muscular arms of animated hip-hop henchman Russel smashed out the four-beat snare-drum introduction to the hit song 'Clint Eastwood'.[9]

Gorillaz – whose first album went on to sell six million copies – is in some ways a rather conventional four-piece: in addition to the two members named above, the band comprises Murdoc on bass, and the Japanese guitarist, Noodle. Their music blends post-punk and reggae with rap and contemporary electronica; but, again, in the early years of the twenty-first century, such a blend is not of itself unique. Even the fact that they are animated characters, first drawn by the cartoon-book artist Jamie Hewlett, does not mark them out as a new phenomenon in popular music; cartoon bands have had number ones before (The Archies, for example, with 'Sugar Sugar'). However, as soon as 2D opens his virtual mouth, the listener hears Damon Albarn, whose voice has been a very familiar part of the British music scene since 1993. That voice brings a history along with it (again, at least for British listeners). Technology might have advanced sufficiently to facilitate the creation of a group of faked holographs (the images projected during the Brits gave the impression of three-dimensionality, and the illusion is sufficiently well-maintained to enable the group to be filmed from the back). But Albarn, the rock star, is still there, present and absent within the apparently virtual environment the band inhabit. Other pop stars have submitted to a version of the same process; in the early 1970s the Osmonds and the Jackson 5 were both the subjects of cartoon series. However, Albarn and his collaborator Hewlett had taken this process a stage further; Gorillaz came into being as a hyperbolic, cartoonised version of insouciant rock cool. Noodle was fed-exed to the band from Japan, for example; and in the interview quoted above, the resemblance between Murdoc and Pete Docherty was pointed out (Albarn replied that Murdoc predated Docherty by a couple of years). Gorillaz existed as an authored simulation; not as a cartoonised version of real performers. The process of reification that Albarn mentions above, in which the performer is necessarily expected to reduce him- or herself to two dimensions, is here taken to and past the point of absurdity.

It might seem as though, in creating Gorillaz, and then by allowing them a 'live' existence, Albarn and Hewlett are obeying a logic defined by Jean Baudrillard as the logic of simulation – a process whereby the imitation is no longer subordinate to the real. In this new schema, any sense that there is an authenticating origin – in live performance, say – is lost; the live performance is the recording which is the performance; the image of the band already available through other media is the image of the band revealed in performance; presentation and representation are inescapably entwined. For Baudrillard, there is no sense in mounting an opposition to this process, because there is no firm ground outside of representation on which such an opposition could establish itself. Far better, as Albarn puts it, to make peace with the cartoon version of themselves – and, in doing so, to mount a more significant challenge to the process of simulation than could be carried out through a full-frontal attack based on an outmoded idea of the real. For Richardson, this is precisely where the value of Gorillaz can be found. He notes Albarn's central role in the band, according him the status of an *auteur*. However:

This is decidedly not … a 1960s-style singer-songwriter *auteur*. If the running call to that generation was Timothy Leary's 'turn on, tune in, drop out', a reversal of these sentiments might be indicated by 2D's final act of the Brit Awards performance. In a gesture as self-empowering yet evasive as man-without-a-name's reluctance to take centre stage in this project, his animated double approaches the camera with haughty indifference at the end of the Brit Awards performance to extinguish his own image.[10]

The absent presence of the star, effaced by his own creation, which then effaces itself; a live performance which is not 'live', and which by implication reveals the mediations which operate even within the mechanisms of something as apparently unplanned as rock music performance.

At this point, it might be worth detaching the event from what might be termed its 'technological dazzle' – the illusion of difference, provided by the utilisation of new techniques and technologies – and to ask oneself what, precisely, is so new about this performance. Pink Floyd, it could be argued, have also used current technologies to efface themselves (see Chapters 4 and 5); moreover, the band also employed surrogates whose appearance commented ironically on the presence and absence of the original band. Adopting an alter-ego behind which the performer is partly subsumed is also standard practice; from Bowie in the 70s, through Kiss, and Alice Cooper, all the way to Slipknot, the discourses of rock performance have found, as I have argued, a way to accept the performative contradiction such practices imply. The idea that a band eventually becomes a mediated cartoon is the very argument espoused by U2, over ten years before. It is unusual – although not unknown – to find a musician with Albarn's background espousing the argument; although even here the idea of self as performance is taken for granted (otherwise, Brett Anderson and Jarvis Cocker would not have developed as performers in the way that they did).

Perhaps a more useful way of thinking through the dynamic that shaped the Gorillaz performance is suggested by Albarn himself, in an interview with the *Observer* at the beginning of the project:

> Everybody who contributed to the album felt that little bit more confident in being expressive in ways they've not tried before, and the results speak for themselves. It's been incredibly liberating.[11]

It could be said that the kind of freedom enjoyed by Albarn and his collaborators, far from allowing them to pursue the implications of virtuality from the inside, is of a piece with Keighley's definition of modernist authenticity in rock, quoted in Chapter 1 (the project displays openness regarding rock sounds; radical or sudden stylistic change; and, most definitely irony, sarcasm and obliqueness). I am more interested, though, in the claim that the process has been liberating; for it is here that Albarn's work with Gorillaz, both in recording and in performance (of which more below) finds some unexpected soulmates. In particular, two bands – Radiohead and The White Stripes – each use one strand of the strategy that Albarn found so useful in Gorillaz: Radiohead mask themselves, on CD and on stage, by transforming the technology which shapes their music; and The White Stripes (and in particular Jack White) adopt a persona which is half ultimately authentic white blues garage rocker, and half consciously created art object.

During the *OK Computer* tour – a moment in Radiohead's development where the kind of uber-stardom enjoyed by U2 and the Stones beckoned – Thom Yorke, the band's lead singer and guitarist, hit a brick wall. Coming off stage after a gig at the Birmingham NEC, he found that he simply could not communicate:

> I came off at the end of that show, sat in the dressing room and couldn't speak. I actually couldn't speak. People were saying, You all right? I know people were speaking to me. But I couldn't hear them. And I couldn't talk. I'd just had enough. And I was bored with saying I'd had enough. I was beyond that.[12]

The radical transformation of both sound and image that followed stems from this communicative breakdown. The following albums – *Kid A* and *Amnesiac* – moved the band decisively away from the guitar-based, anthemic indie rock that had characterised their first three CDs; it also transformed the band on stage. Filmed live at the Astoria after the release of their second album (*The Bends*), Radiohead's performance style could be characterised as that of a typical guitar band; Yorke centre stage, flanked by the band's other two guitarists (Jonny Greenwood on his right, Ed O'Brien on his left), bassist Colin Greenwood and drummer Phil Selway at the back. The focus of the performance is on Yorke as angst-ridden front man; the performance makes extensive use of backlighting, which effectively wipes out the detailed actions of the other band members, and throws the weight of attention on to Yorke. His eyes are closed, his body shakes; his hands, when not playing guitar, are wrapped around the microphone – as though shielding it and him from the intrusive gaze of the audience. There is little variation within the performance; what is most striking is the extent to which Yorke seems trapped – in a small range of gestures, and on a relatively small part of the stage. Adopting a musical form whose performative discourse was radically different allowed Yorke, and the band, not only to escape the musical expectations that had been erected around them, but also to escape the performative straitjacket that seemed to trap him in the mid-90s. As Reynolds (*Energy Flash*, 1998); and Collin and Godfrey (*Altered State*, 1997) noted, dance is a performative discourse that moves its emphasis firmly from the star musician to the dancing crowd: it also elevates the idea of flow over the creation of musical climaxes. As Erin Harde has noted, this has implications for Radiohead's performances:

> There are no surprises when the Rolling Stones perform; the audience expects Jagger to hump his way across the stage in every performance, and he doesn't disappoint. With Radiohead, there are few presuppositions about the performance ... Yorke's performance is remarkable. He is convulsive in the more demanding songs and mystical in the slower, passionate songs as though he is communicating with a supreme entity.[13]

He is also liberated. To perform a track like 'Idioteque' (which has become a live staple) the band has to reconstitute itself: Jonny Greenwood moves from guitar to keyboards, O'Brien plays maracas, Colin Greenwood a keyboard. Phil Selway still plays drums, but he punctuates the rhythm rather than sustaining it. Yorke, no longer required to fill a guitar part, is free to move across the stage, as he does at Glastonbury in 2003; he can dance up to the mike, bounce down from the stage to communicate directly to the audience, and wheel his way across the stage in a dervish dance towards the track's end. The structure of the new music allows the band to break with the solid, front-facing two or three guitar line up, with the focus on Yorke centre stage; now the music allows that rigid formation to dissolve, and the band to take on a far more fluid performance style. Sometimes, the old style is reanimated, both to perform early tracks and material from *Hail to the Thief* (2005); but the band is no longer ruled by it.

It might seem like a substantial leap – from the Warp records-inspired Radiohead to the Son House and Stooges-inspired White Stripes – but here, also, the same impulse towards masking identity is clearly apparent. Jack White makes a great deal of the band's adherence to old equipment:

> East London's Toe Rag Studios (where the band recorded their 2003 album *Elephant*) is as close to the look, sound and smell of a 1967 recording studio as any romantic, sound conscious Detroit two piece can hope for. The lino floor might be a little warped, the sound-proofed walls might buckle a bit in the middle, but in terms of vintage recording equipment, today, the White Stripes are in heaven.[14]

Age confers authenticity; technologically obsolete equipment not only allows the band to explore a particular sonic environment, but it also creates a history for the musicians by default. A commitment to unvarnished, aged technology also makes its way into the band's performances, most obviously in Jack White's choice of guitar (his main instrument is a red and white vintage Airline guitar from the 60s). It also ties into the band's veneration of the blues:

> It's the pinnacle of music. I [Jack White] think everything from the 20th Century goes right back to that (the blues). It's like the correlation we made with our second album *De Stijl* [and the Dutch art movement of the same name]. It was about breaking down visuals into next-to-basic components. The bluesmen have always been doing that, stripping songwriting down to these three components ... storytelling, melody and rhythm. I hate the fact that the bluesman has been parodied – 'Oh I woke up this morning and my baby's gone,' Blues brothers kind of thing – when those guys are the gods of music.[15]

However, as this quote indicates, the band are themselves very aware of the entirely constructed nature of the music they create: it is not posited as the inhabiting of a naturalised musical form, but as a construction which the band adopt. The band in performance are both an entirely fluid performative entity (with no agreed set list, songs running into each other, cued by a constant, tightly focused communicative language shared by both band members) and a mobile abstract artwork (assembled entirely in blocks of red, white and black).

The same dual reading can be applied to the characters of the musicians, as revealed in performance. The White Stripes first promoted themselves as a brother and sister group – Meg as the older sibling, Jack as the younger. However, as the band grew more famous, the real relation between the band members became public. John Gillis had married Megan White in 1996, adopting her last name in the process; he retained the name after the couple divorced. In interview, White has claimed that neither he nor Meg White care particularly that the truth of the relation had become public knowledge; but both have largely maintained the pretence, Jack still introducing his partner as 'my big sister Meg', long after the story had broken. In 2005, Steve Chick reflected:

> Given this knowledge, almost every aspect of the Stripes' phenomenon gains an extra intrigue ... The fictional creation that is Jack White

would disappear in a puff of logic were he ever to acknowledge the existence of John Gillis. Slyly acknowledging that the Stripes' brother/sister angle might be a fiction is as close as we will ever get to a peek behind this Lone Ranger's mask.[16]

It also, understandably, affects our reading of the live event. In performance, the two musicians are placed on a line parallel to the front of the stage; Meg's drum kit is tilted so that it half-faces Jack; Jack alternates between two microphones, one to the side facing front, the other at the drumkit, facing Meg. This stage arrangement allows a peculiarly intense relation between the performers; at some points the performance is directed out to the audience, but at others we seem to be watching a purely personal moment of communication between the two musicians. We move from inclusion to exclusion; but the relationship we are excluded from is partly mythical – the incestuous closeness of the performers is not, in fact, incestuous at all. The relation, therefore, displays the same dynamic as the relation between the music and the stage set; what seems spontaneous is also constructed. In performance this allows the band the same kind of liberty as Radiohead's espousal of new technologies and musical forms, and as Albarn's embrace of the virtual world; the performers are never quite where we think they are; they never remain fixed within one set of stage relations; they have gained the freedom to move, to transform, and to hide themselves in plain sight.

And here is an appropriate place to end; with Gorillaz' performance of the album *Demon Days* at the Manchester Apollo in 2005. The virtual musicians are there, on the video screens behind the onstage band, and as puppets perched Muppet-style in one of the sideboxes. On stage, clearly visible in silhouette, Albarn plays and sings – a hidden presence, not overtly there, but certainly not absent:

> We witnessed the arrival and departure of 87 musicians and singers from the stage in the course of an hour, including Neneh Cherry (looking disarmingly thin as she wiggled her way through the rumbling 'Kids With Guns'), Ike Turner (resplendent in an orange lizard-skin suit), a furry-hooded Roots Manuva and the giggly Manchester Community Choir.
>
> Albarn sat with his knees clamped under a piano, directing the whole thrilling shebang with a succession of impatient hand signals to his band.[17]

Albarn inhabits the persona the virtual band have created for his distinctive voice; but Albarn the person, Albarn the composer and musician, is also there – as Radiohead the suffering indie artists share the stage with Radiohead the purveyors of minimalist electronica, as Jack White and John Gillis move together across the stage. In these examples – and, I would argue, in every example cited in this book – the relation between the performer, the stage persona, and an idea of the real person exists within the performance event. Radiohead, Gorillaz, and The White Stripes are as 4Real as Metallica, The Doors, Bjork, The Smiths et al.; they might prove their 4Real status negatively, by refusing or evading fixed forms and identities, but they partake of the same performative logic. In a recent essay on Radiohead, Davis Schneiderman argues that, in rock music, the idea of authenticity is inescapable precisely because it is difficult to pin down:

> Both the problem and the value of the concept of authenticity in popular music is that the word generates a multitude of implications and sites of authentication.[18]

Indeed, one could point out that there are multitudinous implications within sites of authentication; places where the processes of authenticity are not where they seem to be, but are nonetheless present; and that, even when the fact of performance as constructed mediation seems to clash with the auratic spontaneity of the live event, the ideology of authenticity is still present – within the 4Real logic of the rock gig.

Notes

1. 4Real: Performance and Authenticity

1. Steve Lamacq,'Blood on the Tracks', *NME*, 25 May 1991.
2. Allan Moore, 'Constructing Authenticity in Rock', *Performance Arts International*, No. 1, 2001.
3. Gareth McLean, 'Band of Brothers', *The Guardian*, Saturday, 1 October 2005.
4. Nick Logan and Bob Woffinden (eds), *NME Encyclopaedia of Rock* (London: Salamander, 1977), p. 134.
5. Keir Keighley, 'Reconsidering Rock', in Simon Frith, Will Straw and John Street (eds), *The Cambridge Companion to Rock and Pop* (Cambridge: Cambridge University Press, 2001), p. 127.
6. Ibid., p. 137.
7. Philip Auslander, 'Good Old Rock and Roll: Performing the 1950s in the 1970s', *Journal of Popular Music Studies*, Vol. 15, No. 2, 2003, p. 185.
8. David Buckley, Review of 'Lookin' Through the Eyes of Roy Wood', *Mojo*, May 2006, p. 120.
9. Allan Moore, 'Authenticity as Authentication', *Popular Music*, Vol. 21, No. 2, 2002, p. 220.
10. Ibid., p. 221.
11. Richard Dyer, 'A Star is Born and the Construction of Authenticity', in Christine Gledhill (ed.), *Stardom: Industry of Desire* (London: Routledge, 1991).
12. Bill Flanagan, *U2 at the End of the World* (London: Bantam Books, 1996), p. 54.
13. 'All Along the Watchtower', *Rattle and Hum*.
14. Steve Sutherland, 'Bittersweet Epiphany', *NME* website, 1997.
15. Ibid.
16. Ibid.
17. Ibid.
18. Jon Savage, *Time Travel: From the Sex Pistols to Nirvana – Pop, Media and Sexuality, 1977–96* (London: Vintage, 1997) p. 392.
19. Ibid., p. 267.
20. Ibid., p. 346.
21. Simon Frith, 'Music and Identity', in Stuart Hall and Paul du Gay (eds), *Questions of Cultural Identity* (London: Sage, 1996), p. 121.

2. Performance and Mediaton: Performance, Space and Technology

1. Philip Auslander, *Liveness: Performance in a Mediatized Culture* (London: Routledge, 1999), p. 38.
2. Peggy Phelan, *Unmarked: the Politics of Performance* (London: Routledge, 1993), p. 146.
3. Auslander, *Liveness*, p. 162.

4. Eamon Dunphy, *Unforgettable Fire: Past, Present, and Future – the Definitive Biography of U2* (London: Viking, 1987), p. 145.
5. Richard Schechner, *Performance Theory* (London: Routledge, 1975), p. 15.
6. Diana Scrimgeour, *U2 Show: the Art of Touring* (London: Orion, 2004), p. 257.
7. Ibid., p. 234.
8. Tim Quirk and Jason Toynbee, 'Going Through the Motions: Popular Music Performance in Journalism and in Academic Discourse', *Popular Music*, Vol. 24 (2005), p. 401.
9. Michael Kirby, *A Formalist Theatre* (Philadelphia: University of Pennsylvania Press, 1990), p. 10.
10. John Waters, *Race of Angels: Ireland and the Genesis of U2* (Belfast: Blackstaff Press, 1994), p. 187.
11. Scrimgeour, *U2 Show*, p. 75.
12. Douglas Kellner, *Media Culture* (London: Routledge, 1994), p. 3.
13. Theodore Gracyk, *Rhythm and Noise: an Aesthetics of Rock* (London: I. B. Tauris, 1996), p. 76.
14. Fred Johnson, 'U2, Mythology, and Mass Mediated Survival', *Popular Music and Society*, Vol. 27, No. 1, 2004, p. 95.
15. Scrimgeour, *U2 Show*, p. 238.
16. Daniel Cavicchi, *Tramps Like Us: Music and Meaning Among Springsteen Fans* (New York and Oxford: Oxford University Press, 1998), p. 65.

3. Performance, Gender and Rock Music

1. Simon Frith, *Sound Effects: Youth, Leisure and the Politics of Rock, 'n' Roll* (London: Constable, 1983), p. 227.
2. Susan Fast, *In the Houses of the Holy: Led Zeppelin and the Power of Rock Music* (Oxford: Oxford University Press, 2001), p. 188.
3. Sheila Whiteley (ed.), *Sexing the Groove: Popular Music and Gender* (London: Routledge, 1997), p. 68.
4. Theodore Grayck, *I Wanna Be Me: Rock Music and the Politics of Identity* (Philadelphia, PA: Temple University Press, 2001), p. 199.
5. In Andy Bennett and Kevin Dawe (eds), *Guitar Cultures* (Oxford: Berg, 2001), p. 55.
6. Mimi Schippers, *Rockin' Out of the Box: Gender Maneuvering in Alternative Hard Rock* (New York: Rutgers University Press, 2002), p. 109.
7. Pierre Bourdieu, *Masculine Domination* (London: Polity Press, 2001), p. 11.
8. Ibid., p. 103.
9. John MacInnes, *The End of Masculinity: the Confusion of Sexual Genesis and Sexual Difference in Modern Society* (Buckingham: Open University Press, 1998), p. 3.
10. In Whiteley (ed.), *Sexing the Groove*, p. 114.
11. Ibid.
12. Michelle Fine, Lois Weis, Judi Addelston and Julia Marusza Hall, 'In-secure Times: Constructing White Working Class Male Masculinities', in Michael Kimmel and Michael A. Messner (eds), *Men's Lives* (Boston: Pearson, 2004), p. 76.
13. Gavin Baddeley, *Dissecting Marilyn Manson* (London: Plexus, 2003), p. 8.
14. Ibid., pp. 73–8.

15. Ibid., pp. 92–3.
16. Deena Weinstein, *Heavy Metal: the Music and its Culture* (New York: Da Capo Press, 2000), p. 62.
17. Judith Butler, 'Performative Acts and Gender Constitution: an Essay in Phenomenology and Feminist Theory', in Sue-Ellen Case (ed.), *Performing Feminisms: Feminist Critical Theory and Theatre* (Baltimore: Johns Hopkins University Press, 1990), p. 278.
18. Rebecca Schneider, *The Explicit Body in Performance* (London: Routledge, 1997), p. 7.

4. The 1960s

1. Ian MacDonald, *Revolution in the Head: the Beatles Records and the Sixties* (London: Pimlico, 1998), p. 188.
2. Arthur Marwick, *The Sixties: Social and Cultural Transformation in Britain, France, Italy, and the United States, c.1958–c.1974* (Oxford: Oxford University Press, 1999), p. 17.
3. Dave Marsh, *Before I Get Old: the Story of the Who* (London: Plexus, 1983), p. 20.
4. Stephen Davis, *Old Gods Almost Dead: the 40-Year Odyssey of the Rolling Stones* (London: Aurum Press, 2003), p. 21.
5. Mo Foster, *17 Watts?: the First 20 Years of British Rock Guitar, the Musicians and Their Stories* (London: Sanctuary, 2000), p. 163.
6. Andy Bennett and Kevin Dawe (eds), *Guitar Cultures* (Oxford: Berg, 2001), p. 29.
7. Peter Guralnick, *Last Train to Memphis: the Rise of Elvis Presley* (Boston: Little, Brown, 1994), p. 174.
8. Marsh, *Before I Get Old,* p. 126.
9. Ibid., p. 213.
10. *The Kids Are Alright* DVD.
11. Edward Macan, *Rocking the Classics: English Progressive Rock and the Counter Culture* (Oxford: Oxford University Press, 1997), pp. 17–18.
12. Dennis McNally, *A Long Strange Trip* (London: Corgi, 2003), p. 231.
13. Ibid., pp. 426–7.
14. Blair Jackson, *Grateful Dead: the Music Never Stopped* (London: Plexus, 1983), p. 21.
15. Stephen Davis, *Jim Morrison: Life, Death Legend* (London: Ebury Press, 2005), p. 254.
16. Ibid., p. 264.
17. Clem Gorman, *Backstage Rock: Behind the Scenes with the Bands* (London: Pan Books, 1978), pp. 77–8.
18. Nick Mason, *Inside Out: a Personal History of Pink Floyd* (London: Weidenfeld & Nicolson, 2004), pp. 71–2.
19. Nicholas Schaffner, *The Pink Floyd Odyssey: Saucerful of Secrets* (London: Helter Skelter, 2005), p. 65.
20. Alice Echols, *Scars of Sweet Paradise: the Life and Times of Janis Joplin* (New York: Henry Holt, 1999), p. 230.
21. Ibid., p. 231.
22. Rickey Vincent, *Funk: the Music, the People, and the Rhythm of the One* (New York: St. Martin's Press, 1996), p. 48.

23. Dave Headlam, 'Appropriations of Blues and Gospel in Popular Music', in Allan Moore (ed.), *The Cambridge Companion to Blues and Gospel Music* (Cambridge: Cambridge University Press, 2003), p. 186.

24. Quoted in Chris Welch, *Cream* (London: Backbeat Books, 2000), p. 41.

25. Ibid., p. 120.

26. Annette Carson, *Jeff Beck: Crazy Fingers* (San Francisco, Backbeat Books, 2001), p. 19.

27. Charles Cross, *Room Full of Mirrors: a Biography of Jimi Hendrix* (London: Sceptre, 2006), p. 104.

28. Ibid., p. 109.

29. Ibid., p. 182.

30. Charles Shaar Murray, *Crosstown Traffic: Jimi Hendrix and Post-War Pop* (London: Faber & Faber), p. 111.

31. Cross, *Room Full of Mirrors*, p. 275.

32. Vincent, *Funk*, p. 94.

5. The 1970s

1. Nick Mason, *Inside Out: a Personal History of Pink Floyd* (London: Weidenfeld & Nicolson, 2004), p. 255.

2. Chris Welch, *Yes: Close to the Edge* (London: Omnibus Press, 2003), p. 145.

3. Christopher Sandford, *Bowie: Loving the Alien* (New York: Little, Brown, 1998), p. 125.

4. Quoted in Paul Stump, *Unknown Pleasures: a Cultural History of Roxy Music* (London: Quartet, 1998), p. 76.

5. Ibid., p. 73.

6. Ibid., p. 70.

7. C. K. Lendt, *Kiss and Sell: the Making of a Supergroup* (New York: Billboard Books, 1997), pp. 13–14.

8. Quoted in 'Welcome to my Nightmare', *Mojo*, December 2005, p. 52.

9. Lendt, *Kiss and Sell*, p. 341.

10. Jimmy McDonagh, *Shakey: Neil Young's Biography* (London: Vintage, 2003), p. 417.

11. Ibid., p. 418.

12. Ibid., p. 419.

13. *Rust Never Sleeps* DVD.

14. *Baby Snakes* DVD.

15. *You can't do that on stage anymore*, Vol. 1 CD.

16. *The Last Waltz* DVD.

17. In Brian Hinton, *Celtic Crossroads: the Art of Van Morrison* (London: Sanctuary, 2003), pp. 113–14.

18. Joey Ramone, *End of the Century* DVD.

19. Robert Garnett, in Roger Sabin (ed.), *Punk Rock, So What?: the Cultural Legacy of Punk* (London: Routledge, 1999), p. 23.

20. Nick Kent, *The Dark Stuff: Selected Writings on Rock Music* (Cambridge, MA: Da Capo Press, 2002), pp. 170–1.

21. Kris Needs and Dick Porter, *Trash: the Complete New York Dolls* (London: Plexus, 2005), p. 40.

22. Ibid., p. 103.
23. Ibid., p. 98.
24. Joe Ambrose, *Gimme Danger: the Story of Iggy Pop* (London: Omnibus, 2004), p. 148.
25. Ibid., p. 137.
26. *Lick my Blood* DVD.
27. Ibid.
28. *The Filth and the Fury* DVD.
29. Ibid.
30. Legs McNeil and Gillian McCain, *Please Kill Me: the Uncensored Oral History of Punk* (Harmondsworth: Penguin, 1997), p. 159.
31. Ibid., p. 293.
32. Pat Gilbert, *Passion is a Fashion: the Real Story of the Clash* (London: Aurum Press, 2005), pp. 101–2.
33. Ibid., p. 149.
34. Deborah Curtis, *Touching from a Distance: Ian Curtis and Joy Division* (London: Faber & Faber, 2005), p. 114.
35. Ibid., p. 114.

6. The 1980s

1. Christopher Sandford, *Bowie: Loving the Alien* (New York: Little, Brown, 1998), p. 266.
2. Ibid., p. 269.
3. Lawrence Grossberg, in Simon Frith, Andrew Goodwin and Lawrence Grossberg, *Sound & Vision: the Music Video Reader* (Routledge, London 1993), pp. 206–7.
4. Per Nilsen, *Prince: the First Decade – Dancesexmusicromance* (New York: Firefly Books, 2003), p. 185.
5. Kevin Williams, *Why I Still Want My MTV: Music Video and Aesthetic Communication* (New Jersey: Hampton Press, 2003), p. 158.
6. Carol Vernallis, *Experiencing Music Video: Aesthetics and Cultural Context* (New York: Columbia University Press, 2004) pp. 56–7.
7. Quoted in Nilsen, *Prince*, p. 286.
8. Ibid., pp. 187–8.
9. Ibid., p. 29.
10. Ian Christie, *Sound of the Beast: the Complete Head-banging History of Heavy Metal* (London: HarperCollins, 2004), p. 1.
11. Robert Duncan, *The Noise: Notes from a Rock'n' Roll Era* (New York: Ticknor and Fields, 1984), pp. 36–7.
12. Ed Ward, Geoffrey Stokes and Ken Tucker, *Rock of Ages: the Rolling Stone History of Rock and Roll* (New York: Summit Books, 1986), p. 608.
13. Deena Weinstein, *Heavy Metal: the Music and its Culture* (New York: Da Capo Press, 2000), p. 199.
14. Steve Harris, in Dave Bowler and Brain Dray, *Infinite Dreams: Iron Maiden* (London: Boxtree, 1996), p. 17.
15. Ibid., p. 17.
16. Ibid., p. 124.

17. Martin Huxley, *AC/DC: the World's Heaviest Rock* (New York: St Martin's Press, 1996), p. 17.
18. Bowler and Dray, *Infinite Dreams*, p. 61.
19. Weinstein, *Heavy Metal*, pp. 205–12.
20. Christie, *Sound of the Beast*, p. 154.
21. Ibid., p. 155.
22. Robert Walser, *Running with the Devil: Power, Gender, and Madness in Heavy Metal Music* (Hanover, NH: Wesleyan University Press, 1993), pp. 120–1.
23. Ibid., p. 130.
24. Christie, *Sound of the Beast*, p. 79.
25. Mick Wall, 'It's Only Rock and Roll', *Mojo*, February 2005, p. 55.
26. Paul Stenning, *The Band that Time Forgot: the Complete Unauthorised Biography of Guns N' Roses* (New Malden, Surrey: Chrome Dreams, 2004), p. 42.
27. Ibid., p. 11.
28. Joel McIver, *Justice for All: the Truth about Metallica* (London: Omnibus Press, 2006), pp. 137–8.
29. *OED*, p. 263.
30. Fred Maus, 'Intimacy and Distance: On Stipe's Queerness', *Journal of Popular Music Studies*, Vol. 18, No. 2 (2006), p. 195.
31. Ibid., p. 196.
32. Peter Glick and Susan T. Fiske, 'Gender, Power Dynamics and Social Interaction', in Myra Ferree, Judith Lorber and Beth Hess (eds), *Revisioning Gender* (London: Sage, 1999), p. 382.
33. Mark Simpson, quoted in *Saint Morrissey* (London: SAF, 2004), p. 92.
34. Deena Weinstein, 'All Singers are Dicks', *Popular Music and Society*, Vol. 27, No. 3 (2004), p. 325.
35. Matthew Bannister, *White Boys, White Noise: Masculinities and 1980s Indie Guitar Rock* (Aldershot: Ashgate, 2006), p. 109.
36. David Bret, *Morrissey: Scandal and Passion* (London: Robson Books, 2004), p. 42.
37. Ibid., p. 170.

7. The 1990s

1. Charles Cross, *Heavier than Heaven: a Biography of Kurt Cobain* (London: Sceptre, 2002), p. 201.
2. *Tourfilm* DVD.
3. Joe Ambrose, *The Violent World of Mosh Pit Culture* (London: Omnibus Press, 2001), p. 3.
4. Ibid., p. 20.
5. Ibid.
6. During 'Nookie', Woodstock 1999.
7. Ambrose, *Mosh Pit Culture*, p. 133.
8. Ibid., p. 134.
9. Gina Arnold, 'Review, San Francisco Cow Palace, December 31, 1991', *Rolling Stone*, 20 February 1992.
10. Sheila Whiteley, *Women and Popular Music: Sexuality, Identity and Subjectivity* (London: Routledge, 2000), p. 196.

11. Ibid., p. 9.
12. Mavis Bayton, *Frock Rock: Women, Popular Music, and the Conditions of Performance* (Oxford: Oxford University Press, 1998), p. 13.
13. Anna Feigenbaum, 'Some Guy Designed This Room I'm Standing In', *Popular Music*, Vol. 24, No. 1 (2005), pp. 52–3.
14. Adrian Deevoy, 'Hips. Tits. Lips. Power', *Q Magazine*, May 1994.
15. Ibid.
16. Helen Davis, 'All Rock and Roll is Homosocial: the Representation of Women in the British Rock Music Press', *Popular Music*, Vol. 20, No. 3 (2001), p. 307.
17. Whiteley, *Women and Popular Music*, p. 204.
18. Interview, *Arena* magazine, April 1995.
19. Andrew Billen, 'The Billen Interview: PJ Harvey', *The Observer*, 8 October 1995.
20. Whiteley, *Women and Popular Music*, p. 66.
21. Barbara O'Dair, *Trouble Girls: the Rolling Stone Book of Women in Rock* (New York: Random House, 1997), p. 530.
22. Mark Mazullo, 'Revisiting the Wreck', *Popular Music*, Vol. 20, No. 3 (2001), p. 433.
23. *Showtime* Video.
24. John Harris, *The Last Party: Britpop, Blair and the Demise of English Rock* (London: Fourth Estate, 2003), p. 300.
25. Ibid., p. 87.
26. Kenneth Lunn, 'Reconsidering Britishness', in Brian Jenkins and Spyros A. Sofos (eds), *Nation and Identity in Contemporary Europe* (London: Routledge, 1996), p. 98.
27. A. Blake, 'Retrolution: Culture and Heritage in a Young Country', in A. Coddington and M. Perryman (eds), *The Moderniser's Dilemma: Radical Politics in the Age of Blair* (London: Lawrence & Wishart, 1998), p. 150.
28. Imelda Whelan, *Overloaded: Popular Culture and the Future of Feminism* (London: Women's Press, 2000), p. 5.
29. Rosemary Gill, 'Overloaded: Popular Culture and the Future of Feminism', in Bethan Benwell, *Masculinity and Men's Lifestyle Magazines* (Oxford: Blackwell, 2003), p. 34.
30. Quoted in Graham Fuller, 'Pulp Culture', *Interview*, July 1998.
31. Rupa Huq, *Beyond Subculture: Pop, Youth and Identity in a Postcolonial World* (London: Routledge, 2005), pp. 144–5.
32. *Oasis...There and Then* DVD.
33. Interview by Andrew Smith, 'How Does it Feel?', *Word*, September 2005, p. 92.
34. Murray Forman, *The Hood Comes First: Race, Space and Place in Rap and Hip Hop* (Middletown, CT: Wesleyan University Press, 2002), p. 52.
35. Tricia Rose, *Black Noise: Rap Music and Black Culture in Contemporary America* (Middletown, CT: Wesleyan University Press, 1994), p. 61.
36. Mark Anthony Neal, 'Postindustrial Soul', in Mark Neal, and Murray Forman (eds), *That's the Joint!: the Hip-Hop Studies Reader* (London: Routledge, 2004) p. 378.
37. Foreman, *The Hood Comes First*, pp. 176–7.
38. Fred Durst, Interview, October 1997, http://www.limpsite.com/articles/10.shtml
39. Slipknot biography, http://www.black-goat.com/profiles.php
40. Korney Rockers, *dB Magazine*, 13–26 January 1999.

8. The 21st Century

1. Nigel Williamson, 'More Bangs for Your Buck', *The Observer*, Sunday, 28 August 2005.
2. Review, London Shepherd's Bush Empire, *NME*, 2003, http://nme.com
3. John Strausbaugh, *Rock 'Til You Drop* (London: Verso, 2001), p. 71.
4. Ibid., p. 2: italics in the original.
5. Bryan S. Turner, *The Body in Society* (London: Sage, 1996), p. 234.
6. Review, London Shepherd's Bush Empire, *NME*, 2003, http://nme.com
7. Review, Los Angeles Staples Centre, *NME*, 2003 http://nme.com
8. Damon Albarn, on *Late Night with Jonathan Ross*, November 2005.
9. John Richardson, '"The Digital Won't Let Me Go": Constructions of the Virtual and the Real in Gorillaz' "Clint Eastwood"', *Journal of Popular Music Studies*, Vol. 17, No. 1 (2005), p. 1.
10. Ibid., p. 24.
11. Nick Duerden, 'Gorillaz in Our Midst', *The Observer*, 11 March 2001.
12. Mark B. N. Hansen, 'Deforming Rock: Radiohead's Plunge into the Sonic Continuum', in Joseph Tate (ed.), *The Music and Art of Radiohead* (London: Ashgate, 2005), p. 118.
13. Erin Harde, 'Radiohead and the Negation of Gender', in Tate, *The Music and Art of Radiohead*, p. 54.
14. Andrew Male, 'Basic Instinct', *Mojo*, September 2002.
15. Jim Jarmusch, 'The White Stripes: Getting to Know the Most Interesting Band in Music Today', *Interview*, May 2003.
16. Steve Chick, 'Heart of Darkness', *Mojo*, August 2005.
17. Lynsey Hanley, 'Albarn's Coup de Théâtre', *The Observer*, 6 November 2005.
18. Davis Schneiderman, 'The Aura of Authenticity: Perceptions of Honesty, Sincerity and Truth in "Creep" and "Kid A"', in Tate, *The Music and Art of Radiohead*, p. 50.

Bibliography

Ambrose, Joe, *The Violent World of Mosh Pit Culture*. London: Omnibus Press, 2001.

Ambrose, Joe, *Gimme Danger: the Story of Iggy Pop*. London: Omnibus Press, 2004.

Arnold, Gina, 'Review, San Francisco Cow Palace, December 31, 1991', *Rolling Stone*, 20 February 1992.

Auslander, Philip, *Liveness: Performance in a Mediatized Culture*. London: Routledge, 1999.

Auslander, Philip, 'Good Old Rock and Roll: Performing the 1950s in the 1970s', *Journal of Popular Music Studies*, Vol. 15, No. 2, 2003.

Auslander, Philip, *Performing Glam Rock: Gender and Theatricality in Popular Music*. Ann Arbor: University of Michigan Press, 2006.

Baddeley, Gavin, *Dissecting Marilyn Manson*. London: Plexus, 2003.

Bannister, Matthew, *White Boys, White Noise: Masculinities and 1980s Indie Guitar Rock*. Aldershot: Ashgate, 2006.

Bayton, Mavis, *Frock Rock: Women, Popular Music, and the Conditions of Performance*. Oxford: Oxford University Press, 1998.

Bennett, Andy and Dawe, Kevin (eds), *Guitar Cultures*. Oxford: Berg, 2001.

Benwell, Bethan (ed.), *Masculinity and Men's Lifestyle Magazines*. Oxford: Blackwell, 2003.

Billen, Andrew, 'The Billen Interview: PJ Harvey', *The Observer*, 8 October 1995.

Bourdieu, Pierre, *Masculine Domination*. London: Polity Press, 2001.

Bowler, Dave and Dray, Brian, *Infinite Dreams: Iron Maiden*. London: Boxtree, 1996.

Bret, David, *Morrissey: Scandal and Passion*. London: Robson Books, 2004.

Buckley, David, Review of 'Lookin' Through the Eyes of Roy Wood', *Mojo*, May 2006.

Carson, Annette, *Jeff Beck: Crazy Fingers*. San Francisco, Backbeat Books, 2001.

Case, Sue-Ellen (ed.), *Performing Feminisms: Feminist Critical Theory and Theatre*. Baltimore: Johns Hopkins University Press, 1990.

Cavicchi, Daniel, *Tramps Like Us: Music and Meaning Among Springsteen Fans*. New York and Oxford: Oxford University Press, 1998.

Chick, Steve, 'Heart of Darkness', *Mojo*, August 2005.

Christie, Ian, *Sound of the Beast: the Complete Head-banging History of Heavy Metal*. London: HarperCollins, 2004.

Coddington, A. and Perryman, M. (eds), *The Moderniser's Dilemma: Radical Politics in the Age of Blair*. London: Lawrence & Wishart, 1998.

Collin, Matthew and Godfrey, John, *Altered State: the Story of Ecstasy Culture and Acid House*. London: Serpent's Tail, 1997.

Cross, Charles, *Heavier than Heaven: a Biography of Kurt Cobain*. London: Sceptre, 2002.

Cross, Charles, *Room Full of Mirrors: a Biography of Jimi Hendrix*. London: Sceptre 2006.

Curtis, Deborah, *Touching from a Distance: Ian Curtis and Joy Division*. London: Faber & Faber, 2005.

Davis, Helen, 'All Rock and Roll is Homosocial: the Representation of Women in the British Rock Music Press', *Popular Music*, Vol. 20, No. 3, 2001.

Davis, Stephen, *Old Gods Almost Dead: the 40-Year Odyssey of the Rolling Stones*. London: Aurum Press, 2002.

Davis, Stephen, *Jim Morrison: Life, Death, Legend*. London: Ebury Press, 2005.

Deevoy, Adrian, 'Hips. Tits. Lips. Power'. *Q Magazine*, May 1994.

Duerden, Nick, 'Gorillaz in Our Midst', *The Observer*, 11 March 2001.

Duncan, Robert, *The Noise: Notes from a Rock 'n' Roll Era*. New York: Ticknor and Fields, 1984.

Dunphy, Eamon, *Unforgettable Fire: Past, Present, and Future – the Definitive Biography of U2*. London: Viking, 1987.

Echols, Alice, *Scars of Sweet Paradise: the Life and Times of Janis Joplin*. New York: Henry Holt, 1999.

Evans, Liz (ed.), *Girls Will Be Boys: Women Report on Rock*. London: Pandora, 1997.

Fast, Susan, *In the Houses of the Holy: Led Zeppelin and the Power of Rock Music*. Oxford: Oxford University Press, 2001.

Feigenbaum, Anna, 'Some Guy Designed This Room I'm Standing In', *Popular Music*, Vol. 24, No. 1, 2005.

Ferree, Myra, Lorber, Judith and Hess, Beth (eds), *Revisioning Gender*. London: Sage, 1999.

Flanagan, Bill, *U2 at the End of the World*. London: Bantam Books, 1996.

Forman, Murray, *The Hood Comes First: Race, Space, and Place in Rap and Hip Hop*. Middletown, CT: Wesleyan University Press, 2002.

Foster, Mo, *17 Watts?: the First 20 Years of British Rock Guitar, the Musicians and Their Stories*. London: Sanctuary, 2000.

Frith, Simon, *Sound Effects: Youth, Leisure and the Politics of Rock 'n' Roll*. London: Constable, 1983.

Frith, Simon, Goodwin, Andrew and Grossberg, Lawrence, *Sound & Vision: the Music Video Reader*. London: Routledge, 1993.

Frith, Simon and McRobbie, Angela, 'Rock and Sexuality', in Simon Frith and Andrew Goodman (eds), *On Record*. London: Routledge, 1998.

Frith, Simon, Straw, Will and Street, John, *The Cambridge Companion to Rock and Pop*. Cambridge: Cambridge University Press, 2001.

Fuller, Graham, 'Pulp Culture', *Interview*, July 1998.

Gilbert, Pat, *Passion is a Fashion: the Real Story of the Clash*. London: Aurum Press, 2005.

Gledhill, Christine (ed.), *Stardom: Industry of Desire*. London: Routledge, 1991.

Goodman, Fred, *The Mansion on the Hill*. New York: Random House, 1997.

Gorman, Clem, *Backstage Rock: Behind the Scenes with the Bands*. London: Pan Books, 1978.

Gracyk, Theodore, *Rhythm and Noise: an Aesthetics of Rock*. London: I. B. Tauris, 1996.

Gracyk, Theodore, *I Wanna Be Me: Rock Music and the Politics of Identity*. Philadelphia, PA: Temple University Press, 2001.

Guralnick, Peter, *Last Train to Memphis: the Rise of Elvis Presley*. Boston: Little, Brown, 1994.

Hall, Stuart and du Gay, Paul (eds), *Questions of Cultural Identity*. London: Sage, 1996.

Hanley, Lynsey, 'Albarn's Coup de Théâtre', *The Observer*, 6 November 2005.

Harris, John, *The Last Party: Britpop, Blair and the Demise of English Rock*. London: Fourth Estate, 2003.

Hinton, Brian, *Celtic Crossroads: the Art of Van Morrison*. London: Sanctuary, 2003.

Hopkins, Jerry and Sugarman, Danny, *No-one Here Gets Out Alive: the Biography of Jim Morrison*. London: Plexus, 1989.

Hoskyns, Barney, *Waiting for the Sun*. London: Bloomsbury, 2003.

Huq, Rupa, *Beyond Subculture: Pop, Youth and Identity in a Postcolonial World*. London: Routledge, 2005.

Huxley, Martin, *AC/DC: the World's Heaviest Rock*. New York: St. Martin's Press, 1996.

Jackson, Blair, *Grateful Dead: the Music Never Stopped*. London: Plexus, 1983.

Jarmusch, Jim, 'The White Stripes: Getting to Know the Most Interesting Band in Music Today', *Interview*, May 2003.

Jenkins, Brian and Sofos, Spyros A. (eds), *Nation and Identity in Contemporary Europe*. London: Routledge, 1996.

Johnson, Fred, 'U2, Mythology, and Mass Mediated Survival', *Popular Music and Society*, Vol. 27, No. 1, 2004.

Kärjä, Antti-Ville, 'A Prescribed Alternative Mainstream: Popular Music and Canon Formation', *Popular Music*, Vol. 25, No. 1, 2006.

Kellner, Douglas, *Media Culture: Cultural Studies, Identity and Politics between the Modern and the Postmodern*, London: Routledge, 1994.

Kent, Nick, *The Dark Stuff: Selected Writings on Rock Music*. Cambridge, MA: Da Capo Press, 2002.

Kimmel, Michael and Messner, Michael A. (eds), *Men's Lives*. Boston: Pearson, 2004.

Kirby, Michael, *A Formalist Theatre*. Philadelphia: University of Pennsylvania Press, 1990.

Lamacq, Steve, 'Blood on the Tracks', *NME*, 25 May 1991.

Lendt, C. K., *Kiss and Sell: the Making of a Supergroup*. New York: Billboard Books, 1997.

Logan, Nick and Woffinden, Bob (eds), *NME Encyclopaedia of Rock*. London: Salamander, 1977.

Macan, Edward, *Rocking the Classics: English Progressive Rock and the Counterculture*. Oxford: Oxford University Press, 1997.

MacDonald, Ian, *Revolution in the Head: the Beatles Records and the Sixties*. London: Pimlico, 1998.

MacInnes, John, *The End of Masculinity: the Confusion of Sexual Genesis and Sexual Difference in Modern Society*. Buckingham: Open University Press, 1998.

Male, Andrew, 'Basic Instinct', *Mojo*, September 2002.

Marsh, Dave, *Before I Get Old: the Story of the Who*. London: Plexus, 1983.

Marwick, Arthur, *The Sixties: Social and Cultural Transformation in Britain, France, Italy, and the United States, c.1958–c.1974*. Oxford: Oxford University Press, 1999.

Mason, Nick, *Inside Out: a Personal History of Pink Floyd*. London: Weidenfeld & Nicolson, 2004.

Maus, Fred, 'Intimacy and Distance: On Stipe's Queerness', *Journal of Popular Music Studies*, Vol. 18, No. 2, 2006.

Mazullo, Mark, 'Revisiting the Wreck', *Popular Music*, Vol. 20, 2001.

McDonagh, Jimmy, *Shakey: Neil Young's Biography*. London: Vintage, 2003.

McIver, Joel, *Justice for All: the Truth About Metallica*. London: Omnibus Press, 2006.

McKay, George, *Glastonbury: a Very English Fair*. London: Gollancz, 2000.

McLean, Gareth, 'Band of Brothers', *The Guardian*, Saturday, 1 October, 2005.

McNally, Dennis, *A Long Strange Trip: the Inside History of the Grateful Dead*. London: Corgi, 2003.

McNeil, Legs and McCain, Gillian, *Please Kill Me: the Uncensored Oral History of Punk*. Harmondsworth: Penguin 1997.

Moore, Allan, 'Constructing Authenticity in Rock', *Performance Arts International*, No. 1, 2001.

Moore, Allan, 'Authenticity as Authentication', *Popular Music*, Vol. 21, No. 2, 2002.

Moore, Allan (ed.), *The Cambridge Companion to Blues and Gospel Music*. Cambridge: Cambridge University Press, 2003.

Neal, Mark Anthony and Forman, Murray (eds), *That's the Joint!: the Hip-Hop Studies Reader*. London: Routledge, 2004.

Needs, Kris and Porter, Dick, *Trash: the Complete New York Dolls*. London: Plexus, 2005.

Nilsen, Per, *Prince: the First Decade – Dancesexmusicromance*. New York: Firefly Books, 2003.

O'Dair, Barbara, *Trouble Girls: the Rolling Stone Book of Women in Rock*. New York: Random House, 1997.

Paytress, Mark, 'Welcome to my Nightmare', *Mojo*, December 2005.

Phelan, Peggy, *Unmarked: the Politics of Performance*. London: Routledge, 1993.

Quirk, Tim and Toynbee, Jason, 'Going Through the Motions: Popular Music Performance in Journalism and in Academic Discourse', *Popular Music*, Vol. 24, 2005.

Reynolds, Simon, *Energy Flash: a Journey through Rave Music and Dance Culture*. London: Picador, 1998.

Reynolds, Simon, *Rip It up and Start Again: Postpunk 1978–1984*. London: Faber, 2005.

Richardson, John, ' "The Digital Won't Let Me Go": Constructions of the Virtual and the Real in Gorillaz' "Clint Eastwood" ', *Journal of Popular Music Studies*, Vol. 17, No. 1, 2005.

Rose, Tricia, *Black Noise: Rap Music and Black Culture in Contemporary America*. Middletown, CT: Wesleyan University Press, 1994.

Sabin, Roger (ed.), *Punk Rock, So What?: the Cultural Legacy of Punk*. London: Routledge, 1999.

Sandford, Christopher, *Bowie: Loving the Alien*. New York: Little, Brown, 1998.

Savage, Jon, *Time Travel: From the Sex Pistols to Nirvana – Pop, Media and Sexuality, 1977–96*. London: Vintage, 1997.

Schaffner, Nicholas, *The Pink Floyd Odyssey: Saucerful of Secrets*. London: Helter Skelter, 2005.

Schechner, Richard, *Performance Theory*. London: Routledge, 1975.

Schippers, Mimi, *Rockin' Out of the Box: Gender Maneuvering in Alternative Hard Rock*. New York: Rutgers University Press, 2002.

Schneider, Rebecca, *The Explicit Body in Performance*. London: Routledge, 1997.

Scrimgeour, Diana, *U2 Show: the Art of Touring*. London: Orion, 2004.

Shaar Murray, Charles, *Crosstown Traffic: Jimi Hendrix and Post-War Pop*. London: Faber & Faber, 1989.

Shuker, Roy, *Understanding Popular Music*. London: Routledge, 2001.

Simpson, Mark, *Saint Morrissey*. London: SAF, 2004.

Slaven, Neil, *Electric Don Quixote: the Story of Frank Zappa*. London: Omnibus, 2003.

Smith, Andrew, 'How Does it Feel?', *Word*, September 2005.

Stenning, Paul, *The Band that Time Forgot: the Complete Unauthorised Biography of Guns N' Roses*. New Malden, Surrey: Chrome Dreams, 2004.

Strausbaugh, John, *Rock 'Til You Drop*. London: Verso, 2001.

Stump, Paul, *Unknown Pleasures: a Cultural History of Roxy Music*. London: Quartet, 1998.

Sutherland, Steve, 'Bittersweet Epiphany', *NME* website, 1997.

Tamm, Eric, *Brian Eno: His Music and the Vertical Color of Sound*. New York: Da Capo Press, 1995.

Tasker, Yvonne, *Spectacular Bodies: Gender, Genre, and the Action Cinema*. London: Routledge, 2002.

Tate, Joseph (ed.), *The Music and Art of Radiohead*. London: Ashgate, 2005.

Turner, Bryan S. *The Body in Society*. London: Sage, 1996.

Vernallis, Carol, *Experiencing Music Video: Aesthetics and Cultural Context*. New York: Columbia University Press, 2004.

Vincent, Rickey, *Funk: Music, People, and Rhythm of the One*. New York: St. Martin's Press, 1996.

Wall, Mick, 'It's Only Rock and Roll', *Mojo*, February 2005.

Walser, Robert, *Running with the Devil: Power, Gender, and Madness in Heavy Metal Music*. Hanover, NH: Wesleyan University Press, 1993.

Ward, Ed, Stokes, Geoffrey and Tucker, Ken, *Rock of Ages: the Rolling Stone History of Rock and Roll*. New York: Summit Books, 1986.

Waters, John, *Race of Angels: Ireland and the Genesis of U2*. Belfast: Blackstaff Press, 1994.

Weinstein, Deena, *Heavy Metal: the Music and its Culture*. New York: Da Capo Press, 2000.

Weinstein, Deena, 'All Singers are Dicks', *Popular Music and Society*, Vol. 27, No. 3, 2004.

Welch, Chris, *Cream*. London: Backbeat Books, 2000.

Welch, Chris, *Yes: Close to the Edge*. London: Omnibus Press, 2003.

Whelan, Imelda, *Overloaded: Popular Culture and the Future of Feminism*. London: Women's Press, 2000.

Whiteley, Sheila (ed.), *Sexing the Groove: Popular Music and Gender*. London: Routledge, 1997.

Whiteley, Sheila, *Women and Popular Music: Sexuality, Identity and Subjectivity*. London: Routledge, 2000.

Williams, Kevin, *Why I Still Want My MTV: Music Video and Aesthetic Communication*. New Jersey: Hampton Press, 2003.

Williamson, Nigel, 'More Bangs for Your Buck', *The Observer*, Sunday, 28 August, 2005.

DVD List

Glastonbury (2006)
Woodstock (1997)
AC/DC *Live at Donnington* (2003)
The Band et al. *The Last Waltz* (2004)
Black Sabbath *Never Say Die* (2005)
Bjork *Vespertine Live at Royal Opera House* (2001)
David Bowie *Ziggy Stardust and the Spiders from Mars: The Motion Picture* (2003)
The Clash *Westway to the World* (2001)
Alice Cooper *Welcome to My Nightmare* (1999)
Cream *Farewell Concert: Royal Albert Hall London* (2001)
The Doors *Live in Europe 1968* (2001)
    30 Years Commemorative Edition (2001)
Bob Dylan *No Direction Home* (2005)
Emerson, Lake and Palmer *Beyond the Beginning* (2005)
Genesis *Inside Genesis: The Gabriel Years 1970–75* (2005)
Gorillaz *Demon Days Live* (2006)
The Grateful Dead *The Closing of Winterland December 31 1978* (2003)
    Dead Ahead (2002)
Guns n' Roses *Use Your Illusion 1&2* (1992)
PJ Harvey *On Tour: Please Leave Quietly* (2006)
Jimi Hendrix *A Film about Jimi Hendrix* (2005)
    Jimi Hendrix: Live at Woodstock (2006)
    Jimi Plays Berkeley (2003)
Jethro Tull *Nothing is Easy: Live at the Isle of Wight 1970* (2005)
Korn *Live at the Hammerstein N.Y.C.* (2002)
Korn/ Limp Bizkit/ Ice Cube et al. *Family Values Aug/Oct 98* (2000)
Led Zeppelin *Led Zeppelin* (2003)
Marilyn Manson *Guns, God and Government World Tour* (2002)
Joni Mitchell *Shadows and Light* (2000)
Morrissey *Live in Dallas* (2000)
Van Morrison *Live at Montreux* (2006)
Nine Inch Nails *And All That Could Have Been: Nine Inch Nails Live* (2002)
Oasis … *There and Then* (1997)
Pink Floyd *Live at Pompeii* (2003)
    Pulse (2006)
Iggy Pop *Lick my Blood* (2004)
Prince *Sign O' The Times* (2004)
Pulp *Ultimate Live* (2005)
Queen *Live at Wembley Stadium* (2003)
    Queen on Fire: Live at the Bowl (2004)
Rage Against the Machine *Live at the Grand Olympic Auditorium* (2000)
Ramones *Raw* (2004)

End of the Century (2005)
REM *Tourfilm* (2000)
   Roadmovie (1997)
Rolling Stones *The Stones in the Park* (2001)
   Live at the Max (2002)
   Four Flicks (2003)
Roxy Music *Inside Roxy Music: 1972–4* (2004)
The Sex Pistols *The Filth and the Fury: a Sex Pistols Film* (2003)
Slipknot *Disasterpieces* (2002)
Bruce Springsteen and the E-Street Band *Live in Barcelona* (2003)
   Live at Hammersmith Odeon 1975: Born to Run 30th Anniversary (2005)
Talking Heads *Stop Making Sense* (2001)
U2 *Rattle and Hum* (1988)
   Vertigo (2004)
   U2 Go Home (2003)
The White Stripes *Under Blackpool Lights* (2004)
The Who *The Kids are Alright* (2004)
Neil Young *Rust Never Sleeps* (2002)
Frank Zappa *Baby Snakes* (2003)

Video List

Blur *Showtime*
David Bowie *Glass Spider* (1988)
Metallica *Cunning Stunts* (1998)
Led Zeppelin *The Song Remains the Same* (1976)
Nirvana *Live! Tonight! Sold Out!* (1994)
Radiohead *The Astoria London Live* (1995)
Suede *Love and Poison* (1993)
The Who *Listening to You: The Who Live at the Isle of Wight Festival* (1996)
U2 *Popmart* (1998)

Websites

Allmusic http://www.allmusic.com
Black-goat.com http://www.black-goat.com
Bjork Interviews http://home.concepts.nl/~sinned/2.htm
NME http://nme.com
Sirens Rising: A PJ Harvey Website http://www.room509.net/
Limpsite.com http://www.limpsite.com/
Youtube http://youtube.com

Index

2D   156, 157

Abba   6
AC/DC   113
Aerosmith   108, 117
  'Pink'   108
Albarn, Damon   139, 156–9, 162–3
Almond, Marc   121

Amos, Tori   43, 134–9
  'Me And A Gun'   136
  'Raspberry Swirl'   136
Anderson, Brett   144, 158
Andrew, Sam   73
Angel   90
Anthrax   129
Archies, The   156
  'Sugar Sugar'   156
Arctic Monkeys, The   102
Arnold, Gina   131–2
Ashcroft, Richard   14–17
Askey, Arthur   99
Attali, Jacques   62
Auslander, Philip   vii, 9–10, 21–3,
  25, 27, 32, 36–7, 38, 44

Baddeley, Gavin   51
Baker, Ginger   76
Baldwin, Davarin L.   147
Band, The   70, 91, 93–4
  The Last Waltz (performance/film)
    91, 93–4
Bangs, Lester   92
Bannister, Matthew   55, 124
Bar–Kays, The   73
Barrett, Syd   72
Basil, Toni   84
Baudrillard, Jean   22, 35, 157
Bayton, Mavis   55, 133
Beatles, The   40, 59, 63, 107
  Revolver (1966)   59
  Sergeant Pepper's Lonely Hearts Club
    Band (1967)   59

Benatar, Pat   138
Benjamin, Walter   21, 106
Bennett, Andy   43, 55
Bennett, Roy   109
Berry, Bruce   89
Berry, Chuck   75
Big Brother and the Holding
  Company   73
Bikini Kill   43
Bjork   9, 134–9, 163
  Vespertine (2001)   137
Black Sabbath   110, 111, 113
Bleasdale, Alan   145
Blistan, Matt   109
Bloomfield, Michael   73
Blur   6, 19, 139, 141, 144
  Modern Life Is Rubbish (1993)   141
  Parklife (1994)   6, 141
  The Great Escape (1995)   6, 141
  'There's No Other Way'   139, 141
Bonham, John   83
Bon Jovi   116, 119
  Slippery When Wet (1986)   116
Bono   12, 24, 25, 28, 30–3, 70
Borland, Wes   151
Bourdieu, Pierre   44–5, 55
Bowie, David   8, 53, 84–5, 86, 91,
  95, 104–5, 106, 107, 121, 157
  Diamond Dogs (tour)   84, 86, 104
  Glass Spider (tour)   104–5, 106
  Let's Dance (1983)   105
  Never Let Me Down (1987)   104
  Serious Moonlight (tour)   106
  'Space Oddity'   84
  The 1980 Floor Show (performance,
    made for TV)   105
  'Time'   97
  Tonight (1984)   105
  Ziggy Stardust (tour)   53, 85
Boyer, Bonnie   109
Bozzio, Terry   90
Brand, Russell   155
Brooks, Greg   109

Brown, Ian   17
Brown, James   78, 107
Bruce, Jack   76
Bruce, Lenny   95
Buck, Peter   125
Burns, Bruce   37
Busted   23
Butler, Judith   53
Byrds, The   92
Byrne, David   126

Canned Heat   83
Carey, Mariah   134
Carroll, Dian   134
Cat   109
Cavacchi, Daniel   39, 47
Cave, Nick   70
Cherry, Neneh   162
Chick, Steve   161
Clapton, Eric   22, 61, 73, 74,
    75–6, 78, 79
Clash, The   6, 100–1
Clayton, Adam   24, 25, 28
Clemens, Clarence   46, 48
Cobain, Kurt   14, 103, 127–9,
    131–2, 139
Cocker, Jarvis   140, 142–3, 158
Cohen, Leonard   14
Collin, Matthew   160
Cooper, Alice   52, 87–8, 91, 95,
    112, 113, 151, 158
Country Joe and the Fish   71
Coxon, Graham   139
Crazy Horse   89
Cream   76
  'Spoonful'   76
  'Sunshine of Your Love'   76
  'We're Going Wrong'   76
Curtis, Ian   102–3

Daltrey, Roger   42, 65
Danko, Rick   93
Davies, Bette   87
Davies, Ray   6
Davis, Helen   135
Davis, Jonathan   151
Deacon, John   120
Deadheads   67–8
Dean, Martyn   84

Dean, Roger   84
DeFranco, Ani   134
de la Rocha, Zack   151
Dickinson, Bruce   112, 114–15
Dio, Ronnie   115
Docherty, Pete   157
Dodd, Ken   98
Doors, The   65, 68–70, 163
Dr Strangelove   29
Duncan, Robert   111
Dunphy, Eamon   26
Durst, Fred   55, 129–30, 131, 149,
    151
Dyer, Richard   11–13, 17, 20
Dylan, Bob   7, 59–60, 63, 70,
    78, 91, 93–4, 153
  'Baby, Let Me Follow You
    Down'   93
  'Forever Young'   93
  'Like a Rolling Stone'   59
  No Direction Home (film)   59, 93

E Street Band, The   45–9
Eagles, The   113
Echobelly   144
Eddie (Iron Maiden mascot)   112–13
Edge, The   24, 25, 28, 35–6
Edwards, Ritchie   3–4, 13,
    14, 20
Elastica   143
ELP 85
Emerson, Keith   85
Eno, Brian   7, 61, 85, 136
Entwhistle, John   65
Ezrin, Bob   87

Fast, Susan   41, 83
Feigenbaum, Anna   134
Ferry, Brian   85, 86
Fink, Matt   109
Fisher, Jules   84, 86
Flanagan, Bill   37
Foreman, Murray   146–7, 148, 150
Frampton, Peter   105
Franklin, Aretha   73
Franz Ferdinand   5–6
Frith, Simon   19, 41–2
Frischmann, Justine   143, 144
Furnier, Vincent   52

Gabriel, Peter 85, 86, 91, 108
  'Sledgehammer' (video) 108
Gacy, Madonna Wayne 51
Gallagher, Liam 14, 17, 139,
  144–5
Gallagher, Noel 14, 17, 139, 142,
  144–5
Garcia, Jerry 61, 67
Garland, Judy 11
Garnett, Robert 94
Genesis 85, 104, 108
  'I Know What I Like' 86
  The Lamb Lies Down on Broadway
  86
  'The Musical Box' 86
Gill, Rosalind 142
Gillespie, Bobby 70
Gillis, Jack 161, 163
Godfrey, John 160
Goodman, Fred 6
Gorillaz viii, 156–9, 162–3
  'Clint Eastwood' 156
  Demon Days (2005) 162
Gracyk, Theodore 35–6, 39, 42
Graham, Larry 79
Graham, Martha 137
Grateful Dead, The 60, 65–8, 75,
  91, 92
Grauerholtz, James 100
Greenwood, Colin 159, 160
Greenwood, Jonny 159, 160
Grossberg, Laurence 106, 107, 109
Guns n' Roses 42, 53, 117–18, 119
  'Sweet Child O' Mine' 118
  Use Your Illusion (tour) 118
Guthrie, Woody 7
Guy, Buddy 77

Halford, Rob 113, 115, 116–17, 121
Harde, Erin 160
Harris, Bob 97
Harrison, George 59
Hart, Micky 67
Harvey, PJ 134–9
  To Bring You My Love (tour) 138
Hawking, Stephen 153
Headlam, Dave 74
Hendrix, Jimi 73, 76–80, 102,
  107, 114

Hetfield, James 119
Hewlett, Jamie 156–9
Hook, Peter 102
Hunter, Robert 62
Huq, Rupa 143

Incubus 130
Iron Maiden 112–13, 115
  Powerslave (1985: album and
  tour) 112–13
Isle of Wight Festival, the 81
Isley Brothers, The 77
Isley, Eddie 77

Jackson, Michael 105, 146
  'Beat It' 105
  Thriller 105
Jackson 5, The 157
Jagger, Mick 41, 42, 69, 97, 107,
  153–6
James, Elmore 75
Johanson, David 96–7
Johnson, Fred 36
Johnson, Robert 74, 75
Jones, Brian 70, 75, 102
Jones, Eddie 'Guitar Slim' 76
Jones, John Paul 83
Jones, Mick 101
Jones, Steve 98
Joplin, Janis 73, 83, 102, 137–8
Jordison, Joey 130–1
Joy Division 8, 102–3
Judas Priest 113, 116, 121

Kane, Arthur 96
Keidis, Anthony 129
Keighley, Keir 7–8, 9, 147, 158
Kellner, Douglas 34
Kent, Nick 95, 101
King, B. B. 75
King, Martin Luther 74
Kinks, The 6, 95
Kirby, Michael 32
Kiss 86–8, 112, 113, 115,
  118, 158
KLF, The 9
Korn 149, 150, 151
  Family Values 150
Kraftwerk 7, 102, 107

Lamacq, Steve   3
Leary, Timothy   157
Led Zeppelin   41, 82–3, 113
Lee, C. P.   59
Leeds, Eric   109
Lennon, John   5, 7, 9, 10
Lewis, Jerry Lee   40, 63
Libertines, The   6
Lilith Fair   42
Limp Bizkit   130, 149, 151
Little Richard   20, 77
Live Aid   105, 120
Lofgren, Nils   88
Lollapalooza   42
'Louie Louie'   97
Love, Courtney   128
Lovecroft, H. P.   110–11
Lunn, Kenneth   140
Lydon, John   98

Macan, Edward   66
MacInnes, John   45
MacKay, Andy   85
Madan, Sonia   144
Madonna   152
    Confessions (tour)   152
Major, John   140, 141
Manic Street Preachers   3–4, 14
Manson, Charles   51–2, 88, 95,
    118
Manson, Marilyn   49–55, 87
    'Antichrist Superstar'   52
    'Cruci-fiction in Space'   52
    'The Nobodies'   51
Manuvra, Roots   162
Manzarek, Ray   68
Marr, Johnny   123
Marvin, Hank   61
May, Brian   120
Mazullo, Mark   138
MC5, The   95
MC Hammer   147
Meadows, Punky   90
Melody Maker   14, 97
Melton, Barry   71
Mercury, Freddie   55, 120–1, 123,
    126
Metallica   6, 118–19, 163
McCartney, Paul   5

McFly   23
McKay, George   vii
McRobbie, Angela   41–2
Michael, George   121
Milli Vanilli   22–3
Mills, Mike   125
Mitchell, Joni   91, 92, 107
Mitchell, Mitch   79
Monroe, Marilyn   51–2
Monterey Pop Festival, the   81, 83
Moon, Keith   65
Moore, Allan   vii, 5, 10, 20, 35,
    152
Morello, Tom   151
Morrison, Jim   3, 68–70, 102
Morrison, Van   91, 92–3
    'Cyprus Avenue'   92
Morrissey   8, 124–5, 126
Mothers of Invention, The   9, 90
Motley Crue   116, 117
Mr Bungle   130
MTV 22, 104–10, 116–17, 118, 119,
    127, 131
Mullen, Larry   24, 25, 28, 31
Murcia, Billy   97
Murdoc   156, 157
MX Machine   116
    Manic Panic (1988)   116

Neal, Mark Anthony   148
New York Dolls, The   96–7, 98, 99,
    103
Nice, The   85
Nicks, Stevie   138
Nine Inch Nails   54
Nirvana   5, 6, 23, 127–9, 131–2
    'Love Buzz'   128
    'Smells Like Teen Spirit'   131
NME   3, 7, 14, 153
Noodle   156, 157
Novoselic, Krist   131
NWA   147, 148

Oasis   5, 7, 13–14, 15, 18, 19, 102,
    127, 141, 144–5
    Be Here Now (1996)   13
    What's the Story (Morning Glory)
        (1995)   13
    'Wonderwall'   145

O'Brien, Ed   159–60
Orb, The   6
Osmonds, The   157
Ozric Tentacles   7

Page, Jimmy   41, 42, 83
Palmer, Gareth   47
Pearl Jam   5
Pet Shop Boys   121
Phelan, Peggy   21–3
Pink Floyd   6, 29, 70–3, 81, 115,
    119, 158
  'Astronomy Dominie'   72
  Dark Side of the Moon, The
      (1973)   29, 73, 82
  '14 Hour Technicolour Dream'
      (performance)   72
  'Games for May' (performance)
      72
  Live at Pompeii (film)   73
  Pulse (1995)   29, 73
  The Wall (tour)   82, 119
Pixies, The   101
Plant, Robert   41, 42, 70, 82–3
Plastic Ono Band   9
Pollock, Jackson   101
Pop, Iggy   3, 4, 84, 95, 96, 97–8,
    99, 100, 103, 129, 131
  'I Wanna Be Your Dog'   98
  'Lust for Life'   98
Presley, Elvis   12, 40, 50, 63, 65
  'I Can't Help Falling in Love with
      You'   12
Primal Scream   70
Prince   3, 106–10, 146
  'I Would Die   4 U'   3
  'It's Gonna Be A Beautiful Night'
      110
  'Little Red Corvette'   107
  '1999'   107
  1999 (1983)   107
  Purple Rain (1984)   3, 106–7
  Sign O' The Times (1987)   109
  Sign O' The Times (tour)   109–10
  'U Got The Look'   109
Proby, P. J.   64
Public Enemy   147, 148, 151
Pulp   16, 140, 141, 142–3
  'Common People'   141

Different Class (1995)   143
  'I Spy'   143

Q   134–5
Quatro, Suzi   32
Queen   120, 123, 124, 125
Quirk and Toynbee vii, 5, 30

Radiohead   viii, 6, 14, 19, 102, 119,
    159–60, 162, 163
  Amnesiac   159
  Hail To The Thief (2005)   160
  'Idioteque'   160
  Kid A   159
  OK Computer (tour)   159
  The Bends (1995)   15
Rage Against The Machine   102, 148,
    152
Ramirez, Twiggy   51
Ramone, Dee Dee   99
Ramone, Joey   94
Ramone, Johnny   99
Ramones, The   9, 94–5, 99–100
Ratt   119
Ravitz, Mark   84
Reagan, Ronald   46
Redding, Otis   73
Red Hot Chili Peppers, The   129
Reed, Lou   84, 95–6, 98, 99, 103
  'Heroin'   96
  Live-Take No Prisoners (1979)   95
Reid, Jamie   94
REM   29, 101, 121, 124, 125, 129
  'Country Feedback'   125
  Green (tour)   129
  Monster (1994)   125
Reynolds, Simon   43, 160
Reznor, Trent   53
Rhymes, Busta   108
  'Gimme Some More'   108
Richards, Keith   60, 154–6
Richardson, John   157
Robertson, Robbie   91, 93
Rolling Stones, The   29, 70, 81, 95,
    100, 101, 117, 152–6, 159, 160
  A Bigger Bang (tour)   152
  Forty Licks (tour)   153, 155
  'Satisfaction'   70
  Steel Wheels (tour)   153

Rolling stones – *continued*
  'Street Fighting Man'   155
Rose, Axl   118
Rose, Tricia   146–7, 151
Rotten, Johnny   3, 95, 98–9, 114
Roxy Music   85, 86, 95
Russel   156

S Club 7   10
Safford, Wally   109
Samuels, David   147
Santana   107
Savage, Jon   16
Schechner, Richard   27, 30, 108
Schippers, Mimi   43–4, 55, 116, 138
Schneider, Rebecca   54
Schneiderman, Davis   163
Schwarzenegger, Arnold   46
Seacer Jr, Levi   109
Selway, Phil   159, 160
Sex Pistols   3, 94–5, 98–9, 101
Shadows, The   6
Sha Na Na   9
Shangri–La's, The   99
Sheila E   109
Shuker, Roy   vii
Simmons, Gene   87
Simonon, Paul   101
Six, Nikki   117
Slash   42, 117, 118
Sleeper   143
Slipknot   111, 115, 130, 149, 158
Sly and the Family Stone   79
  'I Want to Take You Higher'   79
Smith, Patti   70, 100, 133
Smiths, The   8, 124–5, 163
SOD   129
  'Milano Mosh'   129
Soft Machine, The   72
Son House   160
Speer, Albert   84
Spice Girls   6, 23
Springsteen, Bruce   6, 7, 39, 45–9, 54–5, 106
  Born in the USA (1984)   46
  Born in the USA (tour)   45–6
  'Dancing in the Dark'   106
  'Independence Day'   47

'Spirits in the Night'   48
The Ghost of Tom Joad (1995)   49
The Rising (tour)   48–9
'The River'   46
Stallone, Sylvester   46
Starr, Ringo   91
Stewart, Jimmy   126
Stipe, Michael   7, 70, 121–2, 124, 125, 126, 133, 136
Stone Roses, The   18, 19, 102
Stone, Sly   107
Stooges, The   3, 6, 160
Strausberg, John   153–4, 156
Strummer, Joe   101
Suede   18, 144
  'Animal Nitrate'   18
  Coming Up (1996)   144
  'Moving'   18
  'The Drowners'   18
Sumner, Bernard   102
Sutherland, Steve   14–17, 19
System of a Down   130

Take That   6
Talking Heads   114, 126
  'Burning Down The House'   126
  'Don't Worry About The Government'   126
  'Life During Wartime'   126
  'Once In A Lifetime'   126
  'Psycho Killer'   126
  Stop Making Sense (film/tour)   114, 126
  'The Good Thing'   126
Taylor, James   92
Taylor, Roger   120
Thatcher, Margaret   140
Them   100
  'Gloria'   100
Thunders, Johnny   96, 98
Townsend, Pete   30–1, 60, 64–5, 73
Turner, Brian S.   154, 156
Turner, Ike   162
Tyler, Bonnie   7
  'Total Eclipse of the Heart'   7
Tyrell, Soozie   49

U2   viii, 24–38, 102, 119, 127, 158, 159

'Bullet the Blue Sky' 29
'City of Blinding Lights' 24, 26
'Elevation' 26
Elevation (tour) 28, 29, 30
'40' 26
How to Dismantle an Atomic Bomb
(2004) 24, 29
'Into The Heart' 26
'Love or Peace or Else' 29
Love Town (tour) 34
'Mysterious Ways' 26
'New Year's Day' 35
'One' 26
'Out of Control' 31
Popmart (tour) 29, 30, 31, 34–8
Rattle and Hum (film: 1988) 31
'Sunday Bloody Sunday' 31–3
'The Electric Co.' 26
The Joshua Tree (1987) 29
The Joshua Tree (tour) 34
'Vertigo' 25
Vertigo (tour) 24–30
'When Johnny Comes Marching
Home' 29
'Where the Streets Have No Name'
37, 38
'Yahweh' 26
'Zoo Station' 29
Zoo TV (tour) 29, 34–8
Zooropa (tour) 37

Vanilla Ice 147
Van Zandt, Steve 48
Velvet Underground, The 95, 96
Vernallis, Carole 108–9
Verve, The 14–17, 19
'Bittersweet Symphony' 14
'Come On' 17
'The Drugs Don't Work' 14
Urban Hymns (1997) 14
Vicious, Sid 98, 103

Waits, Tom 7
Wakeman, Rick 84
Walker, T-Bone 77
Walser, Robert 116
Warhol, Andy 95
Waters, John 33
Waters, Muddy 75, 91

Waters, Roger 82
Watts, Michael 97
WC 150
Weiner, Louise 143–4
Weinstein, Deena 52, 111–12, 114,
115, 120, 123–4
Weir, Bob 68
Westside Connection 150
Whatever Happened to Baby Jane?
(film) 87
Whelan, Imelda 142
White, Jack 5, 160–2, 163
White, Meg 160–2
White Stripes, The viii, 6, 160–2, 163
De Stijl 160
Elephant (2003) 160
Whiteley, Sheila 42, 132–3, 134,
135, 137–8
Whitten, Danny 89
Who, The 60, 64–5, 70, 73, 76, 95,
104, 117
Lifehouse 64
'Won't Get Fooled Again' 65
'Young Man Blues' 30
Wilcock, Dennis 112
Williams, Robbie 8
Intensive Care 8
Wilson, Brian 9
Pet Sounds (1966) 59
Wilson, Peter Wynne 71
Wisdom, Norman 99
Wizzard 9, 10
Womack, Bobby 78
Wonder, Stevie 107
Wood, Ron 91, 155
Wood, Roy 9, 10
Woodstock 65–6, 78, 81, 83, 89,
91, 114
Woodstock (1999) 129–30
Wu Tang Clan 150
'Wu Tang Clan Ain't Nothing to
Fuck Wit' 150

X, Malcolm 74

Yes 84, 152
Tales from Topographic Oceans
(tour) 84
Yorke, Thom 14, 159–60

Young, Alphonso   77
Young, Angus   112, 120
Young, Neil   44, 88–9, 92
   Rust Never Sleeps (tour/film)   89
   'Sugar Mountain'   89
   'The Needle and the Damage
      Done'   89

'Tonight's the Night'   88, 89
Tonight's the Night (tour)   88–9

Zappa, Frank   9, 10, 60, 89–91, 93,
   114
   'Don't Eat the Yellow Snow'   91
   'Punky's Whips'   90